ON PAUL

ON PAUL

Aspects of His Life, Work and
Influence in the Early Church

C. K. BARRETT
Emeritus Professor of Divinity
Durham University

T&T CLARK
A Continuum imprint
LONDON • NEW YORK

T&T CLARK LTD

A Continuum imprint

The Tower Building
11 York Road
London SE1 7NX
UK

370 Lexington Avenue
New York 10017–6503
USA

www.continuumbooks.com

First published 2003

ISBN 0–5670–8902–9

British Library Cataloguing-in-Publication Data
A catalogue record for this book is available from the British Library

Typeset by Waverley Typesetters, Galashiels
Printed and bound in Great Britain by Bookcraft, Midsomer Norton, Bath

Contents

Preface

In preparing this book I have had in mind a project which I hope I may be able to carry out as a supplement to work I have done in the last few decades on the Pauline Epistles and the Acts of the Apostles. The epistles contain the primary, the only contemporary, source for Paul's life and thought. Acts contains, *inter alia*, an account of Paul as he appeared to a sympathetic writer about thirty years after Paul's death. In the introductory essay in this volume I have set side by side the two pictures of Paul (confining myself for the sake of brevity to his relations with the church of Jerusalem) derived from these two sources. Contemporary with Acts and later there are other pictures of Paul, not biographies but references, sometimes historical allusions. I wish to look at these, and at non-Pauline strands in the history of early Christianity, which may be thought of as sometimes rival, sometimes collaborative, forces in theology and church life, and to take this study into the second century, as far as Marcion and Irenaeus. This may teach us something about Paul, it is almost certain to throw some light on the history of the church. It has been suggested to me that such a volume as the present one, in which a few pieces that I have written about Paul are collected and reprinted, may help to introduce the work that is still to be written and also lead to some economy in its presentation.

It will I think be useful to indicate here in a few lines the relevance of the essays that appear below. The introductory essay 'Paul and Jerusalem' has been written because the first step in our investigation must be to gain as clear a picture as possible of Paul

vii

as he saw himself, and the first instrument of comparison will inevitably be the picture of Paul as Luke saw it. In both Paul's own picture of himself and in Luke's picture of him his relations with Jerusalem play a vital part. This essay if it did not stand alone would be the first among those described as **Foundations**. Among these, (1) *'Eidōlothyta* once more' stands first because it shows Paul confronted by two errors (perhaps perversions of his own teaching). We see at once Paul facing two 'Pseudo-Pauls'. (2) 'Christocentricity at Antioch' shows how for Paul practice and theology were related to each other – a relation that would not always be perceived in succeeding generations. The same point is made in (3) 'Paul: Missionary and Theologian'. (4) 'Paul: Councils and Controversies' overlaps to some extent with the Introductory Essay and develops the picture of Paul in controversy with his contemporaries. (5) 'I am not ashamed of the Gospel' shows the relation of Paul with early tradition about Jesus. (6) 'Paul at Athens and to Rome' compares the Areopagus speech ascribed to Paul in Acts 17 with the teaching of Romans, and also serves to introduce a group of Christian missionaries and theologians who were to play an important part in the next stage of Christian history.

This appropriately leads to **Developments**. 'Pauline Controversies in the Post-Pauline period' (7), written nearly thirty years ago, may serve as an introduction to the theme of the Pauline tradition, at least to the controversial aspect of that theme. The Post-Pauline period is clearly entered with (8), 'Ethics in the Deutero-Pauline Literature', a title whose relevance it is unnecessary to point out. The title of (9), 'The Christology of Hebrews', is not so clear, but the essay argues that the distinctive Christology of Hebrews was the work of the group referred to above, under (6). The same group reappears in (10), printed here under the title 'Effective Forces in the Late First Century'. It appeared originally with the title 'What Minorities?' in the Festschrift for J. Jervell, *Mighty Minorities?* It took up Professor Jervell's suggestion of an unexpectedly influential minority in the closing decades of the first century, but identified the minority differently. (11) 'Paul and the Introspective Conscience' differs from the other papers. It takes us first to Luther in the sixteenth century, then to the twentieth. It is, I think, not without its own interest, but it stands here as a witness to the different interpretations of Pauline theology to which different presuppositions may lead, and consequently to the warning that in the first 100 years also different presuppositions and backgrounds must be looked at and allowed for.

C. K. BARRETT

Acknowledgements

Chapter 1, 'Eidolothyta once more'. Reproduced from G. D. Dragas (ed.), *Aksum-Thyateira, a Festschrift for Archbishop Makarios of Thyateira and Great Britain*, London, 1985, pp. 155–8.
Used by permission.

Chapter 2, 'Christocentricity at Antioch'. Reproduced from Ch. Landmesser, H.-J. Eckstein and H. Lichtenberger (eds), *Jesus Christus als die Mitte der Schrift. Für Otfried Hofius*, Verlag Walter de Gruyter, Berlin/New York, 1997, pp. 323–39.
Used by permission.

Chapter 3, 'Paul: Missionary and Theologian'. Reproduced from M. Hengel and U. Heckel (eds), *Paulus und das antike Judentum*, WUNT 58, Mohr-Siebeck, Tübingen, 1992, pp. 1–15.
Used by permission.

Chapter 4, 'Paul: Councils and Controversies'. Reproduced from D. A. Hagner (ed.), *Conflicts and Challenges in Early Christianity*, Trinity Press International, Harrisburg, Pennsylvania, 1999, pp. 42–74.
Copyright © 1999 Trinity Press International. Used by permission of Trinity Press International, Harrisburg, Pennsylvania.

Chapter 5, 'I am not ashamed of the Gospel'. Reproduced from *Foi et Salut selon S. Paul (Épître aux Romains 1, 16). Colloque*

Introduction

Paul and Jerusalem

This introductory essay serves a double purpose. It is intended to introduce the essays that follow – a somewhat miscellaneous collection of pieces which originated for various purposes in the course of several decades of work focused on the Pauline Epistles and the Acts of the Apostles. Some of them deal directly with Paul himself and some of them run over into the period beyond Paul's death. Both those that do this and those in which the living Paul appears introduce from time to time Paul's allies and opponents. Paul continued to be both a creative and a divisive figure, and this essay is intended to introduce also a study that I hope to make of the use, disuse, and abuse, the understanding and the misunderstanding, of Paul up to a point in the second century. Up to a point, or rather points, for I have in mind two stopping-places: Marcion, the arch-heretic, and Irenaeus, the father of orthodoxy. Neither title is fair, especially that applied to Marcion, but conventional brevity may be allowed so far. The period covered is in itself worth study, but it also raises some of the great issues, including not a few controversies that have marked the course of the Pauline tradition through two millennia. The essay on 'Paul and the Introspective Conscience' may illustrate this.

About the essays I have said a word or two in the Preface (pp. vii–ix). The present introductory essay intentionally, the others on the whole incidentally, will show a picture of Paul drawn from his own letters, and a comparable but different picture provided by the author of Acts. What I intend to do in the book I hope to write, is to present a sequence of such contrasting pairs of pictures

1

designed to show what later (but not much later) generations made of Paul. The same process will introduce a number of others who, either in person or as figureheads associated with lines of thought and practice, played an important part in the events of their times.

I say 'a picture of Paul' because the task as I conceive it and must approach it is essentially a historical one: I want to know who did what; but this must, as history, be expanded into 'who did what – and why', and when the persons concerned – Paul at least – were theologically motivated *why* is bound to lead to a certain amount of theology. I recognize fully that there are other approaches to theology, but I know that this is the only one that I am competent to pursue.[1] Of the essays contained in this book some start from the Epistles, some from Acts; most include an attempt to put the two sources together. For many purposes this is a necessary procedure, but from the point of view of history it is not ideal, and here I shall begin by setting out a 'Paul view' and an 'Acts view', only when this has been done attempting to look at the two synoptically. In this essay I shall confine myself to the question of Paul's relations with the church of Jerusalem and other Jewish Christians who may or may not have represented and been supported by that church. Other matters can be added at a later stage.

The story as seen and related by Paul is to be found for the most part in Galatians. We must collect the evidence that the text provides, asking as we go the questions that the text suggests but does not, or does not directly, answer.[2]

The story begins in Paul's pre-Christian days, and – as far as the evidence in Galatians goes – in Jerusalem.[3] Only there could Paul be said to have excelled many of his contemporaries in the study and practice of Judaism. He excelled because of and in his zeal for the ancestral traditions. This zeal for the Law is, for him,

---

[1] For this reason I began my book *Paul: An Introduction to his Thought* (London: Chapman, 1994) with a study of Paul's controversies.

[2] See my book *Freedom and Obligation: A Study of the Epistle to the Galatians* (London: SPCK, 1985), but here as in some other matters I have moved on from conclusions reached there.

[3] See *A Critical and Exegetical Commentary on the Acts of the Apostles*, Vol. 2 (ICC; Edinburgh: T&T Clark, 1998), pp. 1034–6, on Acts 22.3.

the necessary pre-condition for understanding his conversion. He took an active part in the persecution of Christians. At the decisive moment of conversion he was not in Jerusalem but (one infers from Gal. 1.17) in or near Damascus. The essence of this event was an encounter with Jesus which proved to Paul that Jesus, who had been crucified and dead, was now alive, raised by God from death. It is necessary here briefly to turn aside from Galatians. News of the conversion of a leading persecutor, once its genuineness was established, must have been welcome to the Christian leaders in Jerusalem, but it did not in itself confer any particular status on Paul. He regarded it as constituting him an apostle (1 Cor. 9.1; 15.8 – it may have been the last resurrection appearance, but a resurrection appearance it was); others might think him, if an apostle at all, a freak apostle, born too late to be real. There was plenty of scope for controversy here. Paul was sure of apostleship as God's gift, whatever human critics might say (Gal. 1.1).

Paul was an apostle because, in his conversion, God had sent him to preach the Gospel, and to do so specifically among the Gentiles. This involved a new theological understanding of the person and work of Jesus, which this is not the place to discuss. It might perhaps have been wise to discuss this theological advance with 'flesh and blood' (Gal. 1.16), with, that is, the human leaders of the Christian movement, but for Paul immediate obedient action was more important than theological discussion. He did not go up to Jerusalem to those who were apostles before him – an expression that asserts his own apostleship while accepting its posteriority. Instead he went off to Arabia (1.17), some say, to meditate in the desert, more probably, to preach to the (non-Jewish) Arabs. He returned to Damascus. Was this in some sense a base? At least, it suggests independence of Jerusalem.

At length, however, after three years,[4] he did go up (ἀνῆλθον) to Jerusalem. The word, that used[5] with a negative at 1.17, may

---

[4] If, as was usual in antiquity, Paul counted inclusively, the period may not have been much or any more than eighteen months.

[5] But Paul may have written ἀπῆλθον, *I went away*; this word is read by important MSS.

suggest something of a pilgrimage; it may imply no more than that Jerusalem was the capital; it would hardly refer to a merely geographic 'going up'. It may be no more than a subconscious recollection of the Jewish usage of Paul's pre-Christian time. But he went up to 'visit' Cephas. The meaning and significance of ἱστορῆσαι are discussed in Essay 2 (Christocentricity at Antioch). Paul went to Jerusalem to discuss the question that would be raised again years later. What did Jerusalem make of Paul's mission to the Gentiles? Paul was not seeking from the apostolic college an authority that he would not otherwise have had; his apostolate was not from men or through man; it was from a higher authority; it was from God (Gal. 1.1).

It was however important to know how he and his mission stood in Jerusalem. For Paul's purpose there were two men whom it was important to meet. One was Peter, who, somewhat later, undoubtedly was prepared on some terms to consider a mission to Gentiles.[6] The other was James, the Lord's brother, who seems to have stood on the opposite side. What came of their fortnight's consultation we know only from the fact that Paul continued to preach the faith which formerly he had ravaged (Gal. 1.23), and that another fourteen years passed (2.1). They were not trouble-free, but one may suppose that trouble arose and developed fairly slowly, so that it was only at the end of this fairly long period that Paul felt it to be necessary to go up to Jerusalem again, lest his efforts should prove to be in vain. He is evidently concerned in this paragraph in Galatians to show how little contact with Jerusalem he had had; he had not been authorized or directed by those who were apostles before him. But eventually trouble came to a head and he had to go up again to Headquarters.[7] After so long an interval[8] we could hardly suppose that a social or even a devotional motive would have sufficed to bring him to Jerusalem. It was a supernatural monition[9] that prompted the journey; it would be surprising if this did not include,

---

[6] This is suggested by 1 Cor. 1–3; 9.5; also Gal. 2.11. I do not adduce Acts 10; 11; 15.

[7] Here ἀνέβην is used; it will have the same sense as ἀνῆλθον.

[8] See n. 4; perhaps as little as twelve years and six months.

[9] We need not attempt here to interpret κατὰ ἀποκάλυψιν more precisely.

or perhaps reinforce, a rational judgement of a situation of increasing difficulty. Whatever understanding may have been reached on the earlier Jerusalem visit was not working satisfactorily. What was unsatisfactory can only be inferred from the account (in 2.1–10) of what was achieved at the new meeting, and from the fact that Paul thought it appropriate to include the account in his letter to the Galatian churches.

Paul travelled to Jerusalem with Barnabas and Titus; the wording (συμπαραλαβών) suggests that Titus, though a valued colleague, occupied a relatively subordinate position. He was also a Greek, and uncircumcised. This is his importance in Galatians 2.

The narrative of Galatians 2, which we must trace in detail, begins with a statement of Paul's intention in going to Jerusalem. He informed the Jerusalem Christians (who will be further characterized below) of the Gospel which he preached among the Gentiles. They may previously have received biased and incorrect reports. *Informed* is ἀνεθέμην; and this may mean more than *informed*. At Acts 25.14, for example, Festus, seeking help in submitting Paul's case to Rome, and desiring also to gratify his royal visitor, *submitted* (ἀνέθετο) Paul's case to Agrippa II. The word may signify the referring of a matter to an authority with a view to obtaining perhaps not a *judgement* but at least an *opinion*. Which translation should be adopted here? It seems clear that Paul was seeking an opinion, since the outcome of his inquiry would be either that he was and had been, or was not and had not been, running in vain. This does not mean that if Paul had received a negative response he would have changed or suppressed his message. By a negative response those whom he consulted would, in his opinion, have condemned themselves. He would not have changed his Gospel for a No-gospel (1.7), but he and his churches would have been placed in a position of great difficulty. What he would have done we do not know. We may however infer that there was a considerable, probably growing, group that took the view that Paul's Gospel was an intolerable corruption of the original Jewish Gospel[10] and had to be officially

---

[10] This is suggested by Acts 21.15, though the numbers there may well be exaggerated.

disowned – if possible, discontinued. The growth of this opinion would make the journey to Jerusalem necessary.

Paul did not have in mind a public discussion. The question was to be dealt with privately, κατ᾿ ἰδίαν. On one side there would be Paul, Barnabas, and – perhaps an intended provocation – the Gentile Titus; the references to him in 2 Corinthians suggest that he can hardly have been taken along as a mere bag-carrying assistant. On the other side would be οἱ δοκοῦντες. In v. 6 this expression is undoubtedly used ironically – Whatever their reputation may have been it made no impression on me – and in view of this it is hard to think that it can have been used in vv. 2 and 9 without at least a measure of irony. He acknowledges, by his actions rather than by the word (see again v. 6), that they had in fact authority; it was not authority that could make him change his beliefs, but it was authority that could threaten the destruction of his work. It was important to consult the leading people in Jerusalem; it was not important to make a public matter of consulting the whole church. The 'men of repute' were the people who could cause trouble.

In vv. 3–5 the δοκοῦντες disappear and the significance of Titus becomes evident. It is sometimes questioned whether the matter of these verses belongs to a different occasion. But it seems unlikely that Paul should introduce Titus (he is not mentioned in v. 2) in order to say, 'I told you that Titus was a Greek; I ought to add that he was not a proselyte. I had resisted all attempts to have him circumcised and on the occasion of our visit to Jerusalem he was a full representative of the uncircumcised Gentile church.'

The *false brothers*[11] are mentioned in a sentence in which an incomplete grammatical structure is partially remedied by a variant reading, which on the principle *difficilior lectio potior* must almost certainly be rejected. One must infer from the text that the false brothers sought to compel (ἠναγκάσθη) Titus to be circumcised. This means that there were at least two groups of Jewish Christians in Jerusalem: one that insisted on the circumcision of all Gentile converts to Christianity, believing that only Jews (whether by birth

[11] See Essay 2 (Christocentricity at Antioch).

or by proselytization) could have a share in the benefits of the Jewish Messiah, the other while themselves remaining Jewish were willing to accept Gentiles into a kind of associate membership which, though it might be subject to some conditions, did not require full proselytization and therewith circumcision.

It must be added that it is possible to take the *difficilior lectio potior* argument in a different way, in regard not to language but to substance: omit οἷς οὐδέ (with some Western authorities) and put a different stress on ἠναγκάσθη. We then have: Titus was not *compelled* to be circumcised but because of the false brothers we yielded to their demand for circumcision so as to guarantee the Gospel for the future. This however is not a difficult but an impossible reading, impossible because it ignores the vigorous denunciation of the false brothers (and their condemnatory designation), and seems moreover to present the most unlikely means of ensuring that the truth of the Gospel should be safe-guarded. The most that can be said in favour of it is that it might provide an explanation of Gal. 5.11; this verse however can be otherwise explained.

The false brothers must be distinguished from the men of repute (οἱ δοκοῦντες). The issue of circumcision will serve as a clear-cut line of demarcation. Gal. 4.10 may mean that those who taught the Galatians that circumcision was essential may have told them also that they must observe the Jewish calendar. Their existence may well have made life difficult for James and other more moderate leaders – to whom we must now turn. They may have been harder to deal with than the false brothers, who had simply to be contradicted and fought.

Galatians 2.6 is a sentence that does not end as it began. Paul began to write, From the men of repute I received nothing, but after interrupting himself with a disparaging remark[12] (see above p. 6) about 'men of repute' he finishes his sentence, the men of repute contributed nothing to me. Clearly he does not contradict himself; the sense would not have been different if he had written

---

[12] ποτε, *pace* Lightfoot, does not suggest their past record as companions of Jesus. See K. Aland, *NTS* 2 (1956), pp. 267–75.

οὐδὲν προσετέθη. What might they have contributed, or hoped to contribute, to him? The backing of their own authority, expressed in approval of his mission? A fuller theological content for his Gospel?[13] Paul does not suggest that they offered these things, and if they had done so he would not have received them. His calling and his Gospel came directly from Christ himself (1.12); there was no higher authority, and it is impossible to add to a theology which may itself be defined as *solus Christus*. He had not gone to Jerusalem to seek authorization or correction, but to prevent the rupture of nascent Christendom. An offer to share, to take part in, his mission to Gentiles as well as to Jews he would doubtless have been happy to accept. But this, it appears, was not on offer. In vv. 7, 8, 9 the tone of the narrative changes; perhaps the atmosphere in Jerusalem had changed. The aorist participle ἰδόντες may suggest, it is at least consistent with, a change of attitude on the part of the Jerusalem leaders. *They saw* – something that they had not seen before. *They recognized* (γνόντες) something they had not previously recognized. Perhaps Paul should not have stayed away so long. In Jerusalem the authorities now saw that Paul had been entrusted (by whom? – not by them but by the Lord himself) with the Gospel, or, to express the matter more carefully, with a form of the Gospel τὸ εὐαγγέλιον τῆς ἀκροβυστίας. Peter had correspondingly been entrusted with the Gospel[14] of the circumcision, τῆς περιτομῆς. What exactly is the force of the two genitives? Lightfoot quotes Tertullian, *de Praescriptione Hereticorum* 23, Inter se distributionem officii ordinaverunt, non separationem evangelii, nec ut aliud alter sed aliis praedicaverunt. This is true in its positive assertion, not true in its negative. The Christian message to the uncircumcised either did or did not include the requirement that in order to become members of the redeemed people of God they should be circumcised and observe other aspects of the law. If it did, a demand that would change their manner of life their relation

---

[13] The use of the middle προσανέθεντο may suggest *contributed nothing of their own resources* (see Liddell and Scott), but this would have been implied in any case.

[14] It is hardly possible linguistically not to insert this noun.

with their environment was being laid upon the would-be converts; more important, the inadequacy for salvation of the work of Christ was being asserted. If the message did not contain this requirement, the special relation of the Jewish people to God was called in question; if it was not negated it was at least modified. In either case the Gospel of the uncircumcision would differ from the Gospel of the circumcision. It is true that in 1.6f. Paul had virtually said, There is only one Gospel; anything that differs from (my) Gospel is not a Gospel. This conviction was bound eventually to cause trouble, but at least for the present it was an important achievement to have the recognition of 'the Gospel which I preach among the Gentiles' (2.2), even if Peter was preaching something rather different to Jews.

Peter had been entrusted with (the Gospel of) the circumcision: he was a missionary to Jews. This is not quite consistent with the picture of him given in Acts, but this indeed is not quite consistent with itself. In the narrative of Acts 10 Peter does indeed preach to, associate with, and baptize the Gentile Cornelius. It requires however a vision and the voice of God to persuade him to do so (10.15), and he draws attention to the anomalous behaviour involved (10.34–35, 47–48; also 11.2–3, 11–12, 17). In this context Peter may be a missionary to Jews; he is a missionary to Gentiles only under special constraint (and it may be added, to a Gentile who might be said to be half a Jew already). But in Acts 15.7–10 he declares himself to have been the founder of the Gentile mission and that he and his Jewish ancestors have found the Law an intolerable burden. Peter in Acts, however, we must for the moment set aside. In Galatians he is the leader of the Jewish mission.

There can be little doubt that in Gal. 2.7 we must supply the words τὸ εὐαγγέλιον before τῆς περιτομῆς. There is no alternative after πεπίστευμαι τὸ εὐαγγέλιον τῆς ἀκροβυστίας. There is a similar but more difficult ellipsis in v. 8. He who operated on Peter so as to produce (εἰς) an apostolate for the circumcision operated also on me for (εἰς) the Gentiles. εἰς τὰ ἔθνη recalls εἰς ἀποστολὴν τῆς περιτομῆς, and many translations supply or imply 'so as to produce an apostolate for the Gentiles'. This may

9

be correct. The ellipsis would be in Paul's style. But one wonders whether he is reproducing the words of the men of repute, and whether they could not bring themselves to use the word ἀποστολή for Paul's mission because they did not believe Paul to be an ἀπόστολος. The same expression, εἰς τὰ ἔθνη, recurs in v. 9, together with εἰς τὴν περιτομήν. Again there is an ellipsis, or rather there are two. In this case however the omitted but understood words must be verbs because each is introduced by ἵνα (ἵνα ἡμεῖς εἰς . . . αὐτοὶ δὲ εἰς . . .) It may be a very simple verb: *go*, *preach*, *be sent*. It can hardly involve a noun: that we should be an *apostolate* to . . . , that they should be an *apstolate* to . . . It is possible that the form of words was deliberately chosen so as to avoid the suggestion that Paul was an apostle.[15]

There is then in this account of a Jerusalem meeting a recognition, expressed in the two participles ἰδόντες and γνόντες, of Paul and his work. 'They saw that I had been entrusted with the Gospel, they took knowledge of the grace that had been given me.' This recognition must have been welcomed by Paul; his work was not facing destruction. It was however a limited recognition. It came near to implying, if not actually saying, that there were two Gospels, one for Jews and one for Gentiles. This Paul did not believe. There is no distinction, for all have sinned and lack the glory of God. Is God the God of the Jews only? Is he not also God of the Gentiles? Yes, he is God of the Gentiles too, if indeed there is one God, who will justify the circumcision by faith and the Gentiles through faith (Rom. 3.22, 23, 29, 30).

Paul would no doubt have preferred one united mission going simultaneously, as his own did, to both Jews and Gentiles. The division of labour contemplated in Gal. 2.9, however, might have worked on the Jerusalem side, if the Jerusalem apostles were content to confine their work to Jews (though Peter appears to constitute something of a problem and an exception, though in Galatians he is singled out as the apostle of the circumcision). Paul certainly

---

[15] H. Lietzmann, *An die Galater* (*HNT* 10); Tübingen: Mohr, 1932), p. 13: '. . . unlogisch angehängt der Finalsatz ἵνα ἡμεῖς κτλ, abhängig von dem unausgesprochenen Gedanken: "mit der näheren Bestimmung".'

never understood his work to be confined to Gentiles. He cannot have given a *pledge* (if this is what δεξιά means) that he would never preach to Jews. The theological argument of Romans 9–11 does not mean that he had abandoned them to the eschatological mercy of God.

To this agreement – an agreement that each party should go its own way – there was only one addition: μόνον (2.10). This solitary addition was that we should remember the poor (τῶν πτωχῶν ἵνα μνημονεύωμεν). It is impossible to be certain whether the tense of the verb is significant. If it is to be pressed the sense will be, *We were to continue to remember*, with the implication that Paul had already been occupied with the relief of the poor; the famine relief visit of Acts 11 comes to mind. But the verb may express only hope and intention for the future. Paul certainly pursued his work of collecting money for Jerusalem, though he had doubts about its acceptability. Romans 15 shows that he understood πτωχοί both in its literal sense and as referring to the Jewish Christians who by permitting if they did not further the dissemination of the Gospel to the Gentiles has been willing to share their spiritual gifts. It is clear too that he hoped that his collection would help to cement the unity of the church.

Only (Gal. 2.10): unless the word is discounted one is bound to infer that at this meeting nothing was said – at least, nothing was decided – about meals shared by Jewish and Gentile Christians, and that no decrees of abstention were imposed on Gentiles. It must have been agreed that Gentile Christians did not need to keep the Law, or Paul's Gentile mission could not have been approved. The men of repute added nothing to me (2.6): I continued as before; so presumably did they, addressing the Gospel to an already Law-keeping community, and assuming that converts would continue to keep the Law they had always observed. It may go too far to say that this was a step on the way to two churches, or to a church with two authorities, but at least it contemplated a church that included one law-observant and one non-law-observant division. There is no hint of any such thing as the so-called Apostolic Decree of Acts 15.

That the meeting described in Gal. 2.6–10 had produced no regulations to make possible and to control meals shared by Jewish and Gentile Christians is confirmed by the new paragraph, 2.11–14. If there had been a Decree accepted by James and Peter, Paul and Barnabas, it would certainly have been observed at Antioch in the presence of three of its sponsors, and the fourth sponsor, James, would have had no cause for complaint. In fact his complaint was so strongly expressed that it frightened Peter into withdrawing from the common meals. Barnabas too – even (καί) Barnabas – followed him. The meeting of 2.6–10 had recognized two missions,[16] but it did not contemplate any full connection between them. Paul goes on to record his debating rebuke of Peter and its theological supplement,[17] whether this was made at the time or added after subsequent reflection. What happened after this we do not know. What became of the relation between Paul and Peter? In 1 Corinthians there seems to have been at least a partial reconciliation; see 1 Corinthians 1–3; 9.5; 15.5, 11.[18] What became of the relation between Paul and Barnabas? What became of the relations between Paul and the church of Antioch? Does Gal. 1.1 mean that he no longer had a commission from Antioch?

For the present we are dealing with relations between Paul and the Jerusalem church, and there is little more explicit evidence. It is clear that there were in Galatia Jewish Christians who were urging upon the Galatians circumcision and perhaps other Jewish practices (cf. 4.10) These were *those who are troubling you* (οἱ ταράσσοντες ὑμᾶς, 1.7) with their attempt to pervert the Gospel. In 5.10 the corresponding singular is used, ὁ ταράσσων ὑμᾶς, with the added note that he will bear his judgement, *whoever he may be*, ὅστις ἐὰν ᾖ. This recalls 2.6, where Paul says of the men of repute, ὁποῖοί ποτε ἦσαν οὐδέν μοι διαφέρει, whoever they were makes no

---

[16] See M. D. Goulder, *A Tale of Two Missions* (London: SCM Press, 1994), which contains much that is apposite to this discussion.

[17] See Essay 2 (Christocentricity at Antioch).

[18] See my essay 'Cephas and Corinth' in O. Betz, M. Hengel and P. Schmidt (eds), *Abraham unser Vater* (*FS* O. Michel) (AGSU V; Leiden: Brill, 1963), pp. 1–12; also Galatians 2.

difference to me.[19] Were then these *troublers* the Pillars, with James and Peter as their representative heads? In 6.12, 13 Paul says of the motives of those who seek the circumcision of the Galatians that they wish to make a fair show in the flesh, they wish to avoid persecution for the cross of Christ, they wish to glory in your flesh. He adds that they do not themselves keep to the Law. Taken in the ordinary and most natural sense (and not as referring to the law of love – 5.14) this seems very improbable; the two parts of v. 13 must be taken together and understood to mean: It is not the keeping, the honouring, of the Law that is their true motive, but the (very common and natural human) desire to have some visible basis for glorying. This makes us think rather of the false brothers of 2.3–5, with their emphasis on circumcision, than of the Pillars, but it also raises difficult, perhaps in the end unanswerable, questions about the two groups and their relation with each other. Did the false brothers, in Jerusalem, in Galatia, in Corinth (see below, p. 14) claim to have the support of the Jerusalem apostles, to represent them and their authority? It must be remembered that when, in ancient times, agents were sent out to act on behalf of those who commissioned them, the latter had no means of controlling those who were intended to represent them. Means of communication, did of course exist, but an agent sent from Jerusalem into distant parts (say, Galatia or Corinth) could easily, in good faith or bad, misrepresent the one who had sent him. 'Of course Peter and James would expect you to be circumcised; how else could you share in the blessings of the Jewish Messiah?'

The references to Peter in 1 Corinthians suggest that he engaged in wide-ranging missionary travels.[20] There is nothing (except Galatians 2) to suggest that he confined his work to Jews. In 1 Corinthians 1–3 he seems to be somewhat less warmly treated than Apollos, but, even if not above criticism, he is a colleague rather than an enemy. In 9.5, though he makes use of privileges which Paul did not accept, it is recognized that he had a right to them. At 15.5 he is the primary witness to the resurrection. The relative

[19] See n. 13.
[20] See n. 18.

dates of 1 Corinthians and Galatians are not easy to determine.[21] Did Peter fall away from his Corinthian standard to fail (under pressure from James) in Antioch? Or did he, left to himself, return to the practices he had followed before he received the message from James? The psychoanalysis of Peter is hardly a proper task for a historian, but his behaviour, so far as we can observe it, seems to have been somewhat wayward, and, it is probably true to say that (unlike Paul and James) he was not a born leader, rather, a useful figurehead, whom any party might be glad to enrol, if only for a time.

2 Corinthians is important because of the close parallel between the situation disclosed there and that described in Galatians 2. As in Galatians, there are two groups,[22] one of which is dismissed in the strongest terms (they are false apostles, evil workers, servants of Satan: 11.13, 15), whereas the other, the 'super-apostles', ὑπερλίαν ἀπόστολοι, meets with nothing worse than gentle irony. The parallel with the false brothers and the Reputed Pillars is so close that it seems almost certain that we must identify the two pairs of groups. It would not be surprising if Paul's assessment of Jerusalem remained unaltered between the two letters. What must be added here is that the offending group may have been represented by an outstanding leader. Singular pronouns and verbs occur in 2 Cor. 10.7, 10, 11; 11.4, and it is hard to doubt that Paul had in mind a leading adversary of exceptional virulence. Cf. 2.5–11; 7.8–13.[23] One is inclined to suggest that this unnamed person is Peter, but Peter's place must be among the Pillars, even though (see above) he seems to have been a shaky pillar. If not Peter, who? We do not know. But again the question of the relation between the vehemently anti-Pauline group and Jerusalem cannot be avoided.

---

[21] I do not discuss the date of Galatians here; to do so would involve a discussion of the meaning of *Galatia*, which would occupy too much space.

[22] See my commentary on 2 Corinthians (London: A. & C. Black, 1973); also E. Käsemann, 'Die Legitimität des Apostels', *ZNW* 41 (1942), pp. 33–71; reprinted separately, Wissenschaftliche Buchgesellschaft, Darmstadt, 1956.

[23] See the notes in my commentary (n. 22).

So much for Paul's own story of his relations with Jerusalem. We turn to the account given in Acts of the same theme – Paul and the church of Jerusalem.

In the Acts narrative of his conversion Paul is commissioned, as we learn through the instructions given to Ananias, to bear Christ's name before nations (ἔθνη), kings, and the children of Israel (Acts 9.15). He begins without delay to preach, but in the synagogues, and therefore to Jews, (9.20). I say, 'therefore to Jews'; this calls for qualification. The majority of those present in the synagogues of Damascus, as elsewhere, would undoubtedly be Jews by race. There might also be proselytes, fully accepted into Judaism by circumcision (if they were males) and obedience to the Law of Moses in its entirety and equally counting as Jews. The congregation might include also Gentiles whose general acceptance of Jewish theology and ethics had led them to the synagogue service but not, so far, into full proselytization. Whether such persons occupied a recognized, accepted, status in the Jewish community, and were generally known by the designation 'God-fearers', are disputed questions.[24] It is sometimes held that these, whom Paul might hope to win for his new 'Christian Judaism' without imposing the forbidding barrier of circumcision, constituted Paul's main interest in the synagogue. This is doubtful. They may be referred to in Acts 13.16, 43, 50 (Paul at Pisidian Antioch), but this is uncertain. In Acts they are not mentioned elsewhere in relation to Paul's missionary work. There seems to be no reference to them in Paul's letters. Their connection (it there was such a connection) with apostolic Christianity may have arisen through a non-Pauline channel.[25]

Acceptable no longer in the synagogues Paul was soon forced to flee from Damascus and came to Jerusalem (9.25–26). At once he sought to confer with 'flesh and blood' and to join those who were apostles before him (contrast Gal. 1.16–17). He essayed to join the disciples. Naturally suspicious, they were persuaded by

---

[24] See my *ICC Commentary on Acts* (n. 3), Vol. 1 (Edinburgh: T&T Clark, 1994), pp. 499–501, 629–31.

[25] I hope to return to this question.

Barnabas, who brought Paul to the apostles and convinced them that Paul's conversion was genuine. How and why Barnabas came into the matter remains a mystery, but once in he plays an important part. According to Acts, he was a Cypriote, that is, a Jew (indeed, a Levite) normally or at least originally domiciled in Cyprus, but also a member of the earliest Christian community in Jerusalem (Acts 4.36–37). He was trusted by the Jerusalem apostles; in addition to the present passage see 11.22, where he is sent as an envoy to Antioch, where he shared in the extension of mission work to Gentiles (11.23–24). For his later association with Paul see below; there is no apparent reason why he should at the beginning have taken up Paul's cause, accepting him more readily than the Twelve were inclined to do. Perhaps we have to be content to say that the two took to each other; it is the sort of thing that sometimes happens. Accepted by the Jerusalem apostles Paul continued his work as a preacher. This provoked an attack on his life, by the Hellenists[26] and Paul was sent off to Tarsus (9.36). From Tarsus, he was brought by Barnabas to share in the mixed Jewish and Gentile evangelism that was going on in Antioch (11.25–26). The two were sent to Jerusalem with aid from the church at Antioch for the famine-stricken city (11.36). Of Paul nothing more is directly heard till the end of chapter 12, when the mission is completed. In 13.1–3 Barnabas and Paul are sent by the church of Antioch on a preaching mission, which takes them into fully Gentile territory (Acts 13; 14). This mission seems – according to Acts – to have been carried out in complete independence of Jerusalem; at its end (14.26–28) the missionaries report back to Antioch, which evidently was their base.

At this point (Acts 15.1-5)[27] travellers came down to Antioch from Judaea. Judaea can hardly exclude Jerusalem; it may be that Luke did not name Jerusalem because he did not wish to associate

---

[26] For *the Hellenists* (Ἑλληνιστάς) there is a variant reading, *the Greeks* (Ἕλληνας). Luke appears to use the word Hellenist in different ways (6.1; 9.29; 11.20).

[27] Is this the same as the Judaean visitation of Gal. 2.12? The date of Galatians cannot be discussed here; see n. 21.

it too closely with the assertion made by the travellers. This was that the Gentiles cannot be saved unless they are circumcised and observe the Law of Moses. This intervention in Antioch provoked a meeting[28] in Jerusalem, at which James, Peter, Paul, and Barnabas, and others, were present. So far the Acts story is closely parallel to that of Galatians 2. The themes discussed are also related though they are not identical. In Galatians, Paul presented and sought recognition for his mission to the Gentiles and the Gospel on which it was based. This of course included as an important negative element the non-requirement of circumcision. The Acts Council begins from the question whether observance of the Law, including the law of circumcision, was to be required of Gentile converts. The Acts account, however, has so much to do with food laws that it seems to move into a consideration of the terms on which Gentile Christians and Jewish Christians may share meals.

The meeting begins with much discussion (15.7) but none of it is reported till Peter speaks. He recalls that it was through him that the mission to Gentiles began; it was through him that the Gentiles first heard the word of the Gospel and believed. (The reference is of course to the story of Cornelius in Acts 10.) God bore witness to them – that is, to their valid membership of his people – by giving them the Holy Spirit, as he had at the beginning to Peter and his colleagues. To insist on the requirements of the Law would be to tempt God; those requirements had been a burden that neither Peter nor his (Jewish) ancestors had been able to bear. Salvation was by faith, not circumcision. Peter is thus represented as in effect the apostle of the Gentiles, not (as he is in Galatians) the apostle of the circumcision. This – almost Pauline – speech, made by Peter, raises other difficulties. In chapter 10 Peter had taken some persuading to have dealings with the Gentile Cornelius, and professes never to have eaten unclean food. Barnabas and Paul follow, but only report signs and portents done among the

---

[28] A Western variant in 15.2 suggests that Paul and Barnabas were summoned to appear on trial in Jerusalem. It is probably not original; the ensuing narrative is not a trial.

Gentiles.[29] The decisive speech is that of James, who begins with a quotation from Amos which provides biblical authority for the action that Peter had justified in terms of its outcome: if the mission to the Gentiles results in the gift of the Spirit it must be right. It was, James argues from Scripture, always God's intention to acquire a people from among the Gentiles. This however does not mean the immediate unconditional acceptance of Gentiles; there are necessary[30] stipulations: Gentiles must abstain from the defilements caused by (the worship of) idols, from fornication, from strangled food, and from blood.[31] As Acts 15 stands, introduced by 15.1–5, these are conditions of salvation. They constitute basic Judaism, those fundamental articles which a Jew must observe, even at pain of death; and Gentiles if they would be saved must observe them too. It seems however that they could have been understood and were perhaps intended as conditions under which Jews and Gentiles could eat together. This at least would apply to the prohibition of εἰδωλόθυτα (so v. 29; v. 20 is less specific), of strangled food (πνικτά), and of blood (if αἷμα refers to blood not drained out of meat used for food, not if it means *bloodshed*). The prohibition of fornication does not fit this setting.

The conclusion of the meeting was put in a letter (15.24–29), in which the Jerusalem church, headed by the apostles, disavows any connection with those who by demanding the circumcision of Gentile believers had upset the church of Antioch. The letter was sent in the first instance to Antioch, then to the Gentile churches in general (16.4). Paul continued his mission with, as far as Acts tells us, no change in his method or his message. He was however no longer accompanied by Barnabas. The separation between the two is described in Acts 15.37–40. Its cause is quite different from the dispute of Gal. 2.13.

---

[29] A strong case can be made for regarding v. 12 as a Lucan insertion; see R. Bultmann, 'Zur Frage nach den Quellen der Aposteileschichte', in A. J. B. Higgins (ed.), *New Testament Essays: Studies in Memory of T. W. Manson* (Manchester: Manchester University Press, 1959), pp. 68–80.

[30] The significance of ἐπάναγκες should not be underestimated.

[31] So v. 20, in v. 29, from food offered to idols, from blood, from strangled things, and from fornication. See *ICC Acts*, Vol. 2 (n. 3), pp. 730–6.

The story of the Council is on the surface a plain tale, but when closely considered it leaves the reader asking questions, which the text does not, or does not wholly, answer. It is not as clear as at first appears. The most important questions are the following.

(1) Is the outcome of the meeting a statement of conditions which Gentile converts must satisfy in addition to faith in Jesus Christ, or a set of regulations designed to facilitate meals shared by Jewish and Gentile Christians? Does the discussion change course part way through?

(2) If they were conditions of salvation, or even of full Christian fellowship, would Paul have accepted them? Does he ever allude to them?

(3) If, as is often thought, Acts 15 and Galatians 2 refer to the same meeting in Jerusalem, and if that meeting produced conditions of table fellowship, could the dispute of Gal. 2.11–14 have arisen? See above, pp. 11f.

(4) James's quotation of Amos 9.11 (Acts 15.16–18) is relevant and makes his point if it is read in the Greek of the LXX, not if it is read in the Hebrew of the MT. Would James in a Jewish meeting held in Jerusalem, have used the Greek? It seems possible but unlikely; but we do not know.

Paul may have visited Jerusalem at Acts 18.22;[32] it is possible to guess that he did, and possible on the basis of that guess to guess what happened, and thus to guess further why Luke decided not to record the visit. But these guesses need not be allowed to intrude here. The next visit recorded in Acts begins at 21.15. It is more than a guess that on this visit Paul brought with him and delivered the product of the collection for Jerusalem that he had made in the Gentile churches (see Rom. 15.25–28, and other passages), but the only possible allusion to it is at Acts 24.17; one wonders why there is not more. He was received in a friendly fashion by James (apparently now at the head of the Jerusalem

---

[32] See *ICC Acts*, Vol. 2 (n. 3), pp. 880f.

church – there is no reference to Peter or to any other apostle), accompanied by 'the elders' (21.18). All glorify God at the news of Paul's mission to the Gentiles; but a situation has arisen that must be dealt with (21.20, 21). The Jewish-Christian church now numbers many tens of thousands of believers; they are all zealous for the Law, and they have heard that Paul is teaching Diaspora Jews apostasy from the Law, that children of Jewish parents should not be circumcised, and that the legal customs should not be observed. Something must be done to correct this story – which, it is assumed (a charitable assumption?), cannot be true. It is proposed that Paul should prove his innocence of the charge and his loyalty to the Law by taking four men who were under a vow, being purified with them, and being at charges for them (that is, presumably, paying for the necessary sacrifices) so that they may shave their heads and thus be discharged from their vow. The details in relation to the regulations for vows are not clear, but the essential point is that a public act in fulfilment of the Law will prove Paul's good faith as a Jew. He accepts the proposal, but its execution is interrupted by a riot (21.27).

This narrative, like that in chapter 15, raises a number of familiar questions which must be briefly indicated here but need not be discussed.

(1) Paul is informed of the Council's Decree (15.29) as if he had never heard of it. Is this a divergent tradition, according to which, in contradiction with chapter 15, Paul was not present when the Decree was laid down? It is true that 21.25 can be understood as a reminder. 'On the question of believing Gentiles, you know what we decided, namely that . . .' This would imply the introduction of the new problem: 'We decided about Gentile Christians long ago; we now have a new question. What are the implications of the Gospel for believing Jews? Must they give up their Judaism?'

(2) Was the allegation against Paul true or false? We know what he said to Gentiles about circumcision; what did he say to Jews, especially to Jewish parents? Clearly if he was

guilty of the charge he would not have taken the desired steps to establish his innocence.

(3) If he was not guilty of the charge would the proposed plan have been necessary to establish his innocence? Would not a public statement by James have sufficed – 'We are satisfied that our brother Paul is a loyal Jew and does not teach that our sons should not be circumcised'? And would the proposed plan have been effective? What could it prove about Paul's behaviour in the Diaspora?

(4) Would Paul have taken part in a Jewish ceremony which was not essential to his living in company with other Jews, and thus would not be covered by 1 Cor. 9.20?

(5) Was there any connection (I put the matter in the broadest possible terms) between the funds of his collection brought by Paul to Jerusalem and the Temple charges (21.24) incurred in the process proposed by James and (according to Acts) undertaken by Paul?

From this point up to the end of Acts 26 Paul is in Jerusalem and Caesarea, in contact with Jews as well as Romans, but there is no reference to the Jerusalem church. It is not said that his nephew (23.16) was a Christian. This is a silence that permits no firm inference, but invites speculation. Did James and his colleagues, attempt nothing on behalf of the 'brother' (21.20), about whose innocence of apostasy they were now presumably satisfied? The silence in these chapters is matched by ignorance in Rome. The Roman Jews said to Paul, 'We have neither received letters about you from Judaea nor has any of the brothers when he came here reported or said anything bad about you' (28.21). After 28.15 we hear no more about Christians in Rome.

On this negative note, which gives to Paul the opportunity of representing Christianity to Roman Jewry on a clean sheet, the evidence of Acts regarding Paul's relations with the church of Jerusalem comes to an end.

We now have before us two accounts of substantially the same period in early Christian development, the period of Paul's pioneering missionary activity, with our attention focused on the relation between Paul and Jerusalem. It is natural to wish to combine the two accounts, to fit them together with a minimum of discrepancy so as to form a single logically connected narrative.[33] There is a place for this procedure; indeed it may be regarded as the goal of historical study: the formulation, based on all available sources, of a narrative of events that shall be as close as may be to what actually happened. If however this is the historian's final task it is not his first task, and it is not our task at this point.

We thus have two pictures (see p. 1) of Paul in his relations with the Christians at Jerusalem, for the two accounts that we have surveyed are by no means identical. In addition there is more historical raw material; it touches other aspects of Paul's life and work, and I hope later to be able to deal with it. For the present illustrative purpose these two, the fullest that we have, must suffice. They are the earliest and the next in succession, respectively. The Pauline picture of Paul, Paul's own account, is by definition a contemporary source. This does not mean that it is a perfect historical source. Not even an apostle is capable of complete detachment, or of knowing everything that others do, still less of knowing what they thought and how they were motivated. The most honest and self-critical of men will view his own actions differently from those of others. And Paul was not writing history. He was dealing urgently with difficult situations that had arisen in his churches but for the most part in his absence, so that the circumstances were known to him not by observation but only by report.

Over against this we have the Acts picture of Paul, which also must be judged defective. It was not contemporary,[34] though the author may have had some, sources that were more or less contemporary. It must be counted history – popular history written by an amateur historian, who however shows many signs of intelligence and of being well informed. Comparison with Paul's letters suggests

[33] Attempts at various points are made in some of the essays reprinted below; I hope to return to them.

[34] The date of Acts may probably be found in the late 80s or early 90s of the first century.

that he was not capable of entering fully into Paul's thought, greatly though he admired him.

It need not be said that the two pictures of Paul have much in common. In both Paul is an indefatigable traveller and a courageous and effective preacher of the Christian faith. In both he is a founder of churches and a pastor who cares deeply for his people – the children he has begotten in Christ. Names of colleagues and names of places appear in both the letters and Acts. These are all matters of considerable importance and must be weighed against the differences. Differences however do exist and have their own importance. In the letters Paul is an apostle; the last and least of apostles, perhaps not worthy to be called an apostle – but he calls himself one, and is confident of his vocation. It is well known that in only two verses in Acts (14.4, 14) is Paul called an apostle, and in these verses the word may be used, in the sense of evangelist appointed by the church of Antioch.[35] This may correspond with the phenomena noted above (pp. 9f.) in the text of Galatians 2. Does Acts represent a line of tradition that distinguishes Paul from the Founding Fathers?[36] It corresponds with this that though Acts has nothing to tell about the Twelve except Peter and James the brother of John they are to him a significant group, the indispensable witnesses to the resurrection of Jesus (1.8, 22; 2.32; 10.41–42; 13.31). Paul too knows them in this fundamental role (1 Cor. 15.5–7), but in this he counts himself with them (1 Cor. 9.1; 15.8) and speaks of them with a somewhat disparaging irony which is nowhere apparent in Acts. 'Whatever they were makes no difference to me' is very characteristic of Paul's self-portrait; there is no parallel in Acts.

This ironical view of the Jerusalem apostles must have been due in large measure to their failure to co-operate with him in his mission to the Gentiles. He was grateful for the fact that they did not stand in his way, but this was a negative virtue. Peter, in contrast with Paul, was an apostle of the circumcision. In this designation Paul may have done Peter something of an injustice. Acts tells the

[35] See *ICC Acts*, Vol. 1 (n. 24), pp. 666f., 671f., 678f.
[36] We may contrast the Pastoral Epistles, where Paul is the apostle *par excellence*.

story of Cornelius, and makes Peter claim explicitly to have been the first missionary to Gentiles. Was this completely false? Did Paul allow himself to be too strongly influenced by Peter's lapse (as he, Paul, saw it) at Antioch (Gal. 2.11–14)? In 1 Corinthians Peter appears to be an evangelist who did not refuse to deal with Gentiles. Did he perhaps confine himself to devout, God-fearing Gentiles, such as Cornelius? This is historical speculation, for which this is not the place, but it could account for the superficially inconsistent picture of Peter that our sources give us.

Acts describes other sallies into the non-Jewish world: Philip preaches in a (or the) city of Samaria, and Christians, scattered by the persecution that arose over Stephen make their way to Antioch and eventually begin to preach to Hellenists (Acts 8.5; 11.19, 20). It is thus part of the Acts picture of Paul that he was not the only or first evangelist of the Gentile world. This is a matter that must be considered further in another place, but it is a feature of the historical development – indeed it constitutes the outline of the first half of Acts – that is absent from the epistles, in which, of course, Paul makes no attempt to describe the expansion of the church as a whole. This was no part of his pastoral duty and he was not without themes of greater urgency.

The most striking contrast between the Pauline picture of Paul and the Acts picture is in the depth of theological substance in which each is grounded. The matter discussed below in Essay 2 (Christocentricity at Antioch) will provide a good starting point. It is frequently observed that Paul's rebuke to Peter falls into two parts. In the first (Gal. 2.14) Paul makes a logical debating point. 'If you, Jew as you are, live like a Gentile and not like a Jew, how do you compel Gentiles to live like Jews?' Peter's attitude is illogical and inconsistent. Paul continues, in the epistle (2.15–21), with a further argument which draws upon the theological principle of justification, which is by faith and not by works of law, and on the sole sufficiency of the work of Christ in dying for us. We need not here consider the question whether Paul said the whole of vv. 14–21 at Antioch, or said only what is reported in v. 14, adding vv. 15–21 in writing as the result of further reflection. The picture of the event which Paul chooses to give to us (first, to the Galatians) is rooted in profound theological thought and conviction.

It is the presence, in a situation created by the problem of meals shared by Jews and Gentiles, of this theological element that casts doubt upon the narrative in Acts, which depicts Paul as present and not dissenting when the Decree of Acts 15.29 is proposed and adopted, and as subsequently commending it to the churches (15.30; 16.4). Paul's own self-portrait represents him as unaware of the Decree (cf. Acts 21.25); at least he does not mention it and gives advice (e.g. 1 Cor. 10.25, 27) that runs contrary to it.[37] The theological principle involved is that which we have already noted. If faith is the criterion of justification, meat is not; if salvation is in Christ alone, salvation does not turn on the observance of a Decree, even though the Decree be drawn up by a body of apostles.

The epistles represent Paul as living in tension with the church of Jerusalem. He could fight openly with *false brothers, false apostles,* who simply inverted the relation between the Gospel and Judaism, and probably suspected that these opponents might have received some comfort and support from the higher ranks of Jerusalem Christianity. But he never says this in so many words, and of the leaders themselves he never says anything stronger than 'I am as good as they are'. 'Are they Hebrews? So am I. Are they Israelites? So am I. Are they the seed of Abraham? So am I. Are they servants of Christ? I am speaking like a fool, but I am even more.' The 'even more' meant more work, more suffering, more mortal peril. But for him the crucial issue was theological – the content of the Gospel. And they were on the right side. 'Whether then it be I or they, so we preach, and so you believed' (1 Cor. 15.12). They were witnesses of the risen Christ, and they passed on to Paul what they and he believed: 'Christ died for our sins according to the Scriptures, he was buried, he was raised on the third day according to the Scriptures.' (1 Cor. 15.3–4). Paul's theology was bound up with his vocation as a preacher. He could be liberal as regards some aspects of theology and practice (e.g. Rom. 14.5; Phil. 3.15–16),

---

[37] See my commentary on *1 Corinthians* (London: A. & C. Black, 1968, 1971), pp. 240f.

25

but there was only one Gospel (Gal. 1.7). This was constituted by a proposition at once historical and theological; see the passage quoted above from 1 Cor. 15.3–4, and cf. Rom. 10.8–10. He could assert (1 Cor. 15.12) that the Jerusalem apostles preached the Gospel as he did, for they attested Christ's death for sins and his resurrection. This was the base of his own developed and developing theology; that his Jerusalem colleagues did not draw from it all his inferences, both practical and dogmatic, did not disfranchise them, though it could leave him in an unpopular, uncomfortable, and misunderstood solitude. It is on the whole their de-theologized or, better, not yet theologized, version of the Gospel[38] that appears in Acts and determines the Acts picture of Paul. This was in part the result of the passing of time and of events subsequent to Paul's death. The Pauline tradition was always likely to be less theological than its origin; there have been very few theologians of Paul's weight. But it may well prove instructive to take further cross-sections of the tradition in the next hundred years or so of its existence. This is the task for a work on the Pauline tradition.

---

[38] For the positive value of this see *ICC Acts*, Vol. 2 (n. 3), especially pp. cxi–cxviii.

1

Eidōlothyta Once More

I am glad to have been asked to contribute to this volume in honour of Archbishop Methodios, and, knowing his interest in Corinth, to be given thereby the opportunity of returning briefly to Paul's Epistles to the Corinthian church. I recently had occasion to reconsider[1] 1 Corinthians 15, and, noting that Paul refers in two separate places, 15.21–22 and 15.45–49, to the figure of Adam, was able, I hope, to show that though the chapter is undoubtedly a unity Paul had in mind not only two different aspects of the theological significance of Adam but two different groups in the Corinthian church whom he found it necessary to correct in different ways. The first group were responsible for the blunt assertion, There is no resurrection of the dead (15.12). They had not meant to deny the resurrection of Christ, for they had accepted this when it was preached to them (15.11), but they failed to see that Christ died and rose as a representative, and it is this that Paul presses upon them in 15.20–22: As in Adam all die, even so in Christ shall all be made alive. The analogy with Adam enables him to move from the resurrection of Christ, which is accepted, to the resurrection of Christians, which had been denied. Paul turns to the second group at 15.35. They do not deny outright that there is

[1] The reconsideration was published in the proceedings of the ninth Colloquium Paulinum held at S. Paolo fuori le Mura in Rome in 1983. [See now *Résurrection du Christ et des Chrétiens (1 Co 15)*, Série Monographique de Benedictina, Section Biblico-Occuménique, 8; Rome, 1985; ed. Lorenzo De Lorenzi, pp. 99–122.]

to be a resurrection but ask, How are the dead raised? With what kind of body do they come? It is clear – perhaps clearer in the twentieth century than in the first – that these questions can be asked with a sceptical intention. This intention however is not necessarily implied; the questioners may have been genuinely puzzled. In answering both scepticism and bewilderment Paul returns to the story of Adam, this time in order to prove his assertion (15.44) that if there is a σῶμα ψυχικόν there is also a σῶμα πνευματικόν.

Thus one of the major themes of 1 Corinthians, that of resurrection, when carefully examined, leads to the discovery of a more complicated situation than has hitherto been recognized. There is nothing surprising in this complication. The Christian faith can be perverted in many ways and the Corinthians were inventive people. Once this kind of variety has been noticed it is natural to look for it elsewhere. I have already noted an example of sorts in 2 Corinthians,[2] where it seems that Judaizing invaders of the church were obliged in the interests of expediency to adopt criteria of apostleship and churchmanship dictated by the Gentile church on which it was their intention to impose themselves. It is coexistence of these two viewpoints, two programmes, an end along with means to the end, that has led some commentators to describe the invaders as simple Judaizers, others to think them Hellenistic θεῖοι ἄνδρες.

Other examples may be found. One of the most frequently noted features of the Corinthian church is the existence within it of dissensions and divisions. It is not always pointed out that the divisions are themselves divided; that is, the Corinthian church was divided in at least three different ways.

(a) There were divisions based on personal allegiance. Paul has heard through members of Chloe's household that there were such divisions (ἔριδες) and he explains what he means (1 Cor. 1.11–12). Each of you has his party-cry: I belong to

---

[2] See C. K. Barrett, *The Second Epistle to Corinthians* (London, 1973), pp. 28–30, 270–87.

Paul, I belong to Apollos, I belong to Cephas, I belong to Christ. The characteristics of the four groups have been endlessly debated; fortunately there is no need here to enter into the debate. Whatever the tenets, or ways of living, that marked the groups may have been, those who adhered to them attached themselves to persons. It must not be assumed that those whose names were used desired to be leaders of rival factions; it was enough that they existed and had names that could be used as labels.

(b) It is clear from 1 Corinthians 11 that when the church assembled for its common meal those who were present fell into groups which were different in number and probably in composition from those in (a) and were probably quite unrelated to them. The rich formed one group to eat and drink as they pleased; the poor receded into the background to eat with shame their scanty supplies. An assembly of that kind, says Paul (11.17), will do more harm than good. But, he reflects, no doubt there must be parties (αἱρέσεις, 11.19) in order that the tried Christians may stand out. Here then was another kind of division in the Corinthian church.

(c) A third kind of division arose out of the problem of food sacrificed to idols, which is discussed in 1 Corinthians 8–10. This is often referred to as the division between the weak and the strong; it would perhaps be wise to avoid this terminology (which I recognize that I have used myself) since though Paul uses the word *weak*, and this may be said to imply the word *strong*, the latter word does not occur in this part of the epistle (as it does in Rom. 15.1, though in that verse only in the chapter and a half in Romans that deal with a similar division). It is worth while to note that *weak* occurs in the following verses:

8.7: Their conscience, which is weak (ἀσθενὴς), is defiled.

8.9: . . . a stumbling-block to those who are weak (ἀσθενέσιν).

8.10: . . . this weak (ἀσθενοῦς) man's conscience.

29

ON PAUL

8.11: . . . the weak man (ὁ ἀσθενῶν) perishes.
8.12: . . . their conscience, weak (ἀσθενοῦσαν) as it is.
9.22: . . . to the weak (ἀσθενέσιν) I became weak (ἀσθενής), in
order that I might win the weak (ἀσθενεῖς).

It appears that ἀσθενής, ἀσθενεῖν, occur only in chapter 8 and in the summarizing, backward-looking verse 9.22. The word ἰσχυρός does not occur in 1 Corinthians 8–10; the nearest approach to it is the comparative ἰσχυρότεροι at 10.22, which is scarcely relevant since the comparison is with God (Are we to provoke the Lord? Are we stronger than he?). It may possibly allude to a group who thought and spoke of themselves as οἱ ἰσχυροί, but this is hypothetical and not probable. What is certain is that Paul saw fit to use the word *weak* very frequently in chapter 8, not at all in chapter 10; that the word *strong* is not used at all (unless 10.22 is allowed to count), so that it is only stretching the evidence that we can find in either chapter 8 or chapter 10 a group whom we may properly, that is, with some basis in Paul's usage, describe as *the strong*. The point that we must note at present is that terminology does not unite but rather separates the treatments of εἰδωλόθυτα in chapters 8 and 10.

These two treatments have been made the ground for dividing 1 Corinthians into two or more letters written on different occasions. I have tried elsewhere to show that this argument is unconvincing.[3] Chapter 9 is not (as some think) out of place. In Chapter 8 Paul appeals to those who feel free (as he does himself) to eat sacrificial meat to forgo their right of Christian freedom and (when occasion requires it) to abstain in the interests of weaker Christian brothers whose weak consciences might be hurt or even constrained into sin by the unbridled exercise and example of liberty. In chapter 9 he goes on to show that he is not asking of these liberated Christians anything that he does not himself voluntarily do. As an apostle he has even greater rights, but he has

[3] C. K. Barrett, *The First Epistle to the Corinthians* (London, 1968), pp. 12–17; also e.g. H. Conzelmann, *Der erste Brief an die Korinther* (KEK; Göttingen, 1969), pp. 13–15.

abjured them in the interests of the Gospel. He is prepared to become all things to all men, and this includes becoming weak to the weak. All this is by no means irrelevant, so that when in chapter 10 Paul returns to the question of sacrificial food and the Christian housewife's Sunday joint[4] we have no occasion for surprise or for conjecturing the combination of two letters.

I still find this argument convincing and do not wish to retract it, or the fuller statement of it that I have given in the past. There are however two points to which, in the light of the two Adam passages in chapter 15, it seems right to give further attention. The first is the simple fact that Paul deals with food sacrificed to idols twice. If it can be shown that the two treatments are not inconsistent, why did he not put them together, say all that had to be said by way of counsel to the advanced, free Christians, and then proceed to the material contained in chapter 9? It may be that the explanation is simple; Paul believed that he had finished with the subject and then thought of other points that he had omitted to make. Rather than rewrite the whole he added his new points as they occurred to him: Oh, and I forgot to say . . . This is possible, but it is a counsel of despair and not to be accepted unless all other possibilities fail. The second point to be borne in mind is that between the two treatments of εἰδωλόθυτα, there intervenes not only chapter 9, which on consideration proves to be reasonably close to both, but also 10.1–13, which at first sight seems to diverge further from the point, and to be intended to introduce the treatment of the Supper which follows (after an interval) in chapter 11. Can the intervention of 10.1–13 be explained as satisfactorily as that of chapter 9?

Yes, it can; provided that we may suppose that chapter 10 deals with a different group of 'free Christians', who contended for freedom to eat things sacrificed to idols on different grounds, which however Paul could no more regard as satisfactory than he regarded those of chapter 8.

[4] A. Ehrhardt, *The Framework of the New Testament Stories* (Manchester, 1964), pp. 276–90.

For he did not regard as adequate the grounds he described in chapter 8 as adduced by some of the Corinthian Christians. Their conclusion was correct, but their method of proof was mistaken. We all have gnosis, said the Corinthians. The content of their gnosis was that an idol has no real existence. There is only one God; there is only one Lord. They used the formula:

> For us there is one God, the Father, from whom come all things and to whom our own being leads;
>
> And one Lord Jesus Christ, through whom all things, including ourselves, come into being (8.6).

With this statement Paul cannot but agree. Indeed, he probably framed it himself; the Corinthians quote it back at him. But he makes two comments on it. First, gnosis puffs up; it is love that builds up. And secondly, it is not true that we all possess this gnosis. There are some Christians for whom idolatry is intensely real. They are truly Christians; they believe that Christ has delivered them from the evil powers; but they also believe[5] that the powers still exist and still constitute a threat. For these reasons those who feel themselves free will, in the interests of their fellow Christians, use their freedom with restraint. They have overlooked the true ground of freedom, which is not gnosis, not the fact that they are γνωστικοί. Their point of view can be seen behind verse 8 which reveals a Corinthian opinion, to obtain which all that is necessary is to redistribute the negatives. We may infer that the liberated Corinthians said, 'Abstinence from food will not commend us to God; if we eat we lose nothing, nor if we do not eat are we advantaged.' This is true; there is nothing on which we can stand before God but his grace and the faith he grants us to enable us to receive his grace. But this carries with it the proposition that Paul actually writes. 'Food – the food that the free Christian feels at liberty to eat – does not commend us to God; if, like the weak, we abstain from eating, we lose nothing; if, like the strong, we do eat,

---

[5] As did Paul himself, see e.g. Rom. 8.38–39 with its reference to threatening powers.

we gain nothing.' Thus the whole of chapter 8 deals with the position of those who approach the question of sacrificial food from the angle of gnosis. Their conclusion is correct, but it calls for qualification in the light of Christian charity; more fundamentally, it is correct, but vitiated by the fact than it is based on the wrong premises and established by the wrong methods. It depends on gnosis not on faith and love.

What of chapter 10? It begins abruptly. There is a connection with what immediately precedes, but it is not close. The γὰϱ of verse 1 looks back in the first instance to 9.27. I discipline myself, says Paul, because there is in the past history of Israel a shocking case of indiscipline which had disastrous consequences. The real connection however does not appear till we have come round once more to the matter of food sacrificed to idols. The opening paragraph of chapter 10 recalls the story of Israel in the wilderness. Our distant forefathers had a baptism; they were baptized into Moses in the cloud and in the sea. They had also a sacred meal consisting of spiritual food (presumably Paul is thinking of the God-given manna) and spiritual drink (he is certainly thinking of the water made to gush out of the rock). They were thus exceptionally blessed by God; but with most of them God was not pleased. Small wonder: they fell into idolatry, they committed fornication, they put God to the test, they complained against him. For these things they were severely punished.

Commentators for the most part agree that Paul recalled this piece of Old Testament history because the Corinthians misunderstood their sacraments, taking them to be a kind of defence behind which they could safely shelter. 'We have been baptized; we take part in the Lord's Supper; we may do what we please and do it with impunity.' Doubtless this general interpretation is correct. But should not the point be made more precise? Is not the cue for the second discussion of εἰδωλόθυτα the fact that just as some Corinthians argued for freedom in this matter on the grounds of gnosis, so others were saying, 'Because we have baptism and the Supper, and are protected by them, we may eat εἰδωλόθυτα?' Again, the conclusion was correct but the argument faulty.

33

It was faulty in its disregard of the Old Testament. The ancient dipping, eating, and drinking were no guarantees of immunity, and these things 'were written down as a warning for us' (10.11). The argument was faulty also in its understanding of the Supper.[6] Paul therefore found himself obliged to counter the false inference from the Supper by setting forth its true meaning; hence the reference to it in 10.16, 17. 'Paulus ist nun hier wie sonst nicht in der Lage, den Glauben an das Sakrament im Sinn einer modernen Geistigkeit bestreiten und damit zugleich seine Überspannung abwehren zu können, sondern er ist in der viel schwierigeren Lage, aus dem (echten) Sakrament gegen das (unechte) Sakrament streiten, mit dem Sakrament die Sakramentierer bekämpfen, aus dem Sakramentsglauben den Sakramentsaberglauben widerlegen zu müssen.'[7] The Christian Supper, Paul says, is not a religious immunization; rather it will teach you the true significance of sacred eating.[8] The cup of blessing which we bless is (as you yourselves profess) not merely a common cup of wine; it signifies, it is, a joint participation in the blood of Christ, that is in all that his blood-shedding has obtained for us. The broken loaf is not merely a basic part of our diet; it signifies, it is, a joint participation in the body of Christ. These therefore join us to one another, because they join us all to him. You may see an analogous relation between worshippers and that which a material object (the altar) signifies in the religious life of Israel (v. 18). At this point there is contact with

---

[6] Paul does not develop the theme of baptism.

[7] H. von Soden, *Urchristentum und Geschichte 1* (Tübingen, 1951), p. 260. Cf. in the same work p. 259: Certain critical questions 'gehen von einer das theologische Verständnis, von 1 Kor. auch sonst mehrfach hemmenden oder irreleitenden Auffassung der korinthischen Gnostiker als aufgeklärter Libertinisten aus, während sie vielmehr überspannte Enthusiasten des Pneumaglaubens sind. Sie setzen ihr Vetrauen nicht entscheidend auf die rationalististische Erwägung, dass es Keine Götzen gibt . . . sondern darauf, dass die mit den Sakramenten Christi Geweihten gegen alle Mächte gefeit sind und deshalb eine schrankenlose ἐξουσία haben'. Much of this is very well observed, but it fails to recognize that Paul has to deal with two groups. One is not inaccurately described as aufgeklärte Libertinisten, whereas the other consisted of those who put an exaggerated trust in the sacraments.

[8] It is true also that useful inferences can be drawn in the opposite direction.

Paul's argument against the gnostics in chapter 8. The meaning of the rhetorical questions is clear: an εἰδωλόθυτον is nothing – nothing more, that is, than any other piece of meat; an εἴδωλον is nothing – nothing more, that is, than any other piece of wood or stone or metal. But it would never have occurred to Paul to say that a demon was nothing; it was real, evil, and dangerous.[9] And to eat in a context determined by demons was incompatible with eating in a context determined by the Lord. Food will not harm you, but demons, if you let them, will.

Paul was in an awkward and complicated position. Two groups were contending for a view which he believed to be correct, but they were contending for it by arguments that he was bound to reject. Others were taking a view which he knew to be mistaken, but he was obliged by Christian charity to defend them in their error. He could hardly take a step without appearing to say something that he did not mean. Hence he winds up the discussion in the most practical terms, You may buy in the meat-market any meat that pleases you. You may go out to dinner in any company you wish and eat whatever is laid on the table. But you must consider the conscience of others; in all you do you must seek the glory of God; you must never do anything that would prevent another from accepting the Gospel, or, if he has accepted it, would drive him from it. All this[10] is clear enough for anyone. But no doubt Paul was wise, even if it led to some repetition and the possibility of some confusion, to separate from each other two erroneous arguments, the one based on gnosis and the other on an exaggerated sacramentarianism. And we may be grateful that his method contributes one more small insight into the make-up of the Corinthian church.

---

[9] Cf. n. 5.
[10] Except verse 29b, which I have tried to explain in my commentary (n. 3).

2

Christocentricity at Antioch

There have been many studies of the history and theology of the early Christian Council of which we have two accounts, in Acts 15 and Galatians 2.[1] This is not the place to add another comprehensive study; all that will be attempted here will be to look at the Council and its aftermath from the point of view determined by the title of this volume. This involves an examination not so much of the decisions of the Council (so far as these are ascertainable – and they evoke considerable problems) as of the kind of discussion that seems to have taken place and the criteria that were employed. It will be necessary first to look at some particular points, not all of which have always been noted in more general discussions.

I

The Epistle to the Galatians refers to two visits[2] to Jerusalem made by Paul. The earlier visit is seldom brought into discussions of the later, but there is a strong case for considering it. In Galatians 2 Jerusalem is represented by the three 'Pillars', James, Cephas, and

[1] There is no space here, and I think no need, for argument that the two passages refer to the same event. For recent discussion of the Council see several essays by J. D. G. Dunn and his recent commentary on Galatians (J. D. G. Dunn, *A Commentary on the Epistle to the Galatians* [BNTC; London, 1993], with bibliographical information).

[2] Two visits, not, as Acts may suggest, three. Even without Gal. 1.20 one would have to recognize that prudence if not honesty would compel Paul to omit nothing.

37

John. Of these the third seems to have played no notable part,[3] the other two are mentioned in Gal. 1.18–19 as the only Jerusalem figures met on his first visit. It is often argued that the fact that Cephas is mentioned first, with James in second place, in chapter 1, whereas in chapter 2 the order is reversed, bears witness to the supersession of Cephas by James in the leadership of the Jerusalem church. This may well be true, though it is far from certain; what can be affirmed with confidence is that in chapter 1 as in chapter 2 the two were among, and probably were pre-eminent among, the leaders of the church. Is it not likely that the questions raised in chapter 2 were already in the air in chapter 1? It is true that a number of years[4] separated the two meetings and that the former may have taken place before the so-called First Missionary Journey of Acts 13; 14; but according to his own account (Gal. 1.16; cf. Acts 9.15; 22.21; 26.17) Paul knew from the beginning that he was called to be a missionary to the Gentiles, and according to Gal. 1.17 he had already been in Arabia – possibly for meditation and reflection, more probably for mission.

Paul says (Gal. 1.18) that he went to Jerusalem *to visit* (ἱστορῆσαι) Cephas, and stayed with him a fortnight, and that he also *saw* (εἶδον) James. We can hardly suppose that the latter verb means that he was content simply to gaze at James, as one of the notable sights of Jerusalem; it is reasonable to suppose that εἶδον looks back to and repeats ἱστορῆσαι. The meaning of ἱστορῆσαι was discussed by G. D. Kilpatrick,[5] who however emphasizes the distinction between ἱστορῆσαι and εἶδον. The former word (Kilpatrick quotes Liddell and Scott) means to visit a

---

[3] Acts mentions only James and Cephas; in Gal. 2.11–21 only these two are mentioned. Cf. Acts 3 and 4 for John's 'walking-on' role.

[4] There is no need here to consider whether the years of 1.18 have to be added to or are included in the fourteen years of 2.1, and the effect of inclusive reckoning. 'Ten or a dozen years' would do well enough.

[5] G. D. Kilpatrick, 'Galatians 1.18 ΙΣΤΟΡΗΣΑΙ ΚΗΦΑΝ', in A. J. B. Higgins (ed.), *New Testament Essays: Studies in Memory of T. W. Manson* (Manchester, 1959), pp. 144–9. See also O. Hofius, 'Gal. 1.18; ἱστορῆσαι Κηφᾶν', in *Paulusstudien* (WUNT 51; Tübingen, ²1994), pp. 255–67. I do not think that what I have suggested is necessarily inconsistent with Professor Hofius's view.

person with a view to eliciting information. 'St. Paul seeks information from St. Peter and not from St. James. Is there any information that the one had to give him that the other could not provide? St. Peter had been an eyewitness and disciple of Jesus. St. James could not claim to be a comparable informant about the teaching and the ministry. We know then of one kind of information for which St. Paul would go to St. Peter rather than St. James, information about Jesus' teaching and ministry' (148). Kilpatrick finds a difficulty for his own suggestion in Gal. 1.12; neither the difficulty nor Kilpatrick's solution of it is wholly convincing, and the difficulty disappears if the information that Paul sought from Cephas and James was information about the conduct of a Christian mission to Gentiles.

It may be suggested – I do not regard it as proved – that already at the time of Gal. 1.18–19 Paul believed that he had found a *modus vivendi* with the leaders in Jerusalem; it must have been the more disturbing when it appeared that the representatives of the Jerusalem church, claiming, though it may be falsely, the authority of their leaders, were attacking what had seemed to be an agreed position.

II

The last few lines anticipate a further subject of inquiry. If, ten years or more previously, there had been ground for the belief that Paul and the apostolic leadership of the Jerusalem church were in agreement regarding the basis and conditions of a mission to the Gentiles, why was the question raised again? It is sometimes said that Acts and Galatians give different reasons for the convening of a council. In Acts (15.1–5) the church at Antioch, provoked by the demand of visitors from Judaea that all Gentile converts should be circumcised and required henceforth to keep the Law, decided to send Paul, Barnabas, and others to Jerusalem to discuss the matter. According to Gal. 2.2 Paul (accompanied by Barnabas and Titus) went up to Jerusalem κατὰ ἀποκάλυψιν. There is no serious problem here; it could easily be that the same event is being described from two angles. The church meeting at Antioch that decided to send Paul and his companions to Jerusalem would not reach its decision as the result of parliamentary debate, but in some such way as that described in Acts 13.1–3, and what the Holy Spirit 'said' (through the mouth of prophets) could properly be described as an ἀποκάλυψις. What must be taken more seriously is the Western text of the passage in Acts. According to D and other Western authorities those who had come from Jerusalem gave orders (παρήγγειλαν) that Paul, Barnabas, and others should go up to Jerusalem in order to stand trial before them (ὅπως κριθῶσιν ἐπ' αὐτοῖς); 'them' (αὐτοῖς) would be the apostles and elders just mentioned. This gives a different picture of the intention and procedure of the event; it would probably however be a mistake to take this different picture very seriously. The reading is commonly reckoned among those in which the Western text gives a radically different understanding of events from that in the Old Uncial text, but the radically different understanding arises out of the Western text's habit[6] of brightening the colours of the basic narrative. Somewhat in the manner of a modern tabloid newspaper the Western text takes the opportunity of sharpening and embittering conflicts; here, if Paul is to be judged, he on his own side is described as διϊσχυριζόμενος. This however is not to say that the conflict was not sharp; only that it would probably go too far to suggest that Paul was standing in the dock.

Luke is unable here to avoid giving the information that Jerusalem was sending out envoys to convey anti-pauline propaganda to Pauline churches (which at this time would include Antioch). In view of Acts 15.24 (οἷς οὐ διεστειλάμεθα) we must not say, James was sending out envoys; this would perhaps go too far, but it is quite possible that the envoys claimed James's backing for what they did and certain that they carried commendatory letters.[7]

[6] C. K. Barrett, 'Is there a theological tendency in Codex Bezae?', in E. Best and R. McL. Wilson (eds), *Text and Interpretation. Studies in the New Testament presented to Matthew Black* (Cambridge, 1979), pp. 15–27.

[7] See 2 Cor. 3.1; C. K. Barrett, *A Commentary on the Second Epistle to the Corinthians* (BNTC; London, 1973), pp. 40, 106–110, 266.

III

Galatians also bears witness to the existence in Galatia of a counter-Pauline mission which demanded circumcision (and probably insisted also on the observance of Jewish festivals, 4.10). If these appear in Paul's account of the Council they will undoubtedly be the ψευδάδελφοι of 2.4.[8] It will be worthwhile to give these brief consideration. Paul says that they crept in to spy out our liberty (παρεισῆλθον κατασκοπῆσαι τὴν ἐλευθερίαν ἡμῶν) which we have in Christ Jesus. 'To spy out' is the translation usually given to κατασκοπῆσαι. In *Freedom and Obligation*[9] I did not seriously question it, but suggested that '"spying" refers to underhand methods, not precisely defined'. It may be that this is all that needs to be said, but it may be possible to go further. Lightfoot[10] translates 'to act as spies on', and comments 'κατασκοπεῖν generally signifies "to examine carefully", the form κατασκοπεύειν being most frequently used where the notion of treachery is prominent. For instances of the sense in the text however see 2 Sam. 10.3; 1 Chron. 19.3.' This is correct. κατασκοπῆσαι may mean (though it is not the commonest meaning) *to act as spies*; if this meaning is adopted it will be natural to ask, In whose interests were they acting as spies? Spies are usually the agents of an employer, who wishes to make use of the information they can bring. So it is in the passages adduced by Lightfoot; or rather, so it is assumed in the charge of spying that is in these passages falsely brought. In whose interests then were the false brothers acting? It is hard to find any answer other than, the leadership of the church in Jerusalem. There are, of course, free-lance spies who act on their own and sell information they acquire

[8] See 2 Cor. 11.13–26, with my *2 Corinthians* (n. 7) *ad loc.*; also C. K. Barrett, 'ΨΕΥΔΑΠΟΣΤΟΛΟΙ (2 Cor. 11.13)', in A. Descamps and R. P. A. de Halleux (eds), *Mélanges Bibliques en hommage au R. P. Béda Rigaux* (Gembloux, 1970), pp. 377–96.

[9] C. K. Barrett, *Freedom and Obligation: A Study in the Epistle to the Galatians* (London, 1985), p. 11.

[10] J. B. Lightfoot, *The Epistle of St. Paul to the Galatians. With Introduction, Notes and Dissertations* (London 1865 and later editions), p. 106.

to the highest bidder. From whom could they have hoped for a price but the leaders of the Jerusalem church?

It may be however that κατασκοπῆσαι has something more like its usual meaning, especially the nuance found in it by H. Schlier.[11] 'κατασκοπῆσαι ist "spionieren", "in feindlicher Absicht auskundschaften", "belauern", aber auch "inspizieren" und "examinieren". Bei der letztgennanten Bedeutung käme das Instanzenbewußtsein der Gegner zum Ausdruck.' For this meaning Schlier cites Polybius 10.20.2 and POxy 1414.4. In these passages however the middle is used, not as here, the active, and the meaning of *inspection*, in any formal sense, must be considered doubtful – doubtful, but not impossible, for it is no more than a formalized, regularized, purposive development of the more common meaning of κατασκοπεῖν, as when for example Menelaus looks round among his men to see who may be in difficulty.[12] The suggestion of furtive behaviour conveyed by παρεισάκτους and παρεισῆλθον, not to mention the ψευδ-element compounded in ψευδαδέλφους, must be borne in mind, and lends some support to the notion of a privy inspection of Paul's company and his practice.

Where had these false brothers operated? Some think in the Pauline churches generally. So Lietzmann:[13] 'Es handelt sich allgemein um das Auftreten judaistischer Spione und Aufwiegler in den paulinischen Gemeinden, um derentwillen Pls in Jerusalem nun sein Recht verteidigt, nicht etwa um eine Szene zwischen den ψευδάδελφοι und Pls in Jerusalem.' This is probably correct; we cannot say that it is confirmed by the evidence of Galatia and Corinth because Galatians and 1 and 2 Corinthians are later than the Council, but it finds some support in Acts 15.1–5. The aorist παρεισῆλθον however suggests strongly that there was a scene in Jerusalem, at which probably past events came to a head.

---

[11] H. Schlier, *Der Brief an die Galater* (KEK 7; Göttingen, ¹1949), p. 39.
[12] Euripides, *Helena* 1607.
[13] H. Lietzmann, *An die Galater* (HNT 10; Tübingen, 1932), p. 11.

IV

A question that can never be answered with complete confidence is the interpretation of the sentence about Titus, οὐδὲ Τίτος . . . ἠναγκάσθη περιτμηθῆναι. The simplest alternatives are: (a) He was circumcised, but not under compulsion; (b) He was not compelled to be circumcised, and was not circumcised. The problem becomes more complicated when, with the recognition that ἠναγκάσθη means that there was at least talk of compulsion, it is asked who tried to exert compulsion – the false brothers, or the church leaders, James, Cephas, and John. Lightfoot's argument[14] that Titus was not circumcised seems to me as nearly conclusive as may be, though there remain the possibility of laying a different emphasis on ἠναγκάσθη and on τῇ ὑποταγῇ, and the story in Acts of Paul's circumcision of Timothy. Of these however the first must be reckoned an improbable possibility, and the second is a problem primarily for the student of Acts.

The question where the authority to compel lay can be handled only by conjectural inference. There was probably a chain of command. The false brothers made their own conviction and desire clear: they believed that Titus should be circumcised. When they met with firm resistance however they had no means short of physical violence (cf. 2 Cor. 11.26) of achieving their end but could only appeal to higher authority. So one must conclude that either the Pillar Apostles chose not to support them[15] or found that they too were confronted by an unmovable object and retreated before Paul's resolution and arguments.[16] The former alternative would have led to a more harmonious conference, but the latter is the more probable in view of the combative style that Paul adopts – To whom not for one moment did I yield in subjection . . .

V

The combative style is reinforced by the way in which Paul speaks of his opposite numbers in the Council. In Gal. 2.9. they are named,

[14] J. B. Lightfoot, *Galatians* (above n. 10), p. 104.
[15] So J. D. G. Dunn, *Galatians* (above n. 1).
[16] So J. B. Lightfoot, *Galatians* (above n. 10).

James, Cephas, and John. Elsewhere (except in the reference to Peter as the leader of a mission) they are οἱ δοκοῦντες (2.2, 6), οἱ δοκοῦντες εἶναί τι (2.6), οἱ δοκοῦντες στῦλοι εἶναί (2.9). It is hard to miss the irony with which these expressions are used. The first pointer is the use of δοκεῖν εἶναί τι in 6.3: if anyone thinks himself to be something when he is nothing he deceives himself. We are dealing not with public reputation but with men's opinion of themselves. It is they who think themselves to be pillars, though no doubt there were many others who found it profitable, or thought it would be profitable, to use the same terms.[17] The ironical interpretation is powerfully confirmed by the double parenthesis: ὁποῖοί ποτε ἦσαν οὐδέν μοι διαφέρει, and πρόσωπον ὁ θεὸς ἀνθρώπου οὐ λαμβάνει. Others may be impressed by their powerful personalities and their authority, but Paul is not; and he does not think that God is. The paragraph as a whole takes so low a view of the Jerusalem authorities that one is surprised that Paul should consult them and lay before them the Gospel that he preached among the Gentiles (2.2); yet he did so, and feared that not to do so would imperil his mission. They might react in such a way as to bring his work to nought (μήπως εἰς κενὸν τρέχω ἢ ἔδραμον). Their disapproval would not prove him wrong, but it might destroy his work – it is clear, as the letter proceeds (e.g. 4.20), that he feared that this would happen.

The same fear is apparent in 2 Corinthians (e.g. 13.5, 10), together with the same ironical attitude to the Jerusalem apostles. In this epistle they are no longer στῦλοι but ὑπερλίαν ἀπόστολοι – superapostles, but Paul can say (2 Cor. 12.11), I came short of these superapostles in no way – 'nothing' that I am (cf. 11.5). It was noted long ago by E. Käsemann[18] that in 2 Corinthians Paul

---

[17] The term *pillar* may look back to the notion of the apocalyptic foundation stone used of Peter in Mt. 16.18. C. K. Barrett, 'Paul and the "Pillar" Apostles', in J. N. Sevenster and W. C. van Unnik (eds), *Studia Paulina in honorem Johannis de Zwaan* (Haarlem, 1953), pp. 1–19.

[18] E. Käsemann, 'Die Legitimität des Apostels. Eine Untersuchung zu II Korinther 10–13', *ZNW* 41 (1942), pp. 33–71, reprinted Darmstadt, 1956. I have taken a similar line in my commentary on 2 Corinthians (above n. 7), pp. 28–32.

has in mind two groups of opponents. In addition to the ὑπερλίαν ἀπόστολοι, who scarcely count as opponents, for Paul hardly goes further than damning them with faint praise, there are the ψευδαπόστολοι, the deceitful workers, the servants of Satan who disguise themselves as servants of righteousness. These are the real enemy, who correspond the more closely with the ψευδάδελφοι of Galatians in that both groups are accompanied and, it seems, to some extent supported by the relatively harmless Pillars or super-apostles. The agreement between Galatians and 2 Corinthians is too striking to be a matter of coincidence. There was an anti-Pauline mission which sought to undo his work, preaching a different Gospel, another Jesus (Gal. 1.6–9; 2 Cor. 11.1–4), and requiring observance of the Law by Gentiles who would join in the Jewish-Christian movement; this group found a measure of sympathy and possibly some support in the Old Guard based in Jerusalem, who may have provided them with commendatory documents but on occasion withdrew support when their protégés went too far (Acts 15.2–4).

Paul was in a difficult and probably embarrassing position. His own faith[19] was based upon Christ, crucified and risen, and the only contact with the historical Jesus was provided by the original group, now based in Jerusalem, which had accompanied him in his earthly ministry. To break with them would mean, he feared, probably rightly, that he had run and was running in vain; his Gospel would have become no longer a theology but an anthropology, an existentialist reinterpretation of the Judaism in which he had been brought up. But to keep with them at any cost, at the cost for example of imposing circumcision on his Gentile churches, would equally have destroyed his Gospel and his mission. The false apostles had to be fought; the superapostles must not be completely antagonized. He must have gone up to Jerusalem knowing that the Council would be an event that required very careful handling. It would not be easy to defend the Gospel as he understood it and to keep the peace.

---

[19] See further below.

VI

We turn therefore to the two narratives contained respectively in Acts and Galatians. Apart from the narrative and thematic framework, from which it appears that they are dealing with the same event, they are almost entirely different. In Acts there is an exegetically based discussion of the question on what terms Gentiles may be admitted to the saved people of God. Three specific contributions to the discussion are recorded. Peter makes a statement (15.7–11) based on his visit to the centurion Cornelius. God chose him to take the Gospel to the Gentiles; on the basis of nothing but faith God cleansed their hearts and gave them the same gift of the Holy Spirit that he had given to the apostles on the Day of Pentecost; the Law is an intolerable burden even to Jews and should not be imposed on Gentiles since all, Gentiles and Jews, are saved in the same way, namely by faith. The contribution made by Barnabas and Paul[20] is no more than an account of the signs and portents done by God among the Gentiles; it is implied that God thereby showed his approval of the mission to the Gentiles. Finally James, quoting Amos 9.11–12, argues that God has from the beginning intended, and has declared his intention in Old Testament Scripture, to include Gentiles among his people. This inclusion is connected with the restoration of the house of David, an allusion which is not explained.[21]

In Galatians no speeches are quoted. The men of repute added nothing to Paul.[22] They recognized that as God had given to Peter an apostolate to Jews so he had called Paul to preach the Gospel to the uncircumcised. Recognizing this as God's gift, the Pillars had shaken hands with Paul and Barnabas on the agreement that they, Paul and Barnabas, should go to[23] the Gentiles while they, Peter

---

[20] There is not a little to be said for the view that the references in Acts 15 to Paul and Barnabas are additions to Luke's source.

[21] Amos's prophecy may be taken to refer either to the resurrection of the Messiah or to the conversion of Israel.

[22] Either they added no further content to his teaching or they added nothing to his authority.

[23] For the possibility that εἰς may be differently interpreted see below.

and his colleagues, would go to the circumcised. All they asked (μόνον) was that the Gentile missioners should remember the poor.

Anyone who wishes to harmonize these accounts has two good leads. Paul describes a private discussion (κατ᾽ ἰδίαν τοῖς δοκοῦσιν, 2.2), whereas Acts reports a public meeting. Again, Acts describes the process by which a conclusion was reached, Paul reports the conclusion. Harmonization however is not the best approach to historical sources. These two sources represent Christian history as proceeding on different lines. Acts sees the universal mission proceeding in agreement. There are a few necessary (15.28) rules that Gentiles must observe, but given compliance with these there is no objection to their presence. It is true that Acts allows us here and there to see that it was not quite as simple as this, but this is the picture we are intended to see. Paul depicts a partial agreement which was ill-thought out and ill-founded and not surprisingly broke down. That this was in fact the immediate consequence of the Council is proved by the existence of the Epistle to the Galatians (and of 2 Corinthians and Philippians) and in particular by the events at Antioch described in Gal. 2.11–14. Acts looks back at the Council from a date nearer the end of the first century: the more immediate consequences (of the 50s and 60s) have been forgotten and the church is expanding into the Gentile world on the lines of the Decree (contained in Acts but not in Galatians). Acts and Galatians are both valuable sources but they relate to different periods.

VII

Our next step is accordingly to look at Gal. 2.7, 8, 9 and ask what sort of agreement they represent – for that they do represent an agreement is clear. It was an agreement that was important to Paul; hence its place in Galatians; but as is apparent in the second part of the chapter it was not an agreement that ended disagreement.

A number of exegetical questions arise here which are to some extent due to excessive brevity in Paul's style. In v. 8, are we to understand τὸ εὐαγγέλιον again before τῆς περιτομῆς? If we do, is it implied that there are two different Gospels? If this is implied, is the proposition inconsistent with 1.6f., where it seems that a ἕτερον εὐαγγέλιον, a Gospel different from that preached by Paul, is not ἄλλο εὐαγγέλιον, that is, is not a Gospel at all? In v. 8, is it significant that the word ἀποστολή occurs only once, or is εἰς τὰ ἔθνη to be understood as εἰς ἀποστολὴν τῶν ἐθνῶν? If the omission of a second ἀποστολή was intentional does it imply that Paul was not regarded as an apostle? Grace had been given to him (v. 9), but it was not the grace of apostleship.[24] In v. 9, how was the division of missionary work intended to be applied? Would the Pillars never include Gentiles in their churches? Would Paul and Barnabas never preach to Jews? Or does εἰς (εἰς τὰ ἔθνη, εἰς τὴν περιτομήν) mean something other than direction? Lietzmann[25] notes the illogically connected final clause, ἵνα ἡμεῖς κτλ, and interprets it as dependent on the unspoken thought, 'mit der näheren Bestimmung', and translates, 'daß wir für die Heiden und sie für die Beschneidung (seien)'.[26] But this 'für die Heiden' if it means *for the benefit of* is scarcely adequate for εἰς ... εἰς, which evokes the sense of movement; as missionaries Paul and Barnabas will go to the Gentiles, the Pillars to the circumcised.[27]

'Excessive brevity' of style is not the only cause of obscurity here. The propositions marked by obscurity are obscure on account of inadequate theological thinking. It might seem a quick way to reach an agreed solution of a problem to say, 'We have the Gospel for the Jews, you have the Gospel for the Gentiles', but the words are unsatisfactory without a careful definition of the word εὐαγγέλιον. Such a definition could indeed be given: What we mean is that there is one piece of good news which tells of what God has done for the whole human race without distinction through his Son, Jesus Christ, but we recognize that this one piece of good news, this one εὐαγγέλιον, if it is to be understood, must

[24] Contrast Rom. 1.5, Grace and apostleship, possibly meaning the grace of apostleship.
[25] H. Lietzmann, *Galater* (above n. 13), p. 13.
[26] Op. cit., 12; similarly J. D. G. Dunn, *Galatians* (above n. 1), p. 111.
[27] See J. B. Lightfoot. *Galatians* (above n. 10), pp. 107, 110.

be expressed in terms that will differ with differing human groups. We may call these different modes of expression different εὐαγγέλια, but this is a distinct use of the word and is not intended to deny the essential unity of the essential εὐαγγέλιον. This could have been done, though it would probably seem wiser to use a different word to express the different concept. Again, there is no indication in Galatians that serious attention was given to the concept of law. What was its place in the divine purpose, for Jews and for the rest of mankind? Paul finds that he cannot deal with the Galatian situation without raising the question, τί οὖν ὁ νόμος; (Gal. 3.19); and the question should have appeared on the church's agenda paper as soon as there was a single Gentile convert – and indeed before that. There is some reference to the question in Acts 15, though it may well be anachronistic and is in any case unsatisfactory. Peter declares that the Law is intolerable even for Jews (15.10); James says in effect that we cannot ask for the whole Law but we must have some of it. Galatians 2.9 must have been unworkable however it was interpreted. If it meant, 'We will look after Jewish interests, you can look after Gentile interests' it was assuming and perpetuating a division at the heart of what should have been a united body; if it meant, 'We will conduct a mission to Jews, you can conduct a mission to Gentiles', it was asking an impossibility in a world (outside a narrow area in Palestine) of cities with mixed populations, and at the same time was creating two communities unable to meet at a common table. If it was, and was intended to be, no more than a promise not to get in one another's way – 'You are free to take your line and we shall take ours' – then it was hardly more than an agreement to differ and certainly different from a whole-hearted agreement. This was noted long ago by F. C. Baur:

Die κοινωνία war ja zugleich eine Trennung, man vereinigte sich nur dahin, dass die einen εἰς τὰ ἔθνη, die andern εἰς τὴν περιτομὴν gehen sollten, d.h. die Judenapostel konnten zwar gegen die Grundsätze, auf welche Paulus seine evangelische Wirksamkeit stützte, nichts einwenden, sie mußten sie insofern anerkennen, aber diese Anerkennung war eine bloß äußerliche, sie überließen es ihm, nach diesen Grundsätzen auch ferner unter den Heiden für die Sache des Evangeliums zu wirken, für sich selbst aber wollten sie nichts davon wissen.[28]

Ihre Anerkennung erscheint ganz nur als eine Concession.[29]

VIII

That some such analysis of the Council is correct is proved by the sequel (in Gal. 2.11–14).[30] This is complicated by a difficult textual problem. The text of N[26] runs: For before certain people (τινας) came from James he used to eat (συνήσθιεν) with the Gentiles; but when they came (ἦλθον) he withdrew . . . This yields a clear story which makes sense. Peter's practice at first was that of Paul; though a Jew he ate with the Gentiles, evidently not thinking that his mission was to Jews only and that he must leave the Gentiles to Paul. Then came a party from Jerusalem, not necessarily sent by James but representing his point of view. When they came, Peter, frightened, withdrew and separated himself from Gentile company. The textual variants have τινα for τινας, συνήσθιον for συνήσθιεν, and ἦλθεν for ἦλθον. The first of these variants (supported by 𝔓 d gᶜ r*) makes little difference; it matters little whether one messenger or several came from James (except in relation to the other variants). συνήσθιον is not clear, but it could refer to the whole company of Jewish Christians in Antioch – clearly it must refer to Jews or it has no point. ἦλθεν could refer to the singular τινα or to Peter (cf. v. 11); Origen (*Contra Celsum* 2.1) took it to refer to James. συνήσθιον is found in 𝔓[46] and a MS of the Vulgate, ἦλθεν in 𝔓[46] א B D* F G 33 *pc* b – a weighty group. ὅτε δὲ ἦλθεν repeating v. 11 probably means that Peter adopted

---

[28] F. C. Baur, *Paulus, der Apostel Jesu Christi. Sein Leben und Wirken, seine Briefe und seine Lehre. Ein Beitrag zu einer kritischen Geschichte des Urchristenthums* (Stuttgart, 1845), p. 125. See also M. D. Goulder, *A Tale of Two Missions* (London, 1994).

[29] F. C. Baur, *Paulus*, p. 126.

[30] The same observation shows the Acts account to be incorrect. If the Council had ended with such a clear-cut agreed result as is given in Acts the trouble in Antioch could not have arisen.

his secessionist attitude as soon as he reached Antioch and was rebuked for it by Paul, independently of the visitor(s) from James. This would make sense[31] but it would leave the πρὸ τοῦ γὰρ ἐλθεῖν clause in the air, and (especially in view of v. 13, συνυπεκρίθησαν ... ὑποκρίσει, and v. 14, ἐθνικῶς ... ζῇς) it is better to accept the reading that makes Peter guilty (in Paul's view) of a change of practice that did not correspond to his conviction but was induced by fear.

It seems clear that the Council had produced no such Decree as that of Acts 15.29; if it had, all concerned would have known where they stood and there would have been no ground for Paul's outburst. It is true that Acts does not represent the Decree as designed to regulate table fellowship,[32] but it was probably used – and in a secondary sense intended – for this purpose from the beginning. Indeed it is probable that the dispute at Antioch was the occasion of its production.[33] Acts places the question of common meals in a different setting (chapters 10 and 11, not 15).

Peter was κατεγνωσμένος: 'the condemnation is not the verdict of the bystanders, but the verdict of the act itself'.[34] Peter's attitude was inconsistent, and it is the theme of inconsistency that runs through Paul's rebuke of Peter. So for example Lietzmann.[35] The observation is familiar and need not be developed at length. Peter's reaction has been due not to conscience but to fear (v. 12). We need not here ask in what sense Peter feared οἱ ἐκ περιτομῆς or who they were. Such cowardice can only be dishonourable. As such it was ὑπόκρισις, the representation of one thing by a man who truly was another; double-mindedness. The Jewish Christians

---

[31] So essentially T. W. Manson, *Studies in the Gospels and Epistles* (Manchester, 1962), pp. 178–80. Cf. B. Corsani, *Lettera ai Galati* (CSANT 9NT; Genova, 1990), p. 153.

[32] Though many think – wrongly, I believe – that the Council in Acts does change course in this direction.

[33] See n. 38.

[34] J. B. Lightfoot, *Galatians* (above n. 10), p. 111.

[35] Up to v. 14, which seems to mark the end of Paul's historical reminiscence. So, for example, H. Lietzmann, *Galater* (above n. 13), p. 15: 'Zunächst wird die Form der Ansprache an Petrus – aber auch nur die Form – beibehalten'.

who were carried away by Peter's action συνυπεκρίθησαν αὐτῷ. They professed to be brother Christians with their Gentile colleagues but they refused to treat them as brothers. They were not walking straight towards, ὀρθοποδοῦσιν,[36] the truth of the Gospel; in English, they were crooked. Finally, Paul lays Peter's inconsistency before him in plain terms. If you, a Jew, live as a Gentile (so there must have been a period when Peter was eating with the Gentiles at a table not fenced by a Decree), how can you try to compel (conative present) Gentiles to live as Jews?

This is good solid *ad hominem* and *ad homines* argument, and for most purposes it would do. But Paul knew – or if he did not know he acted on theological instinct and his instinct did not mislead him – that there was a better way than this secular putting down of an opponent. The whole debate, so far as we can reconstruct it from Gal. 2.1–10, had been for the most part on a secular level. It was time to make it Christian. Hence 'Christocentricity at Antioch'.

The question whether 2.15–21 continues the report of what Paul said to Peter or is fresh writing addressed to the Galatian situation has often been discussed.[37] For the present purpose it does not greatly matter. Whether at the time or after subsequent reflection Paul saw that the argument as he had so far conducted it was unsatisfactory – the whole affair from his arrival in Jerusalem, though correct in his adamant refusal to yield to any requirement that Titus, the representative Gentile, should be circumcised, was unsatisfactory. Agreeing to a division of mission fields, even to a division of the Gospel into two forms, gave him a kind of tactical success in that it permitted him to go on doing what in all probability he would have continued to do, with or without an agreement; but as soon as the envoys, or the influence, of James divided the church in Antioch it was apparent that the Jerusalem agreement was inadequate. There were two ways out of the unsatisfactory

---

[36] See G. D. Kilpatrick, 'Gal. 2.14 ὀρθοποδοῦσιν' in W. Eltester (ed.), *Neutestamentliche Studien für Rudolf Bultmann zu seinem siebzigsten Geburtstag am 20. August 1954* (BZNW 21; Berlin, 1954), pp. 269–74.

[37] See C. K. Barrett, *Freedom and Obligation* (above n. 9), pp. 18–20.

situation that had arisen. One was the way of the so-called Apostolic Decree, produced not by either of the 'Hebrews', James and Paul, but by the 'Hellenists'.[38] This was a compromise: not the whole Law, and not no Law: the few essentials of Law. The alternative was Paul's way, elaborated in Galatians 3 and 4, but outlined in 2.15–21.

Verse 15 provides the link with what goes before by describing Paul himself and Peter as men who start with the advantages of Judaism; yet they had both as Christians recognized that justification comes not by works of Law but only by faith in Christ. It may be that Paul here (with his εἰδότες) anticipates a conclusion that he will establish in the following verses: if justification is only through (both διά and ἐκ) faith in Christ it is not by works of Law – no one can have it both ways. Problems remain in the exegesis of vv. 19–21 which there is no need here to discuss. What is clear beyond doubt is the drive to the person of Christ, with the ultimate *reductio ad absurdum* of v. 21. If righteousness can be had through Law Christ might as well not have died; for Paul this was unthinkable. It would empty the grace of God of its meaning, for grace is summed up in the fact that the Son of God loved me and gave himself for me. This is the only Gospel there is (1.6–7) and it is the same for Jew and Gentile (cf. 3.28). It is a theological proposition, and at the same time it determines matters at a deeper level, and therefore more effectively, than any Decree could do. The true solution of the practical problem discussed in Jerusalem was a theological, a Christological one. Paul may have been temporarily led astray by the course of the argument, answering theological fools according to their folly; he came back to Christocentricity in time to write Galatians.

There are parallels to this movement of thought elsewhere in the Pauline corpus, for Paul, great theologian as he was, did not always from the beginning see through to the end of a theological argument. The parallels are not as clear as this example because

---

[38] See C. K. Barrett, 'Acts and Christian Consensus', in P. W. Børkman and R. E. Kristiansen (eds), *Context: Essays in Honour of P. J. Borgen* (Trondheim, 1987), pp. 19–33.

nowhere else does Paul give so full and long an account of a sequence of events. They may be left for discussion elsewhere. For Paul, the present is a decisive example of the decisiveness of Christocentricity.

3

Paul: Missionary and Theologian

The starting-point of this lecture is the statement that I once read, 'Paul was not a theologian; he was a missionary' – a statement incorrect both in principle and in history. It is wrong in principle, because there is no Christian theology that is not, in the broadest sense, kerygmatic theology; and it is wrong as a matter of fact, because the historical Paul wrote as a theologian and worked as a missionary.

So much is, in my opinion, clear, and it is not necessary to provide detailed proof of my two counter-propositions. Long ago, while I was an undergraduate, I read an article by Karl Barth on 'The Basic Forms of Theological Thought'. These, Barth said, were three. The *first* was exposition. The theologian quarries in Scripture the raw material of theology: of course, the text requires exegesis, exposition. The *second* form was criticism; by this word Barth meant that the theologian, having discovered biblical truth, will set it alongside the thought and the ethical behaviour, which naturally implies conscious or unconscious thought, of the society in which he lives. He uses it as the criterion by which he judges human systems of thought. The *third* basic form of theological thought, without which the process would remain incomplete, was proclamation. Different theologians at different times would emphasize different elements and use them in different proportions, but always all three, including proclamation, must be present. Barth was right; and it follows that the Christian theologian must be a missionary. Naturally this does not mean that he must be an outstanding preacher or a world-traveller, but his subject requires that he should make the content of his subject known. Conversely, the missionary must be a theologian; this means that he must understand as well as possible what he is talking about. If Christian theology has a missionary content, the message of the Christian missionary has a theological base. It is good news of God; and that is theology.

The historical question also may be answered briefly. It is not necessary to go into the historical problems that are raised by the Acts of the Apostles. The epistles contain sufficient evidence. When Paul does not describe himself as δοῦλος Χριστοῦ (Christ's slave) he calls himself ἀπόστολος (apostle). Everyone knows that this Greek word has a very scanty background in pre-Christian use. We can hardly think that Paul meant to say that he was a naval expedition and must allow him to define the word for himself. The Cynic–Stoic use of κατάσκοπος, the spy, sent out to investigate and illuminate the human situation, is only of limited usefulness. The use in late Hebrew of *shaliaḥ* and its cognates is important (and Paul may himself contribute something to our understanding of rabbinic practice), but in the end it is Paul himself whom we must hear.

He defines himself as doing ambassadorial service, as though God himself were making the appeal through him; 'We beseech you on behalf of Christ, Be reconciled to God' (2 Cor. 5.20). He is not content simply to make a verbal appeal; he will do anything to win men for Christ. 'Though I am free from all I made myself a slave to all that I might win the more . . . I have become all things to all men, so that somehow I might save some' (1 Cor. 9.19–22). This meant preaching, not running an institution. 'Christ did not send me to baptize but to preach the Gospel' (1 Cor. 1.17). He was a pioneer missionary who avoided the easy well-trodden tracks, eager 'to preach the Gospel where Christ's name was not yet known, that I might not build on another's ground' (Rom. 15.20). He was a hardened traveller who covered long distances and endured great hardships. But he was more than this. What he was doing was itself a part of the Gospel that he preached. The Gospel, he said, is the power of God which saves all who believe; in it the righteousness of God is revealed – ἀποκαλύπτεται, present tense (Rom.

1.16–17). When Paul preached the Gospel the saving righteousness of God was revealed, power leading to salvation was in operation. When Paul spoke, the word of Christ was heard (Rom. 10.14).

It would not be difficult to add more, but from this last observation it is easy to take the next step. Was Paul also a theologian? It may be that the author whom I have quoted intended to say, 'Paul was not a systematic theologian'. This has often been said, and it is possible to make a case for it. Certainly it is true that Paul never (so far as we know) wrote a textbook of systematic theology, setting out in regular order the usual chapters: Revelation, God, Christ, the Spirit, the Trinity, Sin, Redemption, and so forth. But it is not necessary to write a textbook in order to be a systematic theologian. It is necessary to think systematically, and one must have the ability to recognize the important traditional themes and to perceive their relation to one another. One must be able so to work with the Christian tradition as to express Christian truth in the light of contemporary philosophical thinking.

If we have here a reasonable definition Paul will qualify not only as a theologian but also as a systematic theologian. One must of course remember that for him the 'Christian tradition' was something different from what it has become for us who have centuries of Christian theology behind us. For Paul the tradition scarcely existed. He became a Christian only a very short time after the resurrection; before him there had been no one capable of handling the story of Jesus in a seriously theological way. Paul had indeed received the outlines of belief, that Christ died for our sins according to the Scriptures, that he was buried and raised on the third day according to the Scriptures, and that he appeared to a number of people whose names could be listed (1 Cor. 15.3–5). The importance of this report is not to be undervalued, but it shows hardly any trace of further reflection. It is asserted that Christ died for our sins; but how could his death achieve anything for the sins of others? He died and was raised up according to the Scriptures. Which Scriptures? And what concept of the fulfilment of Scripture is presupposed? These are questions that arise immediately; but it was Paul who articulated them, and Paul who first gave some indication how and where answers might be sought. Not only as a missionary but also as a theologian Paul was a pioneer. Again, the religious and philosophical atmosphere that he breathed was different from ours, so that it is certain that he provides us with no systematic theology for our own time. Even an apostle cannot do that, for a systematic theology for our time must speak to today's intellectual environment. What the apostle will do for us is of course something more than that; he will provide us with the raw material out of which every later generation can construct a systematic theology for its own time. It is however possible to collect out of the Pauline letters material for the conventional theological themes.

For example, Paul wrote about God. That was not difficult, for at this point he had Judaism and the Old Testament behind him. He had however to modify the Jewish inheritance. God was the creator, and as any artist is known through his creative work, so also is God; at least there is a potential knowledge of God in the things that God has made (Rom. 1.20), even if it remains potential because those who ought to accept it are unwilling to do so on the only terms on which it can be had: they are unwilling to glorify God and give thanks to him (Rom. 1.21). Instead, they choose to pass by their creator and in his place to worship their fellow creatures. The result is the darkening of their morals and of their minds. Creation goes out of joint as Paul sees most clearly in the perversion of human sexuality, and thought, not only moral but metaphysical thinking, is corrupted (Rom. 1.19–25). Broadly speaking, this is Paul's exegesis of the Old Testament story of creation, but it is necessary only to compare it with the parallels in the Wisdom of Solomon to see how much more profound it is than anything that his predecessors or contemporaries achieved. Also Jewish is the belief that God is judge, and that as judge he is righteous and always acts in righteousness (Rom. 2.5; 3.6). Here too one recalls Genesis: Shall not the judge of all the earth do right? (Gen. 18.25). Abraham had asked the rhetorical question; but Paul has a problem. God, as a good judge, will duly distinguish between the innocent and the guilty. What then if there are no innocent? Paul can quote the Old Testament to prove that 'there is none righteous, no, not so much as one' (Ps. 14.1; Rom. 3.10). Paul the theologian has grasped the supreme moral problem about

God, which is not, How can God be righteous and yet permit suffering? but, How can God be righteous and yet fail to inflict suffering upon the whole of universally guilty humanity? How can God at the same time be both just and justifier – when there are none to justify but the ungodly (Rom. 3.25; 4.5)? Paul is aware of the question, and also has an answer, though that is not to be dealt with now. It is at least clear that God loves, as Luther rightly said, with a love that 'non invenit sed creat suum diligibile'. The act of love took place while we were still sinners (Rom. 5.8; 8.38–39). The paradoxical question can be dealt with only by a paradoxical answer. From first to last, from foreknowledge to glory (Rom. 8.29–30), God is the author of salvation.

The conviction that God loves those who have no claim upon his love rests upon the fact that Christ died for us. It is the love of God which is in Christ Jesus our Lord from which nothing can separate us (Rom. 8.38–39). Paul therefore must also write about Christ. And here is perhaps the hardest question of all: How can the death of another person benefit the rest of us? Or (to ask a different though related question), What sort of person is he whose death can benefit the rest of mankind? After the crucifixion and resurrection the conviction arose that it had so happened, and that Jesus was that sort of person. In the earliest days that conviction sufficed; and there are some for whom it suffices still. But for one who had a searching and analytic mind, and therewith a theological responsibility for his fellow Christians, it would not suffice. Here we can with a great deal of probability observe Paul developing the tradition that he had received. If time permitted we could in paragraphs such as Phil. 2.6–11; Rom. 1.3–4 trace how Paul edited Christological formulations. Here we can only note that the theologian who takes his calling with full seriousness has many problems. Paul never ran away from them.

Here we can consider only one more theme, that we may observe how Paul's mind works, and how his thought develops. What has Paul to say about the Law?

Paul was a Jew; he never ceased to be a Jew. He loved the Law, as Jews did and do. It was easy for Paul to say, The Law is good; it came from God, it is spiritual, it gives commands which are still to be obeyed, it carries within itself its own self-transcending summary in the commandment of love; easy for him to say this, and leave it there. Paul was also a Gentile missionary. He knew that Gentiles were acceptable to God as they were, without any legal observance, that the grace of God was free and undiscriminating. It was easy for him to say, If you get yourselves circumcised, Christ will be no good to you. I testify again to every man who is getting himself circumcised that he is under obligation to do the whole Law. You are finished with Christ, you who would be justified by Law; you have fallen out of grace (Gal. 5.2–4); easy for Paul to say this, and to leave it there.

It is characteristic of Paul, the theologian, that he insists on both propositions and refuses to take either easy way out. The key to his understanding of the matter is to be found in Rom. 7.7–25, which handles the outrageous but unavoidable question, Is the Law sin? Here Paul insists most strongly on the divine excellence of the Law, which is holy, righteous, and good. Here he says that in his experience the Law means that the good he wants to do, he does not do; the evil that he does not want to do, he does. And it is here that he states in the plainest terms the answer to the problem. The Law itself is good but an evil power has taken hold of it and twisted it out of its proper use and purpose so as to form a ἕτερος νόμος, a different law, a different kind of law, which makes war upon the good Law that my mind approves. It is not for us at present to trace in detail the way in which Paul works this out; it is enough that we should see with what seriousness Paul wrestles with his problem. We can see too, though again not in detail, how Paul's thought advances. In Galatians the Law appears as essentially an interlude, filling the space between Abraham and Christ. Now that Christ has come we no longer need the παιδάγωγος, the child-minding slave who gets the boy to school. In Romans Paul does not contradict this but says even more explicitly than in Galatians that the Law slipped into this interval in order that transgression might abound (Rom. 5.20); here too however he has seen how the Gospel establishes the Law (Rom. 3.31). God is not contradicting himself; a self-contradicting God would not be God, and the whole theological enterprise would be at an end. The Gospel establishes the Law not as the Judaizers understood it but as God himself understood it. For Paul can now see that the Law is to be understood ἐκ πίστεως, by faith (Rom. 9.30–33). Understanding the Law in this way we can see that it proclaims the righteousness of faith.

We may conclude then that Paul sets us a proper example by being both theologian and missionary. That presents no serious difficulty. More difficult is a second question: How were these two aspects of Paul's life related to and bound up with each other? For he was one man, and his whole life was determined by one conviction: 'All I do, I do for the sake of the Gospel' (διὰ τὸ εὐαγγέλιον, 1 Cor. 9.23). The Gospel was at the same time message and theology; a theological message and a kerygmatic theology. Fresh theological insights furthered the mission; the mission required constantly fresh theological work. A circular relationship; but in this case the circle has a beginning. We call it conversion.

Conversion: but is this the right word? Should we not rather say, Vocation? The arguments for vocation are well known and are not without weight. It never occurred to Paul that, as a Christian, he was worshipping a different God from the one he had served as a Jew. When he describes most clearly the beginning of his Christian life he does so in terms that recall prophetic vocations in the Old Testament: 'God who separated me from my mother's womb and called me through his grace' (Gal. 1.15). On the other hand, at the end of the same chapter he speaks of the most radical of conversions: 'He who once persecuted us is now preaching the faith which formerly he ravaged' (1.23). This is not merely a new course of action; it originates in a changed belief. What had seemed so wrong that it was necessary to use all possible means to stamp it out now seemed so right that it must be not only held but propagated. The fact is that every true conversion, especially in the Christian sense, is at the same time a vocation. And for Paul the vocation was 'that I should preach Christ among the Gentiles' (1.16).

In his conversion Paul was presented with two theological problems, both of which were relevant to his call. I call them 'problems'; they were in fact growing-points from which his thought developed. The content of his conversion was the discovery that the crucified Jesus was now alive. He could only be alive because God had raised him from death, and that God had done this was proof that Jesus had been right; his opponents had been wrong. The first consequence of this was that Paul had to reconstruct the eschatological framework of his Jewish theology. The eschatology was now realized, though only partially. The world, human society, was still subject to sin, suffering, and death. What in these paradoxical circumstances did God expect his people, and especially those who accepted the Messiahship and Lordship of Jesus, to do? Let us for a moment leave that question and notice, secondly, that Jesus had been cast out and rejected by the Law, or at least by its authorized exponents. But he had been right and they had been wrong. Had the Law, not Jesus, led Israel astray? Were the Gentiles, who had no Torah, better off than the Jews? In these two questions there is a great deal of theological substance; here they call for only one observation. Both questions as I have stated them lead us back to the Gentile mission.

We are inclined to take this Gentile mission for granted. To us it seems to be beyond question, but at that time it was a matter of radical questioning. Jesus had left neither a church constitution nor a liturgy, neither a theological system nor a missionary programme. All this had to be improvised. That there should be a Jewish mission was self-evident. Jesus was the Messiah of Israel, and the Messiah was a national figure. True, most Jews had rejected him, but they now had an opportunity to change their minds. 'Now, brothers, I know that you did it out of ignorance, as did also your rulers. But God has fulfilled what he announced through the mouth of all his prophets, that the Christ should suffer. Repent therefore, and turn, that your sins may be blotted out' (Acts 3.17–19). But what of the Gentiles? Probably there were some who said: The End will come soon; then God will do what he will. We have no time to evangelize the Gentiles. It is certain that there were some who said: First we must win all the Jews; after that we will turn to the Gentiles. We can be certain of this, first because it is presupposed by Paul's counter-proposal (to which I shall come in a moment), and secondly because it is confirmed by the speech attributed to James in Acts 15.13–18. James quotes Amos 9.11–12: 'Afterwards I will return, and I will build up again the tent of David that had fallen down, and I will build up again its ruins, and I will raise it up, in order that the rest of mankind may seek the Lord, even all the Gentiles upon whom my name has been named.' The interpretation of these words is disputed, but the quotation was probably taken to mean that Israel must first be re-established in order that others might then be incorporated into God's plan. This makes the best sense of the Apostolic Council. We must (so runs the argument that leads to the Apostolic Decree) retain so much of Judaism that the Jews may be satisfied now, and not so much that the Gentiles will later be offended. The counter-proposal, the third way forward, is set out in Romans 9–11, especially in 11.31–32. There is no way to the mercy of God but the way of unbelief and disobedience. The Gentiles were always unbelieving and disobedient; therefore they may enter immediately into the realm of free, gratuitous mercy. They have deserved nothing from God; his approach to them cannot be based on any merit of theirs and they cannot pretend that it is. This the Jews had to learn through hard experience, as Paul himself had done when he came to regard his credits as debits and his righteousness as dung (Phil. 3.7–8). The Jews' rejection of the Gospel thus served a double purpose. Its immediate result was the Gentile mission; as the Jewish door closed the Gentile door opened. The more remote result was that it gave to the Jews the possibility of understanding the mercy of God and accepting salvation. So the conversion of the Gentiles would make possible the deliverance of Israel.

I have spoken of improvisation. Paul was the great, creative improviser, and as Gentile missionary he had a trump card up his sleeve. For him, Jesus was not only the Christ but the last Adam, not only a national but a universal figure. 'Or is God the God of the Jews only? Is he not also the God of the Gentiles?' (Rom. 3.29). Once more, theology and mission, though distinguishable, form an inseparable unity. It is interesting here to compare the Pauline Epistles with Acts. When Paul writes, 'The Jews first and also the Greeks' (e.g. Rom. 1.16), what he has in mind is primarily a theological proposition. In Acts we have the equivalent of it in a practical missionary programme: Try the synagogue first, and when the Jews throw you out move on to a neighbouring lecture-hall. Between Luke and Paul there is a difference, but no contra-diction: Paul may well have worked in this eminently sensible way. But it is characteristic of Paul to state the matter theologically, and of Luke to like his theology in the form of stories. The result is the integration of theology and mission.

Theology and mission: but we must return to the words with which we began, Theologian and missionary. That is, we must ask, How could Paul hold the two functions together in his one person? What was the relation between the two?

The question is in the first instance a historical one. How did Paul conduct his missionary work? It was his aim to preach only where the name of Christ was not yet known (Rom. 15.20). How was that to be done? How did Paul do it? We know all about this. In Galatians 4, for example, Paul gives a fascinating account of his first encounter with the Galatians and of his reception by them, but in this chapter we have not a word of what Paul said in his preaching. The epistles can indeed be described as written preaching, but they are not mission preaching. There are sermons in Acts, but they give us little help. The sermon in Acts 13 is a synagogue sermon, and assumes a good deal. In the opening words, 'the God of this people Israel' (13.17), it presupposes that there is one true God, who is active in history and especially in the election of the people to be his servant. It presupposes τὰς φωνὰς τῶν προφητῶν, since the prophetic books are publicly read Sabbath by Sabbath (13.27). Perhaps one might hope for more from the Areopagus address in Acts 17, but this address presents us with historical and theological problems. I shall however return to it shortly.

What can we learn from the epistles? The passage usually cited in this connection is 1 Thess. 1.9–10. There is no need for him, Paul says, to give anyone an account of the Thessalonians and their conversion. Everyone already knows how they accepted the Gospel. Their response had been that for which Paul hoped. They had turned to God from idols, to serve the living and true God and to await his Son from heaven, whom he raised from the dead, Jesus, who delivers us from the coming wrath. That seems to confirm, what we might *a priori* expect, that Paul would as a beginning press the Gentiles to abandon their idolatry and turn to the true God, whom he had known from childhood through the Old Testament. But with what sort of proof would he convince his hearers? In 1 Thessalonians he reports the end but not the means. In order to learn more we move to Athens and to the speech in Acts 17. If the speech is read quickly it seems that Paul uses the same proofs that were used by contemporary philosophers. They – some of them – believed in one spiritual universal God, who had created all mankind from one origin, was not confined to material temples, and had no need of material gifts from his worshippers. All this can be found in ancient thinkers, not least in the Epicureans and the Stoics, who are mentioned in the passage. Epicurus (as Lucretius tells us) had delivered men from religion. The gods were distant and much too concerned with the enjoyment of their existence to interfere with ours. The Stoics knew that life had a meaning, a λόγος, and that this λόγος was a sort of god, the reality that lay behind the ridiculous mythologies of the uneducated and credulous. Such a god was not to be found in wood and stone. So did Paul use a philosophical natural theology of this kind when he preached to the Gentiles? Did he follow the philosophers as far as he could, in order at the end to supplement nature by grace, referring to Jesus – though not indeed by name (17.31)?

The objection that is usually – and rightly – brought against this view is that Paul seems to have had no high opinion of natural theology (Rom. 1.18–23). 'They have changed the truth of God into a lie, and honoured and served the creation instead of the Creator' (1.25). Creation could give them at most the conception of an invisible and powerful Other. To this supreme Other they have preferred visible things, so that the only god they had in fact derived from the world of nature was an opposite to the true God. Their natural religion was bringing down upon them not the divine favour but the divine wrath. This is hardly the sort of gambit with which Paul would begin a missionary speech. We observe a difficult historical question with regard to Acts 17 and a theological uncertainty with respect to 1 Thess. 1.9–10.

There are further observations to make. In 1 Cor. 1.18 Paul describes the Christian message as the word of the Cross. For Paul, Christ is God's power and wisdom, but he knows that to the Greeks his Gospel is nonsense. That means that his mission preaching to Gentiles was not constructed so as to be pleasing to the philosophers. 'The word of the Cross is foolishness to those who are lost . . . We preach Christ crucified, to Jews an offence and to Gentiles a nonsense' (1 Cor. 1.18, 23). In the next chapter he repeats the same theme: 'When I came to you I did not come proclaiming my testimony about God with pre-eminent eloquence or wisdom. For I resolved that in the midst of you I would know nothing but Jesus Christ, and him crucified' (2.1–2). We may here recall Gal. 3.1, where we have what is missing in Galatians 4. We know very well how Paul preached in Galatia. Before the eyes of the Galatians he placarded Jesus Christ, the crucified. The difference between these passages and Acts 17 is clear. In the Areopagus speech we have nothing at all about the Cross. Only at the end is Christ mentioned. All men must now repent because God has set a day on which he will judge the world in righteousness by a man whom he has appointed for the purpose (17.30–31). This man must have died, for God has raised him from the dead, but the manner, even the fact, of his death is not mentioned. One wonders, Is the word *difference* strong enough? Should we not say, *contradiction*?

We may note first that though Acts 17:22–29 contains philosophical thought, and a quotation from a Greek poet, it contains also the thought and the words with which Isaiah and Jeremiah attack the idolatry of their contemporaries. For Isaiah also, God is the Lord, the Creator of the ends of the earth, who calls the stars by name. He is not to be confined within material, man-made houses. 'Heaven is my throne and the earth is my footstool, what is the house that you would build for me . . . ? these things my hand has made' (Isa. 66.1f.). The practices of human religiosity are scorned by the prophet as they are by Epicurus. 'He who slaughters an ox is like him who kills a man; he who sacrifices a lamb, like him who breaks a dog's neck; he who presents a cereal offering, like him who offers swine's blood; he who makes a memorial offering of frankincense, like him who blesses an idol' (Isa. 66.3). This paragraph in Acts 17 contains the Old Testament proclamation of the one, true God. In other words (though they put the matter too neatly to be entirely true), we may say that what we read in Acts 17 is not natural but revealed theology. He who wrote Acts 17 learned his theology not from the Greeks but from the Bible. And the result is perhaps not totally irreconcilable with Romans 1. Since the Fall, the *theologia naturalis*, the theology that sinful man draws from nature, is a fallen theology, idolatry, a flight from the true God who seeks from men service and obedience. This is the prophetic message, and the message of Romans 1, where the essential point is that man has set in the place of the true God god-substitutes which can never truly be his Lord and serve only to corrupt his thinking and his moral behaviour. The recognition of the Old Testament influence on Acts 17 throws a different light on the Areopagus speech, though it probably came not from Paul but from a non-Pauline branch of the Gentile mission.

A second observation comes from a return to 1 Thess. 1.9–10. The Thessalonians learned to await Jesus who rescues us (τὸν ῥυόμενον ἡμᾶς) from the coming wrath. So Jesus is a rescuer, a deliverer. How, we may ask, does he deliver us? This question is not answered in 1 Thess. 1.9–10, We must seek an answer elsewhere. We may begin with a passage in the same letter. In 1 Thess. 5.10 Paul writes of Jesus that he 'died for us that, whether we wake or sleep, we may live with him'. Many similar passages can be quoted from the other letters. For example, Jesus 'gave himself up for our sins that he might deliver us out of this present evil age' (Gal. 1.14); the Son of God 'loved me and gave himself up for me' (Gal. 2.20); 'Christ died for our sins' (1 Cor. 15.3). These passages show that Christ had delivered the Thessalonians by dying for them; so we come back to the 'word of the Cross', to the 'nothing but Christ and him crucified' (1 Cor. 1.18; 2.2). If Paul told the Thessalonians to await the coming of God's Son from heaven, he was a Coming One who would be recognized by the marks of his passion.

We may be able to take a step further. Paul proclaimed the Christ, the crucified Christ. A Greek would probably be able to work back from *Christ*, Χριστός, to the verb χρίειν, to anoint, but the word would have no clear content. Who is this person smeared with oil? Paul cannot have preached Jesus as the Christ, the Messiah, without giving his hearers some preparatory instruction in Judaism. Only those Gentiles who had already been in the habit of attending the synagogue would find such instruction unnecessary. Once more the Old Testament is involved in the preaching. This means that the preaching of Christ already contains a requirement to abandon idolatry and turn to the true God. It was the Jewish God, the God of the Old Testament, who had a Messiah, and the concept of Messiahship was inseparable from a God conceived in a particular way: a God who was unique and almighty; a God who was actively at work in history, anything but an Epicurean remoteness, anything other than a Stoic immanence; a God who had strangely set his choice upon that strange people the Jews, so that their history became the special locus of his work and of his revelation; a God who to this special people had made special promises, promises which he would be certain to fulfill; a God who made correspondingly special claims upon those who were his. All this says a good deal about God before one begins to consider the particular person whom Christians recognize as Messiah.

One further observation: Paul preached the crucified Christ. Why crucified? Even if his hearers did not understand the meaning of Χριστός they knew very well the meaning of ἐσταυρωμένος. It meant that the person was either a slave who had made his master unusually angry, or a political or military rebel. If Paul was unwilling to accept any of these explanations he must provide another. Such an explanation would require an account, however short, of the life of Jesus. Kähler was correct in the view that the Gospels grew backwards: first the passion narrative, then stories, controversies, teaching, to make sense of the final scene. We note here questions both historical and theological. Why did they kill him? That is a hard question for the historian. Why did God allow him to die? For the theologian this is an even harder question. It is however no more than a beginning, for the New Testament does not represent the death of Jesus as simply part of the tragic fate of human mortality. It is a hard enough question when we ask, Why do the innocent suffer? But this is not an event that God permitted; it was God himself who caused it. 'God did not spare his own Son' (Rom. 8.32). Isaac might come out of his ordeal whole, but not Jesus. If this tells us anything about God, does it tell us that he is a monster? Certainly not; but what then? It must say something about the complexity of the being of God – at least (since the Holy Spirit is not in question and we cannot speak of a trinity) about God's twofoldness, for if the Crucified is not somehow God, as his Father also is, then the Father is inflicting suffering on an inferior – and this is monstrous. One does not treat inferiors so.

I shall not make the universal negative assertion that Paul never argued in the manner of a Hellenistic-Jewish philosopher. Idolatry and polytheism do expose themselves to philosophical objection, and Paul may have argued that popular religion was mere superstition and that men ought to live in accordance with the Mind, the Logos, of God. He could have done this without enrolling Lucretius and Posidonius among the prophets, for the real prophets had themselves said something of the sort. But it was not necessary for him to do this, for simply to tell the story of the Cross poses all the questions about God, and on this basis the preacher could detach his hearers from their old belief (or unbelief) and lead them in a new direction. The Cross questions all conventional philosophical arguments, including the traditional Christian arguments, for the existence of God. The philosophical problem of verification is a real one, and the Cross means that God refuses to verify himself, to come down from the Cross and so to prove his case. It contradicts the cosmological and the teleological proof, for there is no event so disorderly, none that runs more plainly contrary to the notion of purpose in the ordering of the universe. It is the contradiction of the moral argument too, for the moral argument asks, Who but God can have set within me the voice that cries, I ought? And the Cross means that when it comes to the push, the inward voice cries, I ought, but I won't. There is no God, no President of the Immortals, who can make me surrender the search for my own happiness, comfort, and security.

It is not easy to believe in God. That is why Christian thought about God does not begin with Plato and Aristotle, with the consideration of creation (cosmology) or the consideration of history (teleology), but with the preaching of the Cross. It is in the obedience of Jesus that God is known, in the suffering of Jesus that God is glorified. Every other god is an idol, such a god as the Thessalonians had now given up. The Thessalonians were right. We can never be content with a god who wound up this watch of a universe and left it to tick. We need a God who wrestles with rebellion and overcomes resistance with love, a God who speaks to us from outside ourselves, so remote that we can confuse him with the thunder, yet speaks in language that we can understand, because we see him in one who would rather be the friend of sinners and die than give them up and live.

It is not my intention (as it was not Paul's) to construct a Christian metaphysic, though I do observe that we have come to a point where a true metaphysic is possible, for here we are indeed μετὰ τὰ φυσικά, beyond our normal experience, not in a world of fantasy but in the world of unsearchable divine love. Exegetically (and that is my concern) we must recognize that 1 Thess. 1.9–10 on the one hand and 1 Cor. 1.18; 2.2 do not contradict each other; historically (and that also is my concern) we must say that Paul may well have won the Thessalonians from their false gods by preaching Christ crucified.

In our attempt to understand Paul in his double role as at once theologian and missionary there is one further line of investigation that we may follow. In his book *Jesus and the Transformation of Judaism* [London, 1980] John Riches has admirably brought out the way that must be followed by one who wishes to communicate a genuinely new message. He must use language that is essentially familiar to his hearers. If he uses a totally new vocabulary no one will understand him. If however he uses the old words with their old meanings he will achieve nothing more than a mere re-arrangement of ideas. He must use the old vocabulary but he must also give to the old words a new meaning – a meaning that is related to the old one, so that there may be a point of contact, but also different, so that the new message is communicated. This procedure

Professor Riches has pointed out in the Gospels; it may also be seen in Paul. I give two examples.

In 2 Cor. 4.16 Paul writes, 'Though our outward self is liable to corruption (διαφθείρεται) yet our inward self is renewed day by day'. A non-Christian Corinthian would have taken this up immediately. 'We have heard this from the philosophers and we know what they mean. They are contrasting the frail bodily shell, which will soon perish, with the immortal spirit that dwells within.' That was a commonplace; it was certainly not what Paul meant, but what he meant was not totally different. Paul too knew the meaning of mortality. Earlier in this epistle he had written of an experience that could only be described as a sentence of death (1.9). The bodily shell was indeed wearing out, and within was something that did not share this corruptibility. It was however no immortal human spirit, longing to be delivered from its prison. 'We who are in the tent, burdened as we are, groan, because we do not wish to strip, but rather to put on over our body the habitation that comes from heaven' (5.4). So far as there is in man something that may be called Spirit, it is the Spirit of God which God himself has given.

From this starting-point we could, if time allowed, study a complex group of words used by Paul: the inward and the outward self; the old and the new self; flesh and spirit; the mind, the members, the body. Such study is impossible here; I can only state its conclusion. The new Christian eschatology makes possible a new application of the old terminology, and we perceive an important theological operation that enabled Paul the missionary to speak to the Gentile world.

A second example. Occasionally Paul uses the language and the cosmology of astrology. Powers and authorities, height and depth (Rom. 8.38–39) are at home in this field. Related to astrology is Gnosis, and Paul uses also the language and cosmology of Gnosis, but always with a characteristic difference. This too we cannot study seriously; it is possible only to say, in all brevity, that the criterion Paul uses in Christianizing Gnosis is twofold. His gnosis (or wisdom, σοφία) is the Cross, the foolishness of God, which is wiser than men. And, secondly, Paul recognizes that in this age our knowledge is partial, and that in the end what is partial will be done away. 'Now I know in part; then I shall know, as now I am known' (1 Cor. 13.12).

Gnostic cosmology and the heavenly powers remain, but they serve a new purpose. They make clear that the Gospel is not only the possibility of an inward renewal, an existential transformation of human nature, but the external cosmic event that makes this possibility possible. The language of subjective mythology is reapplied so that it expresses the objectivity of a sequence of historical events.

Here I must close and sum up what I have said about Paul as theologian and missionary. Paul is both: it is hardly possible to read a page of his letters without recognizing him in both roles. As missionary he had a message that was a theology, as theologian, a theology that demanded to be communicated. This inverse relation focuses upon the figure of the last Adam, the universal Man, who was the instrument by which God worked out his plan for his human creatures. He was doubly universal in that he represented the universality of God and generalized the particularity of man and so became the Man for all men, in the breadth of his compassion and in his power to unite within himself every member of the human race. His particularity was a special particularity, for he was the unique representative of the unique race, the Messiah of the Jews. But he was not only Χριστός, he was also κύριος, for God is not the God of the Jews only but of the Gentiles too (Rom. 3.29). Christ vindicates the truth of God by confirming the promises made to Israel, but this he does in such a way that the Gentiles may glorify God for his mercy (Rom. 15.8–9). It is because God is what he is that Paul has both a theology and a mission.

4

Paul: Councils and Controversies

I

Paul was and remains a controversial figure, and there are few better ways of getting at both the man and his thought than by examining the story of the controversies in which he was engaged. It might exaggerate a little to say that these focus upon the great Council in which he and Barnabas, with James, Cephas, and John took part. It is true that this occupies a more than arithmetically central place in Acts, but in this there may be a measure of artificiality. Luke is using on the grand scale one of his favourite narrative forms: a problem arises, the problem is solved, and in addition a great expansion of the church results. It is so here. The Council is caused by the first Christian steps outside Judaism, and it leads to and provides the framework for the great expansion of the church into the Gentile world. Luke's account is to a great extent true in that the Council provided the lines on which the church was to grow, but there is something in the suggestion that Luke, who knew these lines well, produced them backwards in time so as to create, or at least to formulate, his Council story. Be that as it may; we know that the Council was important to Paul and I propose to begin not with Acts 15 but with Galatians 2.

I am assuming that Acts 15 and Galatians 2 are related to the same sequence of events. Lightfoot's argument – the geography is the same, the time is the same, the persons are the same, the subject of dispute is the same, the character of the conference is in general the same, the result is the same – needs a certain amount of

73

qualification, as we shall see, but it carries a good deal of weight. The Jerusalem visit of Acts 11.30; 12.25 need not trouble us. We may then attend to Galatians 2. Verses 1, 2 set the stage and emphasize the importance of the event. The wrong result could have undone Paul's work and brought his mission to an end. Not because disagreement would have proved him wrong – it would (for him) only have proved his opponents wrong; but it could have destroyed his churches, cutting them off from their root in the life, death, and resurrection of Jesus, centred as these were in Jerusalem. So he came to see what the Jerusalem authorities – οἱ δοκοῦντες is what he calls them, but for the present I forbear to translate the word – made of his Gospel. It was as he had already said (1.6–7), the only Gospel there is, though there were those who preached a bogus Gospel.

These had to be dealt with first, and, unlike the acknowledged authorities were the real enemy. Paul has hard words for them. They were false brothers, not genuine Christians at all. They had no right to be there; they had gatecrashed the party – they were παρείσακτοι, παρεισῆλθον (v. 4). They had come as spies κατασκοπῆσαι; the word implies deceitful proceedings. And they wished to have Titus, a representative Gentile Christian, circumcised. To this demand Paul uttered a clear No; not for a moment would he tolerate the plan. Salvation is of God's grace, free and unconditional, God was the God of Gentiles as well as of Jews. The truth of the Gospel must be secured (v. 5).

So much for the false brothers; Paul turns to those whom he had come to consult, notably James, Cephas, and John. It is clear that he had no high opinion of them. The word that is characteristic of 2.1–10 is δοκεῖν:

v. 2: τοῖς δοκοῦσιν
6: τῶν δοκούντων εἶναί τι
    οἱ δοκοῦντες
9: οἱ δοκοῦντες στῦλοι εἶναι

With these, and especially with v. 6, we must compare Gal. 6.3, εἰ γὰρ δοκεῖ τις εἶναί τι μηδὲν ὤν, φρεναπατᾷ ἑαυτόν (if anyone thinks himself to be something when he is nothing, he is deceiving himself). This determines the meaning; δοκεῖν here refers not to the opinion of others (as of course it may do in other passages) but to the opinion of the persons in question. It is clear that it is used ironically. This appears as Paul's attitude in the parenthetical clause, ὁποῖοί ποτε ἦσαν οὐδέν μοι διαφέρει· πρόσωπον ὁ θεὸς ἀνθρώπου οὐ λαμβάνει. Whatever they were makes no difference to me; God shows no partiality. They may think themselves to be something, to be the Pillars on which God's eschatological temple will stand. But Paul is not impressed. He had met them before (1.18f. – Cephas and James). They are however people with whom he can talk, with whom he can make an agreement. They recognized the grace that had been given to Paul (v. 9), that he belonged within the Christian fold and had been equipped for a specific ministry (v. 7). God who had given Peter an apostolate (ἀποστολή) the circumcision had given Paul an apostolate (but they do not use the word – is this an accident?) to the uncircumcision (v. 8). There was a Gospel for each division of mankind (v. 7). Did this run counter to 1.6–7? Not necessarily; perhaps what they meant was that the one Gospel took different forms when presented to different people. So the agreement was struck: ἡμεῖς εἰς τὰ ἔθνη, αὐτοὶ δὲ εἰς τὴν περιτομήν (v. 9: We to the Gentiles, they to the circumcision). This was essentially an agreement to differ. We will go on doing what we are doing; you can go on doing what you have been doing. We shall not interfere, and (as silence shows) we shall not expect Gentile converts to be circumcised. Gentiles will still be Gentiles, and Jews will still be Jews.

It was an agreement; a compromise agreement. Its weaknesses are already apparent. Was Paul an apostle, or not? Are there two Gospels? If Paul's Gospel is true, the whole Gospel is for the whole world; who has the right to say, Jews only, or Gentiles only? And there was another problem just below the horizon; if Jews were won by their Gospel and Gentiles by theirs, how were Jewish converts to be related to Gentile converts? We shall meet this problem in due course. Still, it was an agreement; and Paul could and did go on doing what he had been doing before.

What we must at this point observe is that Paul the controversialist has to operate on two levels: against an enemy, the false brothers who are to be found not only in Jerusalem but also on the ground in Galatia, needing to be fought tooth and nail; and against half-hearted friends, who if they had been really in agreement would have been working – and fighting – at his side. In fact Paul must have often been uncertain whether or not they were secretly aiding the false brothers. This duality is of vital importance for the understanding of Paul's controversies. It can be observed in letter after letter.

From the Corinthian letters we can learn what was for Paul the key issue. In 1 Cor. 15.11 Paul says, Whether then it is I or they, so we preach and so you believed. This statement is sometimes given a fuller meaning than it will bear. Paul is in this chapter arguing about resurrection, and in this verse he makes the point that there is no Christian preaching that does not include the resurrection of Jesus. This indeed will take us further. You cannot believe in the resurrection of a crucified man if you cannot find some interpretation of his death. Such an interpretation appears in 15.3, 4, in a pre-Pauline, and therefore very old preaching tradition: Christ died for our sins according to the Scriptures and he was buried and on the third day he was raised up according to the Scriptures. If Cephas and James preach this – and their names appear among the eye-witnesses; it is because they believed it that others do – they are proclaiming what Paul can recognize as the one Gospel. They may not make as much of 'for our sins' and 'according to the Scriptures' as Paul does but they are on the same side. So in 1 Corinthians we can see the half-friends – on this occasion perhaps three-quarters-friends. Their preaching is right and they are acceptable.

What of the enemies? There in not much sign of them in 1 Corinthians; in chapters 1–4 Peter comes off less well than Apollos, and there may be an unfavourable reference to the notion that he was the foundation stone, or pillar, of the church but he is on the right side. But 9.2 shows that there were some who did not regard Paul as an apostle; so does 15.9; he was an ἔκτρωμα (15.8). Moreover, there were those in Corinth who thought it wrong to eat εἰδωλόθυτα, food sacrificed to idols. They did not learn this from their pagan background, or from Paul. It must have come from Jewish influence, perhaps Jewish-Christian influence, perhaps formulated by the Decree of Acts 15.29 (on which see below). See also 7.19; Paul found it necessary to point out that circumcision was of no importance.

In many ways the situation in Corinth had changed when 2 Corinthians was written. It now becomes clear that strangers had entered the church from without and poisoned its relation with Paul. There were others however whom Paul treats with nothing worse than the irony he had used on those who thought themselves to be pillars; indeed these must be the same persons, though now they are described as ὑπερλίαν ἀπόστολοι, super-apostles. Paul claims to be their equal in status and origin (Hebrew, Israelite, descendant of Abraham), and their superior in the sufferings he has endured in the service of Christ (11.22–23). These are not the enemy; some do not distinguish the two groups, but I think we must. There are false apostles, deceitful workers, servants of Satan. You cannot say of people like that, I think I am as good as they are (2 Cor. 11.5; 12.11); it is with reference to the ὑπερλίαν ἀπόστολοι that Paul says this. The false apostles are, to Paul's sorrow, welcomed by the Corinthians. They preach a different Gospel (this is the absolute criterion), another Jesus, a different Spirit (11.4). They invade other men's territory, and boast of labours not performed by themselves (10.14–16). They launch a disparaging attack on Paul; he knows, they say, how to write strong letters, but his presence is feeble (10.10). They (or others of the same kind) dilute and pollute the Gospel (2.17); they arm themselves with commendatory letters (3.1). Paul's problem is to know what connection, if any, there is between the two groups. Are the ὑπερλίαν ἀπόστολοι entirely innocent of the activities of the ψευδαπόστολοι? Or do they, perhaps secretly, support them? Who has written the commendatory letters that they use? Did Paul know? Did he guess? It may have occurred to him that once an envoy, in ancient times, had passed out of sight of the one who commissioned him the latter had no control over him. Not only could he say and do what he pleased; he could attribute what he

77

pleased to his employer. On such matters one can speculate; what is beyond speculation is that the Corinthian letters, like Galatians, bear witness to a two-level opposition to Paul and his mission.

There is more evidence to collect. Some of the evidence provided by Philippians concerns Philippi, other evidence the place in which the epistle was written. This may have been Rome, Ephesus, or Caesarea. I cannot discuss the question here; I prefer Rome, but the other possibilities should be kept in mind. The same twofold opposition appears.

In Philippians 1 Paul speaks of those who preach out of envy and strife (1.15, 17), thinking to add to the imprisoned apostle's troubles – his imprisonment provides us with an opportunity to add to our reputation as preachers and to gain disciples for our outlook and understanding of Christian truth; that will upset him! They are mistaken; for Paul, what matters is that, for whatever reason, with whatever motive, Christ is being preached; and 'therein I rejoice' (1.18). Here are people who, in the realm of ecclesiastical politics, wish to injure Paul, but they are preaching Christ, using it may be words like those in 1 Cor. 15.3–4. This to Paul was the only Gospel there was, and these men were preaching it. There is no question here of preaching 'another Jesus', a 'different Gospel' (2 Cor. 11.4); hence no room for the anathemas of Gal. 1.8–9.

It is disputed whether the two passages in Philippians 3 that refer to trouble-makers deal with disturbances actually happening in Philippi or are warnings of trouble that may be feared. For our purpose this is of no importance. Paul speaks of trouble-makers whom he knows to exist; whether they have reached Philippi or are still on the way is of no account. In both passages Paul speaks as sharply and vehemently as anywhere in his letters. In 3.2, 3 the readers are warned against teachers who are evidently circumcised Jews, who wish (presumably) to have the Gentile Christians of Philippi circumcised. They are described in a way that recalls and perhaps exceeds 2 Corinthians 11. They are dogs; they are evil-workers; they are given the insulting title κατατομή, while Paul reserves the word περιτομή for himself and his fellow Christians, whom he considers to bear the true marks of the people of God. These opponents have confidence in the flesh, that is, in the literal circumcision that they have. This leads to an important statement of the righteousness that comes from the Law and the righteousness that comes by faith.

At the end of the chapter there is a further warning, this time against adversaries who are described as enemies of the Cross of Christ whose end is perdition, whose god is their belly and whose glory is in their shame (Phil. 3.18–19). It is not clear whether this is a second reference to those mentioned at the beginning of the chapter or deals with a different group. The earlier reference is undoubtedly to Jews or rather to Jewish Christians. The later passage seems at first to refer to liberals in theology – they have no room in their thought for the Cross of Christ, and to libertines in morals – they are gluttons and they boast of their shameful behaviour. A strong case, however, can be made for the view that they also are Judaizers. Their interest in what they put into their bellies, in what they eat, amounts to idolatry; that means perhaps not that they are epicures and gluttons but that they hold fast to food laws. Their shame, αἰσχύνη, could refer to the male sexual organ. There is evidence for this use of the word in Liddell and Scott, but most important is the evidence of the LXX, where sometimes (not always) the Greek word renders ערוה; often of female pudenda but see Isa. 20.4; Ezek. 22.10 for ערוה/αἰσχύνη of the male. The word may thus point to the location and thus to the act and state of circumcision in which they boast. These things recall Gal. 5.11; 6.12–13. Those who wish the Galatians to be circumcised do so in order that they may not be persecuted for the Cross of Christ; their intention also is to 'glory in your flesh' in that part of your flesh in which circumcision is carried out; one might say that their glory is in the 'shame', αἰσχύνη. If these observations are valid it could well be that 3.2–3 and 3.18–19 refer to the same people, to Judaizers. This would be interesting, but whether it is correct or not we may note that in Philippians, as in Galatians and the Corinthian letters, we have to distinguish between two levels of opposition. There is the opposition to which Paul is prepared to give the benefit of the doubt, not simply out of charity but because, whatever its motives may be, it does preach the one Gospel of Christ crucified and risen. This is a party with which he can enter into agreement, even though he may have reason to suspect that it tolerates if it does not actually support the second kind of opposition, which preaches a Gospel which is no Gospel and would, if unchecked, destroy the work that he is doing. It was a complicated controversial situation that formed the framework of Paul's mission, and Paul can hardly have been unaware that the agreements he was able to make were unstable and insecure.

Is there more evidence for this twofold opposition? It is worthwhile to note in Romans the sensitive way in which Paul handles the relation between the Weak and the Strong. There is no question that Paul himself is one of the Strong (14.14; 15.1). He does not think that a vegetarian diet will commend him to God. It is by faith only and not by the observance of dietary laws that he stands before God. But if the Weak should not judge the omnivorous Strong, neither should the Strong despise the Weak (14.10). That is, Paul gives full allowance to the Weak to maintain their position and their practices. He who does not eat, to the Lord he does not eat, and he gives God thanks (Rom. 14.6). Each of us will give account of himself to God (14.12); all may and should live together in peace. The Weak does indeed come somewhere near to perverting the Gospel of *sola gratia* and *sola fide*; but he maintains something of the *solus Christus*, and that is enough. The only place in Romans where there may be a glimpse of the radical opponents of Paul is in chapters 9–11, where Paul argues that it is right to pursue the Gentile mission because when the fullness of the Gentiles has been included in the people of God all Israel will be saved (11.25–26). This may be intended as a counterblast to a Jewish–Christian belief that all Israel must be saved first and that only then will it be legitimate to embark on a mission to the Gentiles. There will be more about this when eventually we look at Acts 15. But James and Cephas seem to have thought that the two missions could be pursued side by side (Gal. 2.9) – a view with which Paul does not disagree.

It is probable that 1 Thessalonians is the earliest extant Pauline letter; for our present purpose there is little that we can learn from it. What we may observe is Paul's repudiation of flattery, or a concealed plan to exploit, of a desire to seek personal glory

(2.5–6). We (himself and Silas?) might have made ourselves a burden (ἐν βάρει εἶναι) to you as apostles of Christ, but instead we were gentle among you (2.7). This may reflect the notion, which if it existed will have had some cause, even if the cause arose out of a misunderstanding, that apostles were expected to be authoritarian, a charge that Paul brings or implies against his opponents – perhaps the Pillars, the ὑπερλίαν ἀπόστολοι. These were apostles who thought it proper to fulfil their office by lording it over the members of their churches, whereas Paul thought of himself as his people's slave (2 Cor. 1.24; 4.5); there is only one κύριος, as there is only one foundation. All this is consistent with what is written in 1 Thessalonians but it cannot stand on its own as independent interpretation of the text of the epistle. It to only because we have evidence elsewhere of this authoritarian attitude that we may suspect it in Thessalonica.

To resume: it seems to me impossible to avoid the conclusion that the evidence collected from the epistles points clearly to the existence of two kinds of trouble-maker in the Pauline churches. It is important to keep the distinction in mind not least because it brings out so clearly the importance in Paul's thought and practice of preaching. If this is right, a good deal of variety can be tolerated. 'Let each one be fully convinced in his own mind' (Rom. 14.5, taken in the whole context). If it is not right, nothing can be right. There are then these who are perhaps better described as unhelpful friends than as adversaries. The authorities in Jerusalem believed in and proclaimed a crucified and risen Jesus, indeed they were the origin and support of this proclamation. They saw in his work the forgiveness of sins. This fundamental faithfulness to what he too understood as the Gospel covered for Paul a multitude of sins. On occasion, even Peter, and (by implication) James, might meet with rebuke; certainly they met with no subservience. But they did not preach another Jesus, a different Gospel, though Peter's position sometimes appears doubtful; he may perhaps sometimes have allowed himself to be drawn in on the wrong side (see below).

There was a wrong side, of those who (to adopt for Christian use the Jewish phrase) 'denied the root'. There is no doubt what was Paul's attitude to them. This second group was marked, as we have seen, by a good deal of variety. Most demanding were those in Galatia and at Philippi who demanded the circumcision of Gentile converts (cf. Acts 15.1, 5). Whether this was to them the most important feature of the Law we cannot be certain, but it probably was, for it was the way into Judaism, an indispensable first step. In Galatia they probably expected also observance of the Sabbath and other festivals (Gal. 4.10): circumcision and the Sabbath were the clearest marks of the Diaspora Jew. Perhaps they insisted on a third socially distinguishing feature, the laws of cleanness and uncleanness and other dietary laws – no doubt they approved of the separation described in Gal. 2.12–13. This was a heavy demand, but it is clear that they did not ask for observance of the whole Law; they exposed themselves to Paul's criticism that anyone who gets himself circumcised is under obligation to perform the whole Law (Gal. 5.3) – he intends that all should recognize that it is not a matter of circumcision, and then nothing more.

At or near the other extreme were those who formulated and propagated the Decree of Acts 15.29 (to which I shall come later). This required only the most basic Judaism: little more than loyalty to the one God, with abstention from fornication and bloodshed. It was however basic Judaism that was required, and those who propagated the Decree were Judaizers. There is thus a wide range of Judaizing activity, ranging from the demand for circumcision and almost (not quite) full observance of the Law to the scarcely noticeable requirements of the Decree.

Another question may be raised – hardly answered – at this point. In Gal. 1.7 (cf. 4.17–18) Paul refers to 'Those who are troubling you (οἱ ταράσσοντες ὑμᾶς) and wish to pervert the Gospel of Christ'. In 5.10 the same expression occurs in the singular, ὁ ταράσσων ὑμᾶς. Does this mean that the trouble in Galatia was caused by a group of Judaizers, but that this group was led and could be represented by a single person? Or is the singular used generically to mean 'Anyone who troubles you'? In 5.10 the warning is given that the trouble-maker will bear his judgement whoever he may be (ὅστις ἐὰν ᾖ). Unfortunately the last three words also are ambiguous. They may be generalizing and mean, Any trouble-maker there is – there is no need to be specific – will bear his judgement. So for example the Grammar of Blass–Debrunner–Rehkopf (293.1.2a.n.5; 303.n.l). Others think otherwise. Thus Lightfoot (*Galatians*, p. 206); '. . . whatever may be his position in the Church, however he may vaunt his personal intercourse with the Lord'. Lightfoot must mean Peter, possibly James. Lietzmann (*Galaterbrief*, p. 38) is more explicit. He thinks that the agitation in Galatia was led by a respected personality ('eine angesehene Persönlichkeit'), and quotes Ed. Meyer for the suggestion that this was Peter, adding that it might have been Barnabas. Loisy (*Galates*, p. 183) thought of James, noting that Paul preferred not to name him – though he does do so in chapter 2. It is worth recalling the clause ὁποῖοί ποτε ἦσαν in Gal. 2.6, in a similar context. At 5.10 the Latin quicumque est (indicative) may support the view that finds here a reference to a particular person rather than a generalization. Peter and James have both already been mentioned as causing trouble at Antioch, and Paul may be saying, in veiled words, Be the trouble-maker even Peter or James he will get the judgement he deserves. If one is to choose between Peter and James as the man on the spot, Peter may be preferred as the one who is known to have travelled from Jerusalem and may have been in Galatia as he had certainly been in Antioch, whereas James may have been content to work through messengers.

There is good reason to think that Peter had been in Corinth too, and there is reason to think that the Corinthian trouble-makers had a leader. But those mentioned in 1 Cor. 1.12 were no more than potential leaders of division, though Apollos was a closer partner to Paul than Peter. The bearing of 1 Cor. 9.5 is unclear. There is more material in 2 Corinthians. In 2.5 there is a person, denoted only by τις, who has caused grief, λελύπηκεν, not so much to himself, Paul says, as to the whole community. This is presumably the person who is taken up in 7.12 as ὁ ἀδικήσας, he who did wrong, with a corresponding ὁ ἀδικηθείς, he who suffered wrong. We know neither who ὁ ἀδικήσας was nor what he had done. It is usually supposed that ὁ ἀδικηθείς was Paul himself, who had been attacked or insulted in some way. There is no indication of doctrinal disagreement, though it is of course possible that such disagreement could have been the cause of personal ill-feeling. Paul minimizes his own sense of hurt. He urges forgiveness, and himself forgives. It is often supposed that Paul's opponent was a member of the Corinthian church; it is more probable that he came into the church from elsewhere. This, if correct, confirms the picture of an anti-Pauline mission circulating in Paul's churches with a view to 'correcting' his, insufficiently Jewish, practice. There is more material in the last part of the letter (chapters 10–13). Particularly to be noticed are the singular pronouns in 10.7, the singular verb in 10.10, and the singular pronoun in 10.11, and the singular substantive participle and finite verb in 11.4. Here the substance of the Gospel is involved, for ὁ ἐρχόμενος, he who comes (from without?), preaches another Jesus, and as a result of his preaching his hearers receive a different Spirit and a different Gospel. Here too the words could be generic, but this does not seem probable; if this had been intended it would have been easy and natural to write εἴ τις ἐρχόμενος ἄλλον Ἰησοῦν κηρύσσει. . . . καλῶς ἀνέχεσθε. If a group of anti-Paulinists came to Corinth it would be natural (though of course not certain) that they should have a leader; he could be referred to here.

There is nothing in Philippians that bears on this matter. The references in chapters 1 and 3 are all in the plural except 3.4b, εἴ τις δοκεῖ ἄλλος πεποιθέναι ἐν σαρκί, ἐγὼ μᾶλλον, and this is a general statement. Paul would have, if he chose to appeal to it, more ground for confidence in the flesh than anyone else.

When all the passages mentioned are surveyed there is only one person who could be named as satisfying the evidence; this is Peter, but the suggestion cannot be made with much confidence. He is named as the leader, but probably the unwilling leader, of a group in Corinth (1 Cor. 1.12). In the same epistle (9.5) he is mentioned as one of those who made use of apostolic privileges which Paul renounced. In Gal. 2.11–15 he takes (under pressure from James) a view opposite to Paul's on the relation between Jewish and Gentile Christians. Gal. 1.18 is worth considering here. Paul visited Jerusalem ἱστορῆσαι Κηφᾶν. Why? The meaning of ἱστορῆσαι has often been discussed, and the word itself is unlikely to tell us much. But we know why Paul made his second visit to

Jerusalem (Gal. 2.2); it was in order that he might not have run or be running in vain. Was the first visit made for the same purpose? He saw the same people – James as well as Cephas. It seems probable that Paul already knew that Cephas and James were a potential threat to his work. It is tempting to follow Goulder (*A Tale of Two Missions*) and to speak of a Petrine and a Pauline mission. But in the place where it matters Peter stands among Pillars rather than the false brothers. It is however not unlikely that his attitude and his position varied. In the gospels he appears as a somewhat unstable figure; the familiar image of the Rock – Πέτρος – Kepha probably means no more than that he was the first to confess the Messiahship of Jesus. The evidence of Gal. 2.11–15 depicts him as an unstable character, and it may be that less reputable figures than James were able to sway him. It must be remembered that in the earliest decades Christians had no clear-cut dogmatic tradition to guide them. Paul was at work establishing such a tradition, but it is not surprising, or blameworthy, that this, and its importance, were not universally perceived. The story cannot be perfectly clear to us because the evidence is not sufficient; for other reasons it was probably less than clear to those who participated in it. In the hope of clarifying it a little we may pursue two further inquiries.

First: we may continue with Galatians, and examine what happened after the Council described in 2.1–10. It is, of course, clear that a determined anti-Pauline campaign, which required the circumcision of all Gentile Christians, was in progress. We cannot suppose that this was confined to Galatia, though the campaigners may have concentrated their efforts there. In any case, we must assume that Paul told the story of what happened in Antioch because he believed it to be relevant to what was happening in Galatia. The existence of the Pauline churches was threatened (2.2). This provides the background against which Paul's rebuke of Peter in Antioch (2.11–15) must be understood. Paul's Gospel asserted the free and all-sufficient grace of God, operative in Christ crucified and risen; to suggest that this needed the complement of circumcision, or any other legal provision, was to destroy its foundation. It is evident that Peter had at first accepted the fact that to both

Jews and non-Jews the decisive condition was their faith in Christ; this was what constituted them Abraham's seed, heirs in terms of promise (3.29). Jewish and Gentile Christians ate together with no regard for food laws. This harmony was disturbed by 'certain people from James', who frightened Peter, followed by Barnabas and other Jewish Christians, into withdrawing from table fellowship. We do not know what the envoys from James said. It is possible that they were really false brothers (2.4), wrongly claiming the authority of James; but we note that they convinced Peter of their credentials. James himself will hardly have revoked the agreement of 2.9, but that agreement must be interpreted by his subsequent actions. He must have said something like, 'We agreed that there should be a Gentile mission, led by Paul, and that Gentile converts did not have to be circumcised; but we did not say that Jewish Christians might so far cease to be Jews as to eat meals where observance of Jewish laws was not guaranteed. Conversion does not obliterate the distinction between Jew and Gentile.' This Peter accepted. Previously he had behaved (by eating non-Jewish meals) as if he were a Gentile; now he was requiring Gentiles, if they wished to eat with their Jewish Christian brothers, to behave like Jews (2.14). This was ὑπόκρισις (2.13); Peter had been frightened into playing a part – though it is not impossible that Peter was now reverting to what he truly believed, and that it was with a bad conscience that he had been playing a part when he ate with Gentiles. The evidence about Peter provided by Acts is unclear and in part contradictory. According to Acts 10.14 he had never in the past eaten prohibited food, but (after his vision and the gift of the Spirit) did eat with Cornelius (10.48; 11.3); but Cornelius may have observed Jewish regulations. According to Acts 15.10 Peter had found these regulations intolerable, and presumably had not observed them; yet in the Decree he consented to the prohibition of improperly slaughtered food (15.29).

Paul begins by pointing out the inconsistency in Peter's attitude, and no doubt in doing so became aware of the inadequacy of the agreement that had been reached in Jerusalem (Gal. 2.9; see above). The incident at Antioch may have ended at this point. It is often held that somewhere between Gal. 2.11 and 2.21 Paul, in writing his letter moves from narrative to theological reflection. This may well be true. The transition from debating point to Christ-centred theology undoubtedly takes place in the text before us. It will be appropriate to consider it more fully when we turn from the historical to the theological aspects of Paul's controversial life. The Christocentricity here achieved dominates the rest of Galatians as it dominates Paul's thought as a whole.

We turn secondly to the alternative account of a Jerusalem Council that is contained in Acts 15. It will he impossible here to discuss it in detail, but there are three questions which it will be profitable to consider.

The first is the place of Paul and Barnabas in the Council. They were, according to Acts 15.2, deputed to go to Jerusalem in order to represent the Antiochene point of view in opposition to that of those who had come from Judaea and maintained that it was impossible to be saved without circumcision (Acts 15.1; cf. 5). But the two Antiochene representatives make practically no contribution to the Council (15.12). They narrate the signs and portents that God done through them among the Gentiles, and this was in fact not a bad practical argument: Would God have permitted, have actually performed, such acts of power and benevolence if he had disapproved of what was going on? But would Paul have been content to leave unspoken the theological argument about grace and faith and works? It seems improbable. We may note also the Εσίγησεν δέ at the beginning of v. 12 and the Μετὰ δὲ τὸ σιγῆσαι αὐτοὺς at the beginning of v. 13. There is a case (made for example by Bultmann) for regarding the intervening words (v. 12) as an insertion into a narrative that did not originally contain them. Did Luke, who certainly knew – rightly – of a Council at which Peter and James, Paul and Barnabas, had been present introduce Paul and Barnabas into a Council story in which they played no part?

The second question arises out of the quotation of Amos 9.11–12 ascribed (in Acts 15.16–18) to James. There is a famous and often discussed problem here. If read in the Hebrew text Amos's prophecy speaks of the supplanting by Israel of what is left of Edom. This is of no use or relevance to anyone at the Council. Only if Amos is read in the Greek of the LXX do we hear that the rest of mankind (those who are not Jews) shall seek the Lord. Did James, of all people, in a conference conducted presumably in Hebrew (or in Aramaic – where the Amos passage is even less usable) use an argument that depended on a Greek misreading (as it very probably was)? It seems unlikely; there is no sign of the *'al-tiqre'* formula (used to introduce a deliberately chosen variant reading). This however is not all. Is James's quotation, in its LXX form, relevant? Relevant to what? It may be enough to say that if James simply claims that this passage of the Old Testament supports Peter's assertion that God is interested in taking to himself a people from the Gentile world. The quotation however includes also a reference to the re-erection of David's tent as leading to the incoming of the Gentiles. This could be taken in two ways. The re-erection of David's tent could mean the vindication of David's family in the coming, and in the resurrection, of his heir, the Messiah. This is something that has already happened; the mission to the Gentiles may begin at once. Alternatively: the re-erection of David's tent could mean the restoration of the Jewish people, that is, to a Christian, the conversion of the Jewish people to Christ, a successful mission to the Jews must precede the mission to the Gentiles. This would imply that Amos 9.11–12 was a text whose interpretation was argued about in discussions of the legitimacy of the mission. This is the theme of the Council described in Galatians 2, but it is not the theme of the Council described in Acts 15, which assumes the presence of Gentile converts and considers how much of Judaism they should be required to accept.

This leads to the third question: the Decree. I shall not here discuss its contents; it must suffice to say that it is treated throughout Acts 15 not as a device intended to facilitate table fellowship between Jewish and Gentile Christians but as giving the conditions on which Gentiles may be saved, and that the conditions may be regarded as basic Judaism (without circumcision) and include both ethical and ceremonial provisions. It is also to be noted that it received a good deal of modification in the textual tradition, so that at times it seems to be purely ethical; the evidence is familiar and need not be related here. The evidence of Rev. 2.14, 20 is also relevant, and suggests a decree that forbade only fornication and the eating of sacrificial food. From Paul's letters one would never deduce that the Decree existed, and it is hard to believe that he would ever have accepted it unless he met it in the form in which it simply forbade idolatry, fornication, and bloodshed and enjoined an attitude of general love and kindliness. This is not the form in which the original text of Acts represents Paul as approving and propagating it.

These questions, which are all that can be considered here though there are others that arise, are sufficient to show that behind the narratives contained in Acts there was a complicated sequence of events. Paul's story we may take more or less as it stands; I cannot follow the now fashionable tendency to defend the historicity of Acts by questioning the veracity of Paul. Luke seems to have built up his story out of materials which, on the whole sound in themselves, are in some respects mistakenly connected. Luke knew that there were important discussions in Jerusalem which dealt with the question of the Gentile mission and the terms on which Gentiles might be admitted to the saved people of God. He knew that Paul and Barnabas as representatives of the church of Antioch had taken part in such discussions, but the traditional account of a Council that he had received did not refer to Paul and Barnabas. He should have drawn the conclusion that there had been two meetings, at one of which Paul and Barnabas were present whereas in the other they were not. Instead he inserted a reference (Acts 15.12) to Paul and Barnabas in the one story he had to tell. He may have supposed that only one such meeting took place or he may have compressed the two into one to save time and space in his book. Writing twenty or more years after the deaths of Paul, Peter, and James, at a time when a Gentile mission was almost universally accepted and Gentiles probably outnumbered Jews in the church, he supposed that the three martyrs (as probably all three were) had been closer to one another than in fact they were and that they had been united in taking the Gospel to the Gentile world, so that the only question that had to be solved was the relation of the Gentiles to Judaism, of the Gospel to the Law. Either he was ignorant of the confrontation between Peter and Paul in Antioch or he chose to ignore it. We know that he had a different account

(Acts 15.36–40) of the rupture between Paul and Barnabas. The event in Antioch marked the inevitable failure of the compromise reached at the first Council (that of Galatians 2), and neither James (backed by Peter) nor Paul was in a compromising mood. The position was a serious one. The church of Antioch was split in two, and the same could have happened in every church that contained both Jewish and Gentile elements. Another conference met; Paul was not present. It was of this second conference that Luke preserved a somewhat confused tradition; into this he introduced Barnabas and Paul, who he had reason to think had attended a Council in Jerusalem. It was however a different group of missionaries that took part in this new Council. This was the group, originally headed by Stephen, often called Hellenists, though this is not Luke's use of the word. They are perhaps better called Diaspora Jews; some of their work may be seen in the speeches of Acts 7 and 17. If Luke knew of the presence of such people he may have thought that they were represented by Paul and Barnabas. It was probably these Greek-speaking Jews who introduced the use of the Greek Old Testament, quoting Amos 9.11f. to justify the two-pronged mission to Jews and Gentiles, and devising in the so-called Apostolic Decree a better compromise than that of the earlier Council. It was a better compromise because it was flexible, capable of modification (as we have seen), and of application to practical circumstances, in which Gentiles out of courtesy had no wish to hurt the feelings of Jewish fellow Christians. Paul, it seems, had either to be informed or reminded of its contents on his final visit to Jerusalem (Acts 21.25), when, on one interpretation of the story, his relations with James fell to a still lower level. Perhaps only he recognized the new arrangement as a Judaizing compromise until a comparable theologian, Augustine, arose to be embarrassed by it.

Other events at this final visit cannot he discussed here. Luke's narrative leaves the reader with many questions. Paul had reached Jerusalem bearing the fruit of the collection he had made among the Gentile churches for the benefit of the poor saints in Jerusalem. What happened to the money? Was it used for the relief of poverty, or for the discharge of dues incurred by men who had taken

Nazirite vows? Would Paul have associated himself with such men in the Temple rite, and done so in order to prove about himself a proposition that was only doubtfully true? What did the church of Jerusalem do to aid the prisoner of Christ? Why did he repeatedly find better treatment among Romans than elsewhere?

The story in which the Councils play a prominent part is a complicated one, and it can be given continuity only with the aid of a few guesses but those that have been given here seem to agree not only with one another but with such evidence as there is. It remains to look at the evidence from the point of view of theology.

II

History and theology are as a rule inseparable in the New Testament. Theology could not be completely excluded from the first part of this discussion and the theology that will be considered in this second part arises out of and is presupposed by the history, of which a sketch is attempted above. It will be convenient, and I hope not unduly repetitious, to set out some of the main points afresh. They may in fact appear more clearly if given in briefer form and without the arguments by which they were reached.

The New Testament contains two accounts of a meeting in Jerusalem. In each account the main actors – speakers – are Peter (Cephas) and James, Paul and Barnabas. Both are concerned with the legitimacy, method, and basis of the mission by which Christianity spread out from Jerusalem into the Gentile world. They are not however identical. The narrative contained in Acts 15 arises out of contention in Antioch, where missionaries (including Paul and Barnabas) had won converts from the Gentile as well as from the Jewish world. Travellers from Judaea had asserted that it was necessary to circumcise the Gentile converts and require them to observe the Law of Moses. Only if they did this could they be saved. So important a matter could be properly discussed only in Jerusalem, and Paul and Barnabas, with others, went up to Jerusalem for the purpose. The conclusion was embodied in a letter and in a Decree, which laid down that circumcision and full observance of the Law were not to be required, but that it was necessary that Gentiles should observe, if they were to belong to the saved people of God, certain basic Jewish requirements: they must abstain from food sacrificed to idols, from fornication, from blood, and from strangled meat. Of this Decree neither Galatians nor any other Pauline letter shows any awareness.

According to Galatians 2 Paul (accompanied by Barnabas and Titus) went up to Jerusalem (in consequence of a revelation) to lay before the authorities there the Gospel that he was preaching among the Gentiles. The story of the visit falls into two parts. In the first Paul encounters false brothers, who wished to have the Gentile Titus (and presumably all other Gentile converts) circumcised. Paul is adamant in his refusal to allow this. In the second part his dealings are with James, Cephas, and John, who evidently regarded themselves as the Pillars on which the church was built. Paul was not favourably impressed by their opinion of themselves but was able to reach an agreement with them. Each party recognized the other as preaching a valid Gospel, Paul the Gospel for the uncircumcision (who need not be circumcised), the Pillars, especially Peter, the Gospel for the circumcision. It was agreed that God had been at work in each mission, but Paul and his colleagues would confine themselves to the one, Peter and his colleagues to the other. In addition Paul had no hesitation in agreeing to a request to keep in mind the needs of poor Christians in Jerusalem. This was an agreement, and as such to be welcomed; but it is evident that it was essentially an agreement to differ, a compromise. Paul would continue to do what he had been doing, and so would Peter; and neither would interfere with the other. This was better than nothing, but it was by no means a whole-hearted acceptance of one Gospel (cf. Gal. 1.6) intended for the whole world. In this narrative we see an uneasy peace, and a division of the non-Pauline part of the church into two parties. So it must have seemed to Paul, not necessarily to others. Over against him were on the one hand the Pillars, whom elsewhere (2 Cor. 11.5; 12.11) he describes ironically as the super-apostles. He accepts them because he accepts their Gospel, the proclamation of Christ crucified and risen. Indeed as witnesses they were themselves the origin, the first preachers, and the guarantee of this Gospel, and they found in it the forgiveness of sins (1 Cor. 15.1–11), though, as this passage shows, their position enabled some to sneer at Paul as an untimely birth, unworthy to be called an apostle. They failed to draw adequate inferences regarding both the breadth and the depth of their own Gospel, but their adherence to it was sufficient for Paul. On the other hand, there were those – false brothers, false apostles, dogs – whose 'Gospel' was no Gospel at all. These were the enemy; the distinction can be observed in many parts of the Pauline corpus. They covered a considerable range of what may be described as Judaizing activity, sometimes including (for example, in Galatia) the demand for the circumcision of all Gentile converts, sometimes asking much less. There is some evidence that suggests that they had a leader, conceivably Peter, though it is more probable that his position varied; all were keen to have him on their side, and he was, perhaps, easily persuaded.

The Council reports that we have in Acts and Galatians may refer to different aspects of one event; it seems more probable that they refer to two events, though Luke has assimilated his account by introducing the mention of Paul and Barnabas. The question of the Gentile mission may well have been raised (by Paul, with Peter and James) on Paul's first visit to Jerusalem (Gal. 1.18); it was discussed more fully, with the result described above on his second visit (Gal. 2.1–10). That the compromise agreement reached on this occasion was unsatisfactory was quickly displayed in the division of the church in Antioch, when the Jewish Christians led by Peter and Barnabas refused to eat with the uncircumcised Gentile Christians. The two gospels of Gal. 2.7 led to the existence of two churches, with no real fellowship between them. It was to remedy this situation that the Council, of which we have an edited account in Acts 15, was called, and the Decree (Acts 15.29), another compromise, composed. It is hard to believe that Paul accepted and propagated it, harder still to think that he had a hand in composing it. It was probably the product of a Gentile mission distinct from his, operated by Diaspora Jews who followed a line different in some respects from Paul's but increasingly influential in the later decades of the first century. They were probably responsible for the use of the Greek Old Testament in Acts 15.16–18. Acts 21.25 may mean that Paul was officially informed of the Decree on his last visit to Jerusalem.

We may take up the theology of the history at the point where the first compromise agreement failed. This might work when the two missions were separate from each other, in districts that were wholly Jewish or wholly Gentile. But Antioch was mixed, both as a city and as a church. If Jews were (as James evidently wished) to stand firm as Jews, and if Gentiles refused to become Jews, the church was bound to split. Only a radically theological review of the situation could put it right.

Paul's first reaction however was to fasten on the change, the inconsistency, in Peter's behaviour. 'If you, born and bred (Lightfoot's suggestion for ὑπάρχων) a Jew, live as a Gentile and not as a Jew, how can you seek to compel Gentiles to live as Jews'? The present tense, ζῇς, is perhaps not quite fair to Peter, for he had now under pressure – perhaps threats – ceased to live as a Gentile and was presumably expressing penitence for ever having done so. But Paul's point is clear enough. Fear was compelling Peter to do something that was inconsistent not only with his past position but also with what appeared to have been his conviction; he was, for James's benefit, acting a part; and this was ὑπόκρισις, play-acting. The word made a good debating weapon, and it fitted with all that we know of the Council. Its decision regarding the missions was a compromise; the attitude of Jewish Christians to Gentile Christians, the attitude of James – they may be Christians but not of our sort – was a compromise. And the compromise was dishonest and in the end unworkable uneven when the Jewish Christian demand was reduced to nothing more demanding than the Decree.

At this point the story could end, and perhaps did end. Most commentators agree that at some point between 2.14 and 2.21 Paul ceases to recount an event that took place in Antioch and goes on to develop his subsequent thinking on the question. For us it does not matter whether Paul developed his thought, thinking on his feet in Antioch or took it further as he worked out his argument in writing to the Galatians. He develops the argument from a debating point – 'Be consistent, man!' – to one of his most profound theological statements. In v. 15 he is still addressing Peter – ἡμεῖς, We, you and I – but he soon moves beyond this.

What was wrong with the Council, with Jewish demands, with the Decree, which, though not yet enacted at the time of the trouble in Antioch, was in existence when Paul wrote Galatians? It was that they left out the central figure who should have controlled the whole discussion. In the question about Paul's Gentile mission they did not say, 'Christ died for the Jews, Christ died for the Greeks, therefore there is one mission to all the world, in which all play their part.' They said rather, 'We will go our separate ways, and agree not to tread on each other's toes.' When the question was about Christian fellowship, about Christians' eating and drinking together they did not say, 'We all live by the bread which is Christ's body and the wine which is his blood.' They said rather, 'You give up this and we will give up that.' It may be that I exaggerate somewhat in the interests of clarity and brevity, but that is essentially how Paul saw – came to see – the matter.

For we can trace movement in his thought. Start with ourselves, Paul says to Peter; we are Jews, not sinners picked up out of the Gentile world. But does that make any difference, such as would justify our taking our supper in a different place from Titus, the Gentile? What is our basic conviction as Christians? It is faith in Jesus Christ. We put our faith in him in order that we might be justified by this faith in Jesus Christ, for no one is justified by works of law. The great words, πίστις, πιστεύειν, δικαιοῦν, ἔργα νόμου, all occur here, and it would take a long time to discuss them all seriously. The important thing to note in a brief discussion is that though in this short paragraph Paul's thought spreads out far beyond the immediate situation it begins within that situation. It follows that works of law are, for example, the things that a Jew will do (or abstain from doing) in obedience to God when he sits at table to take a meal. The context of the epistle on a whole supplies circumcision as another representative work, or 'thing done'. 'Works of law' (ἔργα νόμου) are the negative element, mentioned three times (with νόμος, law, another four times) in this short paragraph; the corresponding positive term is the name (Jesus)

Christ (Jesus), mentioned eight times. These are for Paul different ways by which men may think they can be rightly related to God (justified). The alternatives are twice starkly stated in v. 16, and the false alternative is excluded by a (mis)quotation of Psalm 143.3, ἐξ ἔργων νόμου οὐ δικαιωθήσεται πᾶσα σάρξ, By works of law shall no flesh be justified. The quotation is presumably made from memory; it is interesting that πᾶσα σάρξ, all flesh (instead of πᾶς ζῶν, every living person) slips in to describe the inability of man to justify himself; ἐξ ἔργων νόμου, by works of the law, is there not only to suit the context but because the Law, and works done in obedience to it, constitute the highest conceivable, though still inadequate, human claim. Paul is arguing not merely that Gentiles are not to be obliged to observe the rules of purity; it is wrong for Jews, who also are justified by faith and not by works, to insist that such rules should be observed in order that they may be able to join in a meal. It is this, or a Jewish reaction to it, that underlies and explains the protasis of v. 17. If by seeking to be justified in Christ we ourselves also were found to be sinners . . . Seeking to be justified in Christ (without works of law) will involve the Jew in sharing meals with his Gentile Christian neighbour. This will make him, in the technical sense, a sinner. Does this mean that Christ becomes a minister of sin, the effect of his action being to make us sinners? Paul takes this thought into a different context: No, if anyone makes me a sinner I do it myself (παραβάτην ἐμαυτὸν συνιστάνω). And I do this (as Peter has done) when I build up again distinctions which previously I had destroyed. All this results from the Law, or rather from the insistence, We must have from Gentiles if not the whole Law at least part of the Law, a token of the Law. We Jews must continue to observe it, and if we are to do so and also to have fellowship with Gentiles, then the Gentiles must observe it too, at last in part. To this Paul replies with the most absolute of negatives. The Law? I am dead to it. I do not exist for it, and it does not exist for me. This is emphatic and clear enough. But Paul elucidates (though many would say that he obscures) his point by adding two words: διὰ νόμου νόμῳ ἀπέθανον, Through law I died to law. What does 'through law' mean? Paul continues his statement with the words, 'I have been crucified (and this certainly means death) with Christ'. Are 'through Law' and 'with Christ' to be regarded as synonymous? It does not seem probable. Crucifixion with Christ is a death that has a positive outcome already hidden within it; sooner or later it will lead to life with Christ. A parallel saying in Rom. 7.4 is often adduced: You were put to death to the law (ἐθανατώθητε τῷ νόμῳ) through the body of Christ. This is itself a difficult saying. If it means through the dead body of Christ, the dying of Christ, it is a good parallel to the Χριστῷ συνεσταύρωμαι of Galatians but it does not explain διὰ νόμου (though this is not to deny that there is a connection between the death of Jesus and the Law). In our passage Paul gives the goal of death to Law as ἵνα θεῷ ζήσω, that I may live to God, suggesting that this dying is in his mind connected with the death and resurrection that are the beginning of the Christian life; but we still have no explanation of 'dying through law'. There is in Romans a closer and more useful verse, 7.10: The commandment that was intended to lead to life (ἡ εἰς ζωήν) proved to be death (εἰς θάνατον) for me. This indeed (Paul explains) was not the Law's fault; the fault was sin's fault, and sin was shown more clearly for what it is by the fact that it could so pervert and misuse that good, holy, and spiritual thing, the Law. In Galatians also, though in a context determined by sin death comes through the Law, Paul defends the Law. It is not in itself contrary to the promises of God. But it could not give life (3.21), and it served God's purpose only during the interlude between Moses and Christ.

Discussion of the problematical διὰ νόμου in 2.19 has deflected us from the main observation which comes to light in that verse, as v. 16 is taken up again. As long as we allow ourselves to be dominated by Law and to work in the field determined and defined by Law we can do no better than reach compromises, which may at best provide temporary solutions for our problems but only at the risk of creating new ones. The only answer to the problems that councils seek to solve is given in one word – Christ. The one name, the one person, is considered first subjectively, then objectively. Subjectively, Christ means for Paul his own death and resurrection. He has been crucified with Christ; there is now a new, risen life, which is not to be thought of as his own but as the life of Christ within him. He moves here on the edge of mysticism, and his words have often been taken to have a mystical meaning. They are however immediately and starkly interpreted by the word *flesh*, and, in a different way, by the word *faith*. Paul's present life is in the flesh, lived in the context of, lived indeed as part of the ordinary world of material existence, circumscribed by both physical and moral considerations; and he does not live by sight, the vision of heavenly things, but by faith, trusting as Abraham did in a promise which is only a promise and not a possession. 'Christ in me', like 'I in Christ', is not mysticism but eschatology, an anticipation of the life that lies beyond death and resurrection and can be known only by faith. With this we have already moved from the subjective to the objective. Faith is directed to a historical event, which is so stated as to be given thereby an immediate interpretation. I have been crucified with Christ; he was crucified for me, manifesting his love and acting on my behalf. The full conclusion is drawn in v. 21. To do as Peter and Barnabas are doing, drawing distinctions and separating believer from believer by the application of dietary and purity laws, is to make void the grace of God, which is free and for all, a gift to be received, unfettered by legal provisions. This is not the way to secure a right relation with God; this is given by Christ crucified, and if it were achievable in any other way, Christ might as well not have died. Paul may have joined in the debating, compromising process for a while, but here he comes home to the fact that settles all arguments.

In Galatians 3 Paul resumes the argument in the context of Galatia, rather than of Antioch. It had been important to set the record straight and in particular to show his amicable, though hardly deep, relation with the Jerusalem apostles and the Jerusalem church, a relation that persisted until they (represented by James) showed their dependence on legalism by attempting to force it on the Gentile element in the church of Antioch. Paul now goes on to take up scriptural arguments, some at least of which his adversaries had used – probably in Galatia but no doubt also elsewhere. The material is set out so as to tell the story of God's dealings with his people; these reach a climax at the end of the chapter and in the first verses of chapter 4.

The story begins with Abraham, with whom God entered into a covenant. This was based on faith, the ground on which Abraham was accounted righteous. Abraham believed God, and it was counted to him as righteousness. This means that it is not race that determines a relation with God, but faith. Moreover it was specifically stated that the Gentiles were to be included in the process. God announced the good news (the Gospel) in advance: In thee shall all the Gentiles be blessed – and as Gentiles, that is, as those who depend solely on faith. The corollary of this follows, and is expressed in biblical language. Those who depend on works of law, trusting in their legal achievements, receive not a blessing but a curse. This is the curse promised for all those who do not abide in all the provisions of the law. That no one does abide in all the things that are written in the law is proved by another Old Testament verse: It is those who are righteous by faith who shall live. Here Paul pulls up for a moment: Does not this mean that all will be cursed, none blessed? Who has done the whole law? No, this is not the consequence, for the sinless Christ, who was hanged on a tree, has taken the curse for us, so that we are free. This is how the cross comes to mean righteousness for those who in faith accept it. The end of the story is now anticipated. The promise was made to Abraham and his seed. That might seem to mean not to the Gentiles but only to the Israelites, Abraham's descendants. No, says Paul, the word seed is singular, σπέρματι, not σπέρμασι. Thus the climax of the story lies not with ethnic Israel, but with Christ, and (in Christ) his people.

But Paul has been going too fast. Verse 17 is most clearly understood as a reply to an opponent who makes the point, 'Yes, this may be all very well as far as Abraham and God's covenant with Abraham are concerned. But after Abraham came the even greater figure of Moses, and the basis of the covenant is changed. It is no longer a matter of promise and faith but of Law and works. Only those who perform the works that the Law requires will now inherit.' To this Paul answers, playing on the word διαθήκη, which means both covenant and testament. 'When a testator has sealed his will no one can alter it; the Law vas given 430 years after the covenant and cannot change it.' A reply comes back, 'There is one person who can change a testament; the testator.' But Paul still has a shot in his locker. 'The Law was not given directly by God (who made the covenant), but by angels.' The covenant of promise and faith still stands. Paul's interlocutor now has a question. If the Law cannot change things, what is it for? Why was it given? A good question. The answer is that the Law is not to be thought of as a bad thing. It is not itself the conveyer of promise, but it is not against God's promises. It comes through angels but from the same gracious God and is itself a gift of grace. But the covenant of law was a covenant of obedience (Exod. 19.5, 8; 24.3, 7, 8), and the Law was a temporary measure. From 3.19 to the end of the chapter the text is full of temporal clauses: might be given; before faith came; till faith should be revealed; up to the time of Christ; now that faith has come, no longer. These all emphasize the temporary character of the Law. It was not there at the beginning of the process and it will not be there at the end. It has therefore not altered the fundamental character of the original covenant, which (on man's side) is not secured by works (of law) but received by faith. The Law in addition to providing guidance for the conduct of life had the effect of imprisoning mankind – of imprisoning the whole universe if we are to give full weight to the neuter τὰ πάντα in v. 22 – under the sovereignty of sin. The thought is taken up again in v. 24 where the image of the παιδαγωγὸς is used. The παιδαγωγὸς is not a teacher who will in due course lead to the supreme teacher, but the slave who will prevent the schoolboy from playing truant. As long as the Law ruled, where the Law ruled, there was no escape from the dominion of sin, until the possibility of faith in Christ came into being. Once faith came on the scene the παιδαγωγὸς was gone. Looking back through chapter 3 we may well ask what had become of faith since the time of Abraham. It is a question Paul does not ask; not surprisingly there is no answer. If Paul meant that faith was banished by the Law he was being unfair both to the Law and to many who lived under it. The question arises again at the end of Romans 9 and the beginning of Romans 10. Notwithstanding Israel's zeal for God they had misunderstood the Law, thinking that it asked for nothing but works and not perceiving that the true response to it was faith. The recognition of this truth about the Law marks not a contradiction of Galatians but an advance, in that it answers a question which in Galatians was not asked.

The climax of the chapter, which may be regarded, within the epistle, as the climax of Paul's rejection of the temporizing compromise and legalism of Jerusalem, comes in 3.26–29. Faith means being in Christ Jesus. You were baptized into Christ, you put on Christ, you belong to Christ. It makes no difference whether you are Jew or Greek, slave or free, male or female; he is the seed of Abraham, heir of the promise, and those who are in him receive in him their share of the promise, themselves the seed of Abraham, that is, the people of God.

We may note briefly that Paul continues for another paragraph, probably because he remembers that he is writing for Gentiles who, though they seem to be taking up the Jewish law, began their lives outside it. This does not mean that they escape bondage, though bondage under the Law has been replaced by bondage under cosmic powers (στοιχεῖα τοῦ κόσμου). Paul uses a new image, that of the heir, who is the rightful owner of the whole estate but, as long as he is a minor, is no better off than a slave. The end of the story is the same: when the fullness of time came God sent forth his Son to redeem – and he still says, those who were under the law, for indeed all mankind, not only Jews, owe obedience to their Creator. There is an important parallel between 3.29 and 4.9. It is the same person, now presented for the benefit of Gentile readers not as Christ, the fulfilment of Judaism, but as the Son of God, who makes compromise impossible and himself constitutes the alternative to compromise. One does not ask, Can we give a little here and gain a little there? One asks, What does it mean to have Christ the Son of God as Lord and Redeemer? When the question is so put there is no doubt what the answer will be.

This is, I think, the clearest example in Paul of the way in which a more commonplace argument is replaced, or hammered home, by an emphatic Christological assertion. It is clear because here Paul begins by quoting what he said to Peter and continues either with his second thoughts on the occasion itself or with his subsequent more mature thought. Elsewhere in the epistles we have, as one would expect, the argument as Paul, having thought the matter over, decided it should go. There are however other examples of this change of approach; there is a notable one in 1 Corinthians 11, where Paul deals with the disgraceful behaviour of Corinthians at the church supper, for which at this time we have no reason to presuppose an established eucharistic liturgy – or indeed a eucharist. In 11.17–22 Paul berates his readers as one might any society holding an accustomed supper party and behaving badly: '. . . one is hungry, another gets drunk. Haven't you houses for eating and drinking? . . .' But then (vv. 23–25), 'Remember the Lord Jesus at his supper party . . . You proclaim the Lord's death until he comes. How can you do that and mock your poor hungry brother?'

Another notable example is found in Philippians 2, modified by the fact that the first verse of the chapter contains already a reference to Christ; after that however Paul appeals to the Philippian community for unity on the secular ground that it will give him pleasure: Complete my joy by having the same mind, the same love, united in soul. Immediately after this follows the Christological passage: '. . . Who, though he existed in the form of God, thought life on equality with God no prize worth keeping, but humbled himself, took the form of a slave . . .'. Commonplace exhortations to humility are nothing in comparison with this account of the Lord's humiliation.

These are outstanding examples of the way in which Paul will sidestep, or sometimes sweep aside, other arguments and considerations in order to concentrate on the figure of Christ. This becomes explicit in the most vital of contexts when he declares, with reference to his first preaching in Corinth, I decided to know nothing among you except Jesus Christ, and him crucified (1 Cor. 2.2). No doubt this would include the addition made in the words of Rom. 8.34, Christ Jesus who died, or rather was raised, who is at the right hand of God, who makes intercession for us. The whole is summed up in the formula, the word of faith, which is a preaching rather than a baptismal formula, though it would serve both purposes, If you confess with your mouth Jesus as Lord, and believe in your heart that God raised him from the dead, you will be saved (Rom. 10.9). These were propositions on which, for Paul, no compromise was possible; conversely, it was agreement on these that made agreement with others (Pillars, super-apostles) possible. Even here, however, if my reconstruction of the controversies of the apostolic age is correct, Paul learned by the hard way that compromise did not work. It would have worked to say, Jesus is the Jewish Messiah. He himself worked among Jews; he fulfilled the Jewish Bible, his message is for Jews, and what God has done through him he has done for his own people. If others are to join them and share with them in the blessings of the Messianic age they must first become Jews in the manner laid down long ago and consistently practised. I say, 'It would have worked.' It would have produced a united community. It would not have worked very well; not many converts would have been made. The church (though it would not have borne that name) would have been a sub-set of Pharisaism. The name of Jesus would today be no better known than that of Sabbatai Zevi, the seventeenth-century Messiah. It did work, as we know, to throw the barriers down, proclaiming Christ as the sole and all-sufficient author of salvation, a salvation free and accessible to all, whether Jews or Gentiles. But the account of the Council in Galatians 2 seems to present the Jerusalem Pillars as saying: Very well, you may understand the Gospel in that way and take it to the Gentiles; we agree that your converts need not be circumcised; they will be the Gentile, uncircumcised, part of the people of God. We for our part will go our own ways preaching to Jews and accepting only those Gentiles who are willing to become Jews. That this did not work appeared speedily in Antioch. James in the interests of Judaism called for and obtained a separation into two churches which could not sit together at table and eat in fellowship the same food. So much for the right hand of fellowship in Jerusalem. Peter and Paul who had shaken hands in Jerusalem could only oppose each other in Antioch. Paul – at that time or after later reflection – found his way to the solution of the problem. There was no way but by a reference back to the one first principle. We agree on the preaching of Christ crucified and risen; if righteousness comes through the Law this proclamation is a waste of time and its content is a wasted life. Christ need not have died. Since this is absurd we must conclude that he is our righteousness and that – as a means of achieving righteousness – we are dead to the Law and the Law is dead to us.

It was not this conclusion that was reached in a new council at Jerusalem but a new compromise. And it must be admitted that this compromise worked. The Decree produced by the Council (Acts 15.29) proposed a basic Judaism, which Gentile sympathizers with Judaism probably already kept. For them the Decree asked nothing fresh, and they would have no difficulty, either in theology or in practice, in accepting it. It has been maintained that it was these sympathizers, already to be found in the synagogue, that Paul for the most part addressed, and that it was among them that his Gentile converts were found. This seems doubtful. The Gentile Christians in Thessalonica had turned to the living and true God from idols (1 Thess. 1.9); this could not be said of men who regularly attended the synagogue. The converts in Corinth included (1 Cor. 6.9–11) fornicators, idolaters, adulterers, catamites, sodomites, thieves, the rapacious, drunkards, revilers, robbers; this does not sound like a synagogue congregation. 1 Cor. 12.2 speaks explicitly of a past in which Corinthians were driven to dumb idols. The vices listed in Gal. 5.19–21 were probably not unknown to the Galatians. It seems, however, that as Christians these Gentiles also were prepared to accept so much of Judaism, and the Decree was taken (by Luke for example) as the basis of the Gentile mission, which all eventually accepted, and it was observed for centuries. It demanded the bare minimum of Jewish custom and rule; even so, the rules were often bent. I have referred in my first, historical, lecture to the version of the Decree found in Revelation 2, and to the Western text of Acts 15.20, 29; 21.25. This means that there were many churches which understood the Decree to have required no more than abstention from idolatry and fornication, together with a general Christian kindliness. To this no one would object; certainly not Paul. The Western variants however remain variations from Luke's understanding of the Decree; and it must be remembered that Acts 15 is fundamentally concerned not with the question, With whom may I have supper and what shall we eat? but, Who may be saved and on what conditions? From the conditions circumcision is excluded, probably not because it was one outstanding piece of legalism but because it was so repulsive to the Greco-Roman mind that to insist on it would have prevented altogether the spread of Christianity into the Greco-Roman world; not circumcision, but elements of Jewish law taken for the most part from its ethical provisions.

Luke in Acts, written probably in the 80s, presents to us the basis on which the church was organized and its mission conducted in the immediately post-apostolic period. So Paul lost, and the Stephen party, with its *via media* and its Gentile base in the synagogue fringe, won. The church owed, and Luke at least knew that it owed, not only its establishment in a substantial part of the Roman Empire but its independence of Judaism, and therewith its universal scope, to Paul. The author, or authors, of the Pastoral Epistles knew this too, and for them Paul was the apostle *par excellence*, a step that even Luke does not take. But they like Luke fail to state with unambiguous clarity Paul's radical Gospel of radically unconditional grace. The message was based on a compromise, and so was Christian society.

So what are we to say about the theology of the Council, of the post-apostolic age? If you will, of Acts? The period was one in which the Gentile element in the church was increasing, but Jervell has argued, not without force, that the Jewish Christian minority exercised a surprising and disproportionate influence, putting the Decree into circulation and observance, maintaining the Matthean element in the gospel tradition, and, in its early stages, affecting Paul himself to the extent of drawing from him the discussion in Romans 9–11 of the ultimate destiny of Israel. It is better however to see these things, at least the Decree and the influence of the Jewish Christian party, as arising from the Jews of the Diaspora who were at home in the Hellenistic world. These forces had permeated Luke's mind to such an extent that he told the story of his hero Paul in terms of them. He could even make Paul a member and an agent of the Decree-making body, and attribute to him the Areopagus speech of Acts 17.

For the most part it will suffice to say that Luke was a less profound theologian than Paul; if this is a sin it affects us all, and none of us can afford to throw stones at Luke's glasshouse. Again and again Luke stops short of the point Paul had reached a generation earlier. It is so for example in Christology. Luke can write (in Acts 2.36) a sentence that, taken on its own, appears to mean that the man Jesus became Lord and Christ when God vindicated him after his crucifixion. That Luke himself believed that Jesus was Christ and Lord from his birth is shown by Luke 2.11. Did Luke himself not see the difference? Did he think it unimportant? There can be no doubt of Luke's personal loyalty to Jesus, but he had not grasped the fact that a serious Christology, indeed an absolute loyalty, demands something like pre-existence. This is to be seen with special clarity in passages, such as Phil. 2.6–11, where Paul appears to modify less well thought-out Christologies. Luke, one supposes, would have been quite satisfied with the Philippian hymn before Paul edited it. Again, there is in Acts virtually no doctrine of the atonement. One verse is always pointed out as the exception to this theological silence – 20.28. The exception is important, but it is not followed up, and Luke's word (περιεποιήσατο) has no other theological use in the New Testament. Elsewhere Luke is content to say little more than that the crucifixion was a bad thing – a mistake, even a sin – but one that God put right by means of the resurrection. It goes with this that Luke is fully aware of Christian baptism, baptism into the name of Jesus, but does not think of it as specifically baptism into Christ's death; he knows that Christians meet to break bread, that is, to have a meal together, but he does not find it necessary to say that at their meal they may proclaim the Lord's death with a view to his future coming. All this, however, is a matter of omission, and omission does not necessarily mean disagreement. Acts is indeed a vindication of the Christianity of the ordinary man in the pew: see how well you can do without a great deal of theology!

But there are vital points at which you cannot do without theology; one (and it has arisen more than once in the history of the church) is the confrontation of law with grace and faith. If to be saved it is necessary to abstain from food sacrificed to idols, can we believe that Paul was saved? Of course, such a question reduces the matter to absurdity; but that in turn underlines the importance in theology of saying exactly what you mean and not using compromise formulas which can be interpreted in more ways than one, or attempting to let everyone have at least a bit of his own way. 'To become as a Jew to the Jews' is good as a matter of social courtesy; as a way of salvation such occasional obedience would be worse than no obedience at all. The church on the whole accepted the Decree and the church did not disintegrate, but it did turn into something more like an institution and less like a family. Two things however secured the persistence of Christianity. One was the adaptability of the Decree. With some textual variation, or even without that expedient, it could be reduced to an elementary moral code, which rejected idolatry and so maintained faithfulness to the one God of Scripture, and regarded fornication and bloodshed as evil. The other was the faithfulness of all parties, including the heirs of James and of Stephen, to the one Gospel of Christ crucified and risen, ultimately incompatible as it was with any form of legalism. To these may be added the lasting influence of Paul. He may have been imperfectly represented in Acts, in the Pastorals, in 1 Clement and Ignatius, but even untheological hero-worship helped to preserve the letters, with their power to revive and reform the church. And with these we must count the influence of the only indirectly Pauline but no less profound theology of the Fourth Gospel.

5

I am not Ashamed of the Gospel

'I am not ashamed of the Gospel.' Many commentators on Romans have explained these words in a psychological sense. At the beginning of his letter Paul reflects upon the splendour and significance of the place to which his words are addressed, and on its manifest commitment to an understanding of man's existence radically different from his own, and consciously thrusts away the natural feeling of shame which comes upon him at the thought of the figure that he, an obscure provincial bearing a message which must inevitably have appeared unacceptable even if it proved intelligible, must cut in the eyes of the capital. This kind of interpretation has a respectable history. Chrysostom works out at considerable length the contrast between the son of the carpenter and the rulers and gods of Rome. Bengel, more succinctly, writes: 'Mundo evangelium est *stultitia* et *infirmitas*. Quare mundi opinione esset erubescendum, Romae praesertim: sed Paulus non erubescit.' There is no need to underestimate such psychological factors in the situation, and I should not wish to unsay my own statement of them in my commentary. Paul had probably not read those lines of Vergil's which impressively close J. Weiss's *History of Primitive Christianity* –

> Verum haec tantum alias inter caput extulit urbes
> quantum lenta solent inter viburna cupressi (*Eclogue* I, 24f.) –

but now that ninety years of empire had passed since Vergil wrote them the sentiment they contained must have become common property. Of this Paul cannot have been unaware.

True however as observations of this kind may be, they are not adequate as an explanation of Paul's words. He had not been invited to address the Roman Senate, and neither Vergil's poetry nor imperial building projects had altered the fact that the back streets of Rome were pretty much the same as those of other large towns with which Paul was already familiar – Antioch, Ephesus, Athens, Corinth; and it was in these that his work, if he reached Rome, would probably lie. In Rome, too, it would probably prove true that the elect did not number many wise (by this world's standards), many powerful, or many nobly born. No doubt Paul would feel at home among them. Moreover, the construction of his sentence is to be observed. He has just stated (Rom. 1.15) that he is ready to preach the Gospel in Rome, and then adds (1.16) the ground on which his readiness rests: οὐ γὰρ ἐπαισχύνομαι τὸ εὐαγγέλιον. That is to say, the not being ashamed of the Gospel is an antecedent condition which is not in itself necessarily connected with the particular circumstances Paul has in mind, though when it is applied to them it constitutes a basis on which his willingness to undertake Christian activity even at the centre of the Empire may rest. That Paul was not ashamed of the Gospel was a proposition that had particular relevance and point in a letter addressed to Rome, but it was not a proposition specially thought out for the occasion.

This is borne out by the fact that the content of these words in Rom. 1.16 is paralleled elsewhere. Paul does not in any other passage use the word ἐπαισχύνεσθαι in a similar context (it occurs only at Rom. 6.21, in a quite different setting). The simple verb αἰσχύνεσθαι however occurs at Phil. 1.20, where I take the context to be a situation in which Paul is awaiting trial. Whatever happens he will not be put to shame. This is a safe proposition, for Paul knows that Christ can and will be glorified in his, Paul's, body, εἴτε διὰ ζωῆς εἴτε διὰ θανάτου. Such a ground of confidence is in itself a clear indication that not being ashamed is an antecedent, Christian, rather than a social, condition; its cause lies not in Paul's relation to his environment but in the nature of the Gospel. The same verb (αἰσχύνεσθαι) occurs in 2 Cor. 10.8, which describes a situation which differs, in that Paul is here confronted not with pagans but with rivals inside the church; the situation is the same however in that his apostleship and his Gospel are being put to the test. In these circumstances, Paul affirms confidently, οὐκ αἰσχυνθήσομαι. His apostleship and his Gospel, rooted as they are in God, will stand the test successfully; his authority, positively exercised, is real, because it springs not from his own capacity to control his environment but from a divine message and commission. Paul also uses the verb καταισχύνεσθαι. Rom. 5.5; 1 Cor. 11.4, 5, 22 are clearly not relevant. 2 Cor. 7.14; 9.4 are relevant only in that they illustrate the use of the simple verb in 10.8: Paul's boasting about the Corinthian achievement in regard to the collection would reduce him to shame if it were shown to have no substance in it – just as his boasting about his apostolic ἐξουσία would do, if his authority proved to be no more than an empty and baseless claim. In Rom. 9.33; 10.11 however Isa. 28.16 is quoted, in substantial agreement with the LXX: ὁ πιστεύων ἐπ' αὐτῷ οὐ καταισχυνθήσεται (at 9.33, D G make the agreement complete by substituting οὐ μὴ καταισχυνθῇ). The Hebrew differs, having לא יחיש (shall not make haste, or better, get alarmed). Again, the sense is that of having a firm standing ground; the metaphor refers now not specifically to the position and authority of a preacher and apostle, but to the standing of any Christian. 1 Cor. 1.27 puts the same theme as it were in reverse. Judged by normal standards the Christian mob in Corinth might well feel ashamed in the presence of those who, by these standards, were wise, powerful, and nobly born; but these were not God's standards, and in due course it will be the wise, powerful, and noble who are exposed to shame in their frailty and folly. In the same context, 1 Cor. 2.3 is only an apparent exception to Paul's unashamed confidence in proclaiming the Gospel. When he speaks of his weakness, fear, and trembling, this is not because he had in Corinth lost his confidence in the Gospel and become ashamed of it, but rather because of his sense of responsibility, in proclaiming it (so e.g. Schlatter).

The Deutero-Pauline literature also affords plenty of material of a similar kind which is conveniently disclosed by study of the same words. 1 Pet. 4.16 is the classical example of the use of αἰσχύνεσθαι. I must not digress to consider the problem of the persecutions implied by this epistle, and inquire whether ὡς Χριστιανός means that persecution 'for the name' had already been set upon a legal footing. It is at all events clear that the profession of Christianity was likely to lead to grave consequences (otherwise expressions such as πύρωσις in 4.12, and the 'roaring lion' of 5.8, would be ludicrous), and the author urges his readers in these circumstances not to be ashamed of the faith and of the society that had led to their suffering. The use of the cognate noun, αἰσχύνη, in Heb. 12.2 is equally striking, for the example of Christ himself, who thought nothing of the shame of crucifixion, is invoked to encourage Christians. Paul's ἐπαισχύνεσθαι reappears in important passages in 2 Timothy. Paul himself is represented as not ashamed of his sufferings (1.12); Timothy must not be ashamed either of the testimony of the Lord (that is, he must not through shame draw back from bearing this testimony), or of Paul as a prisoner (1.8); in the latter respect Onesiphorus has set a good example (1.16). 1 Pet. 2.6 contains the same quotation from Isa. 28.16 that appears in Rom. 9.33; 10.11; and in 1 Pet. 3.16 there is an interesting inversion that reflects though it changes the familiar usage: so far from themselves being ashamed of their Christian profession Christians should so live that their attackers may be put to shame (ἵνα ... καταισχυνθῶσιν οἱ ἐπηρεάζοντες). Another important inversion occurs at Heb. 11.16: God is not ashamed of those who trust in him.

Hermas (*Similitudes* 8.6.4; 9.21.3) uses ἐπαισχύνεσθαι of the apostates, traitors, and double-minded (ἀποστάται, προδόται, δίψυχοι), who because of their cowardice deny – are ashamed of – the name of their Lord (with a probable allusion to the use of this name in baptism), but outside the Pauline and Deutero–Pauline writings the most important passages are Ignatius, *Smyrnaeans* 10.2 and 1 Jn 2.28. In the former, Ignatius, noting that the Smyrnaeans have not despised or been ashamed of (ὑπερηφανήσατε, ἐπῃσχύνθητε) his bonds, adds, Neither will our perfect hope, Jesus Christ, be ashamed of you (ὑμᾶς ἐπαισχυνθήσεται). In the latter, John urges his readers to abide in Christ, so that at his manifestation they may have confidence (παρρησία) and not be put to shame (μὴ αἰσχυνθῶμεν) before him (so as to be repulsed from him, ἀπ' αὐτοῦ).

These passages in Ignatius and John are important because they connect a state of things at the present time (which in Ignatius is described as being – or not being – ashamed of the circumstances of Christ's representative) with being put to shame in the presence of Christ, that is (if we may interpret John by Ignatius), through Christ's own being ashamed, at the judgement, of those whose action at an earlier stage had been unworthy of him. These sayings, which are both fairly late in date, thus point with particular clearness to a saying ascribed to Jesus himself in Mk 8.38:

> Whoever is ashamed of me and of my words in this adulterous and sinful generation, of him will the Son of man be ashamed when he comes in the glory of his Father with the holy angels.

In view of the variety of passages we have just considered it should immediately be clear that, whatever the origin and history of this saying may be, it is hardly adequate to say with Loisy (*Les Évangiles synoptiques*, II, 26), 'L'esprit et même le langage de Paul se reconnaissent encore'. There are Pauline parallels, but the background is wider than Pauline, and in fact this verse sets before us a very complicated and much disputed problem in *Traditionsgeschichte*.

We must begin by noting the synoptic parallels at this point. Mt. 16.27 offers a piece of formalized apocalyptic:

> For the Son of man will come in the glory of his Father with his angels, and then he will repay each man according to his behaviour (πρᾶξιν).

From this saying almost everything distinctive in the Marcan verse has been removed; in particular it lacks the contrast and parallel between being ashamed of Jesus, and the Son of man's being ashamed. That the Matthean form is secondary is clear; that Matthew was actuated in his editing by the desire to remove the apparent Marcan distinction between Jesus and the Son of man, and to show that Jesus as Son of man was himself the Judge who would hand out rewards and punishments (cf. e.g. 25.31) is also clear.

Lk. 9.26 does little more than rearrange the Marcan form of the warning:

> Whoever is ashamed of me and of my words, of him will the Son of man be ashamed, when he comes in his glory and that of the Father and of the holy angels.

The adulterous and sinful generation drops out, for Luke is not thinking of one generation only, but of conditions of Christian life that will stretch into the distant future; and the glory is not only the Father's – the Son of man and the angels have their proper glory too. But this is not a point Mark would have wished to contradict; the 'great power and glory' of Mk 13.26 are the power and glory of the Son of man.

So far then we find a primary Marcan saying, which Matthew and Luke have modified under no other motivation than their own editorial presuppositions. There is however much more to consider. A similar saying occurs in parallel but not identical forms in Matthew and Luke.

Mt. 10.32f.: Every one who shall confess me (ὁμολογήσει ἐν ἐμοὶ) before men, I too will confess him (ὁμολογήσω . . . ἐν αὐτῷ) before my Father who is in heaven. And whoever denies (ἀρνήσηται) me before men, I too will deny (ἀρνήσομαι) before my Father who is in heaven.

Lk. 12.8f.: I tell you, everyone who confesses me (ὁμολογήσῃ ἐν ἐμοὶ) before men, the Son of man will confess him (ὁμολογήσει ἐν αὐτῷ) before the angels of God. But he who denies (ὁ ἀρνησάμενος) me before men shall be denied (ἀπαρνηθήσεται) before the angels of God.

Here is a divergent Q form of the Marcan saying. Of this Q form Matthew and Luke give versions that are not identical, but they agree in differing from Mark in the following points: (a) they contain not only a negative warning saying, but also a promise – the confessor will not lose his reward; (b) in the negative saying they speak not of being ashamed but of denying. They both agree with the Marcan saying however in that the language they use is appropriate to the situation of Christians in time of persecution. For confessing (ὁμολογεῖν, ὁμολογία) compare Jn 9.22; 12.42; Rom. 10.9–10; 1 Tim. 6.12–13; 1 Jn 2.23; 4.2, 3, 15; 2 Jn 7; Heb. 3.1; 4.14; 10.23 (and cf. Rev. 3.5); and for denying (ἀρνεῖσθαι, ἀπαρνεῖσθαι), in addition to the narratives of Peter's denial, 1 Tim. 5.8; 2 Tim. 2.12; 2 Pet. 2.1; 1 Jn 2.22–23; Jude 4; Rev. 2.13; 3.8.

Matthew's is the smoother form of the Q saying, and shows its parallelism most completely:

He who confesses me	He who denies me
I will confess	I will deny.

Each clause consists of two precisely parallel members, and the two clauses are parallel with each other. In the Lucan form the parallelism is imperfect in the saying as a whole, and at each stage. The first clause shows the same change from 'I' to 'Son of man' as the Marcan saying –

He who confesses *me* . . .
The *Son of man* will confess . . .

The parallelism is broken in the second clause also, though not in the same way; an active verb is followed by a passive –

He who denies me . . .
Will be denied . . .

In Matthew, confessing and denying take place before 'my Father who is in heaven', in Luke, before 'the angels of God'.

It is unnecessary to point out that controversy has raged over the relative originality of these sayings, and quite impossible even to outline the course of the discussion; it will however be useful to illustrate it. I am not in this paper concerned with literary criticism and form criticism for their own sake, but some attention to them will serve to bring out theological points of value for the comparison of Paul with the synoptic tradition.

The modern phase of the discussion of such questions may be taken to begin with Bultmann's *Geschichte der Synoptischen*

115

Tradition. On p. 117 (cf. p. 134) of the 1931 edition he says that Mark and the original form of the Q saying agree in distinguishing between Jesus and the Son of man; this distinction is primary in comparison with Matthew's direct application of the saying to the person of Jesus; Mark has abbreviated the full (positive and negative) form of the saying under the influence of the context in which he places it; one cannot deduce from Lk. 12.9 that the saying originally contained no reference to the Son of man, since Luke elsewhere destroys the parallelism of sayings he transmits. Probably therefore (though he does not explicitly say so) Bultmann would take the primitive form of the saying to be something like

> Whoever confesses me . . .
> The Son of man will confess . . .
> Whoever denies (or, is ashamed of) me . . .
> The Son of man will deny (or, be ashamed of) . . .

When Bultmann returned to the issue in the light of later discussions (*Ergänzungsheft*, 1958 and 1962) he drew attention to the views of C. H. Dodd, E. Käsemann and P. Vielhauer. Dodd (*Parables of the Kingdom*, pp. 93f.) thinks the Q form, because of its parallelism, more original, and notes that in it the reference to the Son of man is less secure; in any case, the Son of man is not as in Mark described as 'coming' – he simply confesses, or denies, in heaven. 'Those who acknowledge Christ on earth thereby possess the sign that they are eternally accepted by Him' (p. 94).

Käsemann considers Mark's ἐπαισχύνεσθαι to be a Grecized version of Q's ὁμολογεῖν ἐν and ἀρνεῖσθαι. Matthew on the other hand is secondary to Mark in that he identifies Jesus and the Son of man. The Marcan distinction however (and here Käsemann appears to go beyond Bultmann) is not sufficient to show that the saying in this form (or with ἀρνεῖσθαι instead of ἐπαισχύνεσθαι) goes back to Jesus. It has its place in the sacred law of the early church. 'Dieser Spruch hat den eigenartigen Charakter der palästinischen Prophetenrede bewahrt, welche Sätze heiligen Rechtes für die Gemeinde verkündigt und an die irdische Bedingung im eschatologischen Futur himmlische Verheissung oder göttlichen Fluch knüpft' (*Exegetische Versuche und Besinnungen*, I, 211; cf. II, 102; *New Testament Studies* 1 (1954–5), p. 257 = *Versuche* II, 78f.). According to Vielhauer (*Festschrift für Günther Dehn*, pp. 68ff.) 'der ursprüngliche Wortlaut des Spruches ist nicht mehr zu rekonstruieren' (p. 69). The Marcan form is secondary in that it is shortened and contains only the threat and not the promise, and in its use of ἐπαισχύνεσθαι. It is at least possible that the passive (ἀπαρνηθήσεται) in Luke's second member is original, and points to God as the subject of the active verb. If this is so, it means that God will be the agent in the first member also, and that the reference to Son of man will be a Christological variation – the beginning of a process carried logically through by Matthew.

Bultmann records these suggestions without giving any hint that he is convinced by them. They are well chosen in that they cover between them a good deal of the most important thinking on the subject of recent years. A few additions however should be made.

G. Bornkamm (*Jesus von Nazareth*, p. 200) thinks it can be asserted with confidence that Jesus spoke (in the manner of Mk 8.38) of the future coming of the Son of man. The distinction between Jesus and the coming Son of man is striking, and gives to Lk. 12.8f. and Mk 8.38 a strong claim to authority. H. E. Tödt and F. Hahn also follow Bultmann in this respect.

E. Haenchen (*Der Weg Jesu*, pp. 298ff.) stands close to Käsemann. He agrees that Mk 8.38 represents a relatively early stage in the use of Son of man, 'nach der Jesus der Menschensohn noch nicht ist, sondern erst sein wird' (p. 299). This however does not make the saying authentic. Both in Mark and Q it presupposes a situation in which one is asked whether he belongs to the *Jesusgemeinde*. Some will deny this in order to save their lives. This sort of situation arose in the church after Easter, but cannot have occurred among the disciples before the crucifixion. 'V. 38 ist also eine prophetische Mahnung innerhalb der nachösterlichen Gemeinde' (p. 299).

J. Jeremias (*Zeitschrift für die neutestamentliche Wissenschaft* 58 [1967], p. 170) brings a different kind of criticism to bear upon the view that Mk 8.38 has as it stands a high claim authenticity, and thus strikes out on a line different from those we have noted so far. He sets out side by side sayings containing Son of man and parallel sayings in which Son of man is replaced by the first person pronoun singular. Discussion shows that the form without Son of man is regularly the older. This observation may be applied to Mt. 10.32–33, Lk. 12.8–9; and the result is that the Matthean form cannot be dismissed (as many have thought) as secondary to the Lucan.

Some have defended the substantial authenticity of Mk 8.38. V. Taylor thinks it less original than the Q form, and that it may originally have lacked the apocalyptic colouring now visible in v. 38b ('when he comes'). It was nevertheless eschatological. 'If the saying is original' (and Taylor certainly suggests that he thinks so), 'one of two possibilities must be true: either, at some point in His ministry, Jesus spoke of the coming of a supernatural Son of Man other than Himself, or by '"the Son of Man" he meant the Elect Community of which He was to be the Head' (*Commentary*, p. 384). Taylor evidently prefers the latter alternative, and draws the conclusion that Mk 8.38 is at present out of place.

Miss Hooker thinks that 'we can perhaps trace the development of the saying from Lk. 12.8–9, through Mk 8.38, to Mt. 16.27' (*The Son of Man in Mark*, p. 119), but thinks that the apparent distinction between Jesus and himself and the Son of man can be defended and explained without recourse to Taylor's pair of alternatives. In both 34 and 38a (which together form a complete counterpart to the Q pair) Jesus speaks of himself because 'he is speaking to those who wish to follow him as they know him in his earthly life' (p. 119). In 38b this shifts to the Son of man because the reference is now to 'some future point of time when Jesus will recognize publicly those who are his followers' (p. 120). The term Son of man is now used because in the future Jesus' authority as Son of man will be generally acknowledged. 'At present, his authority is veiled, but when it is revealed, then the paradox which has brought suffering and shame to both the Son of man and his disciples will cease, and he will be recognized as the rightful ruler' (p. 121). It is difficult to see how Jesus could have proclaimed another Son of man and have left room for himself, and 'extremely unlikely that the Church would ever have created a saying in the form found in Mk 8.38' (p. 189). A somewhat similar view is taken by E. Schweizer in his commentary on Mark. In the Marcan saying, the last clause (in the glory of his Father with the holy angels) may be discounted as an explanatory comment from the church, and Lk. 12.8–9 may be regarded as the oldest form of the saying. But 'die merkwürdige Unterscheidung von "ich" und "Menschensohn" wird auf Jesus zurückgehen, da die Gleichsetzung ja für die Gemeinde selbstverständlich war' (p. 100). By the Son of man however Jesus means himself. 'Die Formulierung ist aber natürlich, wenn betont werden soll, dass die Entscheidung der Hörer dem vor ihnen stehenden, irdischen Menschen Jesus gegenüber schon das letzte Gericht entscheide, von dem Jesus in zurückhaltender, seine Funktion objektiv darstellender Terminologie spricht' (pp. 100f.).

It is now possible finally to make a brief reference to the article on υἱὸς τοῦ ἀνθρώπου in *Theologisches Wörterbuch zum Neuen Testament*, VIII, by C. Colpe. Colpe (p. 459) thinks that the Marcan saying has been exposed to a good deal of editorial rewriting. His usage shows, however, that Mark had no objection to the words ἀρνεῖσθαι, ἀπαρνεῖσθαι; ἐπαισχύνεσθαι is not Pauline but comes from the common tradition. Mark has added καὶ τοὺς ἐμοὺς λόγους, expanded 'before men' into 'in this adulterous and sinful generation', and described the coming of the Son of man in traditional apocalyptic terms. In accordance with his general position he has identified the coming Son of man with the earthly Jesus, as his addition of τοῦ πατρὸς αὐτοῦ shows. Colpe agrees with Jeremias in preferring the form without 'Son of man' (p. 450).

It will be clear from what has been said that the last word on this question has not yet been spoken – nor will it be spoken in this paper, which after all is primarily about Paul and must soon return to its main theme. When the discussion (of which I have reviewed only a fragment) is surveyed, it appears that some at least have attempted to decide too quickly which is the most primitive form of the saying we are dealing with, and whether this primitive form was spoken by Jesus, or originated in the post-Easter community.

It may be affirmed without hesitation that the saying was current in the church, probably in several forms, from an early time; the church, even when not persecuted in a formal sense, was almost always subject to pressures which made it difficult rather than easy to admit one's adherence to the crucified Jesus and his followers, easy rather than difficult to turn one's back on the whole disreputable lot. The use of the odd Greek ὁμολογεῖν ἐν points to a Semitic-speaking background; and it is not impossible (see Colpe, *Theologisches Wörterbuch zum Neuen Testament*, VIII, 450) that behind the variation of ἀρνεῖσθαι and ἐπαισχύνεσθαι lies the Aramaic pair כפר (to deny, renounce) and חפר (to be ashamed). The absence of the positive member of the Q saying in Mark becomes less striking when, with Miss Hooker, we observe that its substance is contained in 8.34 – he who denies himself and takes up his cross is in fact recognized as a disciple. This does not answer the question whether Mark has accommodated the parallel saying to his context, or Q has produced the parallelism out of material in the Marcan form. Fortunately however this is precisely the kind of question this paper need not attempt to settle.

The widest divergence of opinion has been expressed over the question whether or not the reference to 'Son of man' is original. Two arguments have to be weighed against each other. (a) The primitive church would not have made up a saying in a form that distinguished between Jesus and the Son of man, whom it identified. (b) 'Son of man' is never replaced by 'I'; therefore 'I' must be original. Neither of these arguments is or can be entirely satisfactory. On the one hand, we do not know what the primitive church could or could not do except by observing what it did; and it is a fact that, in its records, when Jesus speaks of the future coming of the Son of man he does so in the third person. On the other hand, it can be alleged that the 'Son of man' is never replaced by 'I' only when all parallels have been discussed and it has been proved in every case that 'I' is original and 'Son of man' secondary; one must not therefore use the argument, 'Son of man' is never replaced by 'I', therefore it is not so in this case. The one really firm point is that Matthew, in 16.27, though he does not substitute 'I' for 'Son of man', does remove the distinction between Jesus and the Son of man; to remove this distinction thus was an editorial tendency, even if not a universal tendency.

There is in fact no form of the saying that has not been edited. 'In the glory of his Father with the holy angels' reflects Mark's Son of God Christology. 'Before the angels' recalls Luke's interest in angels. 'In the presence of my Father who is in heaven' contains a common Matthean idiom. This editorial process, through which this early saying has passed, is all we need for the moment observe. Some of the theological motifs discernible in the editing will be mentioned later.

One fact stands out clearly: Rom. 1.16 stands in close relation with the tradition of the sayings of Jesus, and with a characteristic and early stage of this tradition, when Paul declares that he is not ashamed of the Gospel he is not simply putting on a bold front in face of the imperial capital, but expressing solidarity with the early communities which framed their essential discipline in terms of loyalty to Jesus, and saw the Son of man as the one who would execute judgement upon those who by apostasy transgressed this discipline. This fact raises a question which it would be wrong for this gathering to attempt to avoid. If Christianity be defined as the religion that takes its origin in Jesus of Nazareth, what is Paul's place within it? How is he related to Jesus? He has been seen as a second founder, and as a perverter, of the original religion of Jesus. He himself would have regarded neither description as valid. According to him, the church could rest on one foundation only – Jesus Christ himself; and he had a low opinion of those who built unworthily on that foundation. How does he fare when judged by his own criteria?

This is not a new question, and many of our fathers and grandfathers were convinced that Paul had made of Christianity something that Jesus had never intended. They discussed the question, Jesus or Paul?, and its almost synonymous variant, Jesus or Christ? But the question has often been wrongly put, and when a question is wrongly put a wrong answer is likely and an irrelevant answer certain. Sometimes what may on the surface appear to be the right answer has been given on the wrong grounds. One look into the past may illustrate this point. Wrede (*Paulus*, p. 90) writes:

Julius Wellhausen, der Bahnbrecher der alttestamentlichen Kritik, hat sogar mit Betonung ausgesprochen, Paulus sei in Wahrheit derjenige gewesen, der das Evangelium Jesu verstanden habe. Adolf Harnack und viele Andere haben es wiederholt. Ich vermag diesem Urteil jedoch nicht zuzustimmen, sehe darin vielmehr einen nicht geringen geschichtlichen Irrtum.

Wrede seeks to establish his point by first examining supposed connections between the teaching of Jesus and the teaching of Paul. 'Verbindungslinien lassen sich ohne Frage vielfach vom einen zum andern ziehen; ein Einfluss Jesu ist damit aber noch gar nicht erwiesen' (p. 90). That Jesus and Paul were both Jews is sufficient to account for a good deal of similarity. The fact that Paul like Jesus emphasized the supreme command of love is reduced in significance by the consideration that Paul lays less stress on love of the enemy and more on love of the brother, that is, of the fellow-member of the church; love becomes a *Gemeindetugend*, and this virtue may already have been more emphasized in Diaspora Judaism than we know. It is mistaken to argue that Paul's freedom from the Law was due to the example of Jesus. In all his arguments on the subject, Paul never appeals to this example; on the contrary, he states that Jesus lived in accordance with the Law (Rom. 15.8).

Having destroyed the case for resemblance between the teaching of Jesus and the teaching of Paul, Wrede goes on to demonstrate the differences in a series of contrasting quotations, which, he says, are central on either side. I give only the first pair (p. 93).

Jesus says, You shall be perfect, as your heavenly Father is perfect. Paul says, He who spared not his own Son, how should he not also with him freely give us all things?

The fact is that the message of Jesus takes the characteristic form of an imperative addressed to the individual; Paul on the other hand speaks of a divine act, or rather of a series of divine actions, on the basis of which salvation, as a goal already achieved, is offered to all men. 'Jesus weiss von dem, was für Paulus das ein und alles ist, – nichts . . . Paulus andrerseits zeigt sicher eine Reihe Berührungspunkte mit den Sprüchen Jesu. Aber all dergleichen gehört bei ihm zu den Dingen zweiter Ordnung, der Kern seines Evangeliums liegt anderswo' (p. 94).

Wrede is here making a comparison between the recorded and reconstructed teaching of Jesus, and the writing of Paul. Those of his generation who reached conclusions opposite to his did the same thing. Both were wrong, for this was not the kind of connection with Jesus that Paul would have been anxious to claim. H. J. Schoeps (*Paulus*, p. 51) quotes aptly from Kümmel: 'Paulus fühlt sich nicht als Schüler des geschichtlichen Jesus, sondern als Beauftragter des Auferstandenen. Und darum ist es nicht seine Aufgabe, weiterzugeben, was er über den geschichtlichen Jesus und seine Worte gehört und uberliefert erhalten hat, sondern Christus zu verkündigen.' This is undoubtedly true. Schoeps has himself, in a chapter heading, rightly described Paul 'als Denker der postmessianischen Situation'. It is not necessary here to discuss how far the crucifixion and resurrection may have been foreseen and foretold in the teaching of Jesus, and in what ways, if foreseen, they may have been interpreted. Certainly they were, from that point of view, future events; and equally certainly for Paul they were events of the past, and they were eschatologically interpreted. An hour had struck on the clock of history, battle had been joined and a victory won, and things could never be the same again. Paul lived in a new – a postmessianic – situation. It was unthinkable that he should simply transmit the teaching of Jesus. That this teaching was given in a Palestinian setting whereas Paul lived and preached in the Hellenistic world, is significant enough, but it is far less important than the fact that Paul lived and preached in an eschatologically different world. All the promises of God had been fulfilled in Jesus; old things had passed away, new things had come into being.

I have argued this point elsewhere, especially in relation to the different viewpoint adopted by B. Gerhardsson, and I do not intend to elaborate the theme again. Nor do I mean to retract what I have said if I now add that it seems to me that there is a further point to consider. The question we have to ask about Paul is not whether, in relation to Jesus, he played the role of the plastered cistern, losing not a drop of his master's teaching but faithfully handing it on, and, if interpreting it, interpreting it only in accordance with the decisions of the authorized Christian Sanhedrin in Jerusalem. We have rather to ask whether in his theology he affords a valid interpretation of the total event of Jesus Christ. We must not expect Paul to use the terminology that Jesus used, or be surprised when he drops the vivid pictorial language of the Palestinian parables, and speaks never of the Son of man and seldom of the kingdom, but instead of justification, the Spirit, and the church. Again, if we are to speak of the 'total event of Jesus Christ' we must not be surprised if Paul lays heavy weight on the crucifixion and resurrection. To one who looked back at the story of Jesus through the Easter events and the passion these must inevitably have appeared not only the nearest but also the most significant elements in the total event. Moreover, if the Easter faith was true, nothing could conceivably be of greater importance, not simply because it meant a staggering and unprecedented act of divine power, but because it meant the dawn of the age to come. Representatively, the messianic affliction was ended in the cross; representatively, the new age had begun with the resurrection. But – and this is the new point I now want to make – though crucifixion and resurrection were evidently the outstanding elements in the total event, they are not the only elements. Jesus was a teacher, and even if his teaching activity is thought of as in part a façade behind which something more profound was concealed it is hard to think of a faithful and satisfactory interpretation of the whole that failed to do justice to this part of it. Hence the special importance of the contact between Paul and that piece of the gospel traditional material that we are here investigating.

Paul says, 'I am not ashamed of the Gospel', and though he attaches to the word Gospel a meaning that is very different from 'an account of the life and teaching of Jesus', there are a few passages where it seems that he is aware of a relation between the two. Foremost, perhaps, of these is Gal. 2.2. Why did Paul submit his Gospel to the Jerusalem authorities? With this question we may put another: Why did he take the trouble to visit (ἱστορῆσαι) Cephas (Gal. 1.18)? It is surely evident that he did not regard Cephas and his colleagues as ecclesiastical authorities who had a right to exact obedience in virtue of their office (2.6, 11). It is part of an answer to this question that they were the leaders of the Jewish branch of the church with which he was anxious to keep the peace; if we ask for any further qualification on their part it can only be that they knew what Jesus had taught. Presumably we may add to this observation that since these witnesses added nothing (2.6) to Paul they at least did not consider that his preaching was inconsistent with what they had heard Jesus say.

Other passages indicate that what Paul understood by 'the Gospel' was capable of being formulated in terms that could be believed, obeyed, accepted, or rejected, 1 Cor. 9.14 is interesting, though it actually says less than it hints at. The Lord himself gave charge for those who preach the Gospel, that they should live by the Gospel. This is presumably a reference to

Mt. 10.10:   ἄξιος . . . ὁ ἐργάτης τῆς τροφῆς αὐτοῦ
Lk. 10.7:   ἄξιος . . . ὁ ἐργάτης τοῦ μισθοῦ αὐτοῦ

– a saying in the Q account of the mission of the disciples. Paul does not here describe the teaching of Jesus as εὐαγγέλιον, but he shows that he participates in the process (which can be seen clearly in Mark, and was pointed out by Wellhausen – *Einleitung in die drei ersten Evangelien* pp. 110ff.) by which the word εὐαγγέλιον was read back into the narratives as a description of the preaching of Jesus. This means that Paul saw – or believed that he could see – a relation between the content of his preaching and the content of the preaching and teaching of Jesus.

It is not possible, nor would it necessarily be profitable, to examine this conviction of Paul's in general terms. Our attention is directed to a particular passage of his (Rom. 1.16), and this in turn has led us to a parallel group of passages in the teaching of Jesus – more accurately, to one sector of the tradition of the teaching of Jesus. It will take us all the time at our disposal to examine this contact and assess its importance, and this examination will suggest representative material that may lead to general conclusions. The next step is to return to Mk 8.38 and the parallels, and make use of our earlier studies, and other methods, to assess the theological content of the tradition.

125

The Marcan saying opens: ὃς γὰϱ ἐὰν ἐπαισχυνθῇ με καὶ τοὺς ἐμοὺς λόγους. The Q saying has no reference to 'words': it is only the person of Jesus that is confessed or denied. In Mark the noun λόγους is omitted (according to Nestle's apparatus) by W k* cop Tert. In the Lucan parallel there is similar evidence for omission in D a e l syᶜ Or; but since Luke is certainly secondary to Mark we need not pursue this variant. The effect of the omission is that the masculine adjective ἐμούς is left without a noun, and must therefore refer to persons: 'Whoever is ashamed of me and mine . . .'. In both Gospels this reading has been taken seriously and indeed preferred by the New English Bible, and it may therefore be reasonable to consider it for a moment. In fact it will not stand up to examination. It is best to begin with the patristic evidence. Tertullian appears to refer to Mk 8.38 in three places, and to Lk. 9.26 in one (it is not clear why the apparatus does not refer to Tertullian at Lk. 9.26 as well as at Mk 8.38). It is clear what is happening at *De Fuga* 7.2. The main point is drawn from the positive element in the Q saying:

> Qui confessus fuerit me, et ego confitebor illum coram patre meo.
> Quomodo confitebitur fugiens, quomodo fugiet confitens?

Having made this point, Tertullian goes on to quote the negative member, evidently from memory and under the influence of the passage just cited:

> Qui mei confusus fuerit, et ego confundar eius coram patre (meo) .

This is not to be taken as a serious witness to a variant, and in any case it does not support the reading καὶ τοὺς ἐμοὺς. In *De Carne Christi* 5 the argument turns upon the reality of Christ's human nature, and it is not surprising that again interest focuses upon the person of Christ to the exclusion of καὶ τοὺς ἐμοὺς λόγους (the whole phrase):

> Qui me, inquit, confusus fuerit, confundar et ego eius.

In *De Idololatria* 13 the point is that to commit idolatry is to be ashamed of God. You may be known to be a Christian or not; it makes no difference.

> Certe sive hac, sive illac, reus es confusionis in Deo. Qui autem confusus super me fuerit penes homines, et ego confundar super illo, inquit, penes patrem meum, qui est in coelis.

Here Tertullian has confused Mark with Matthew. In *Adversus Marcionem* IV.21 Tertullian must be quoting not Mark but Luke, since his argument is intended to confound Marcion with Marcion's own gospel. The theme is the shame Christ endured through accepting the conditions of ordinary human birth, life, and death.

> Qui confusus, inquit, mei fuerit, et ego confundar eius. Quando nec confusionis materia conveniat, nisi meo Christo: cuius ordo magis pudendus, ut etiam haereticorum conviciis pateat, omnem nativitatis et educationis foeditatem, et ipsius etiam carnis indignitatem, quanta amaritudine possunt, perorantibus.

There is no room here for a reference either to *my words* or to *my people*, and they do not appear.

It is worth noting that at Mk 8.38 the extraordinary Old Latin MS. k actually reads:

> Qui autem me confessus fuerit et meos in natione adultera et peccatrice et filios (sic) hominis confundetur illum cum venerit in claritate patris sui cum angelis sanctis.

A corrector has erased *et meos*; and of course, *confessus* is an error for *confusus* (arising under the influence of Mt. 10.32; Lk. 12.8). On this reading see J. Wordsworth, W. Sanday and H. J. White, *Old-Latin Biblical Texts*, II, p. xci.

Study of these texts not only suffices to make it impossible to take 'me and mine' as the original text; it also throws light on the way in which the saying has developed. In the first place, it is evident that conflation and assimilation have been at work. Passages such as Mk 8.38; Mt. 10.32f.; Lk. 12.8f. invite confusion, and are in patristic quotations often confused. In the second place, there was a natural concentration of interest upon the person of Christ, not only because this was for Christians the centre of loyalty, but also because it was the point of attack for non-Christians, who naturally found the crucified sophist not merely unimpressive but offensive to their natural theological presuppositions. For the same reason this was also the point of dangerous modification for unorthodox Christians who wished to accommodate Christian belief to current objections by denying the full offensive reality of the human person Jesus of Nazareth.

With these considerations in mind we can accept without hesitation as the earliest form preserved in the extant gospels the Marcan με καὶ τοὺς ἐμοὺς λόγους. Compare Mk 10.29: ἕνεκεν ἐμοῦ καὶ ἕνεκεν τοῦ εὐαγγελίου. Rom. 1.16, however, was written before Mark, and we may ask whether Paul does not suggest an earlier stage of the tradition which referred only to 'words' or 'Gospel', and contained no 'me'. This is not impossible, and it is worth noting that it would not have the effect of reducing the Christological significance of the saying. Paul was certainly not a less Christological thinker than Mark. To suffer on behalf of Jesus might indicate no more than the measure of personal affection and loyalty that any one of us might feel for another; but to suffer on behalf of the words of Jesus, or of the Gospel (whether one thinks of this as the Gospel he preached, or as the Gospel which has him at its centre) means recognizing that he was the bearer of the word of God, and thus the unique agent of God – a more profound belief than the conviction that he was a lovable person possessed of the powers of leadership. Thus, 'I am not ashamed of the Gospel' carries with it, 'I am not ashamed of Christ and the Gospel'. This is not to say that 'I am not ashamed of the Gospel' was not an earlier formulation than 'I am not ashamed of Christ and the Gospel'; Rom. 1.16 may suggest that it was, though this earlier formulation has left no trace in the gospels. This reflection must add weight to the argument that in the second, retributive, clause, 'Son of man' is original. To this clause we now turn.

I shall not pursue further the question whether or not this clause originally contained a reference to the Son of man, but inquire what sort of event is implied by the denying, or being ashamed, referred to. Future verbs – ἐπαισχυνθήσεται, ἀποδώσει (cf. μέλλει ἔρχεσθαι), ἀρνήσομαι, ἀπαρνηθήσεται are used throughout, but those in the Q saying are capable of a different interpretation from those in the Marcan. Q can be taken as a simple logical future: If A does X, B will do Y. B's action is future in that it is contingent upon what A does, but it is thought of as essentially a continuation of A's action in the present. Deny Christ, and you will be denied – as in 2 Tim. 2.12 (εἰ ἀρνησόμεθα, κἀκεῖνος ἀρνήσεται ἡμᾶς). Mark (followed by Matthew and Luke) clearly goes beyond this, and describes an event that will take place at a specific time in the future. Retribution is indeed directly and necessarily connected with the offence, but does not follow immediately in point of time. The offence takes place in this generation, and the retribution at a time specified by a temporal clause, ὅταν ἔλθῃ – certainly not now.

Of all the five passages concerned, Mt. 16.27 gives the clearest picture of a judgement scene: the Son of man will come in glory and recompense each man according to his behaviour. The scene is familiar and indeed formalized (cf. Mt. 25.31). Matthew has clarified but not misunderstood what Mark intended to convey; Mark too, followed closely by Luke, thinks of a judgement scene. The only difference is that in Matthew the Son of man is the judge, whereas in Mark and Luke it is not clear whether he is judge, witness, or counsel for the prosecution. ἐπαισχύνεσθαι is perhaps a word that suits a witness better than a judge. There is a somewhat similar problem in 1 Enoch, especially in 62 and 63, where the kings and the mighty appear for judgement. 'They shall be downcast of countenance' (62.5), 'their faces shall be filled with shame' (10), 'their faces shall be filled with darkness and shame before that Son of man' (63.11). But it is not clear precisely what role that Son of man plays. At the beginning of 62 the Lord of Spirits seats him on the throne of his glory and the spirit of righteousness is poured out upon him (62.2); apparently he is to act as judge. This view of the Son of man lasts up to 62.9, where the kings and the mighty petition him and supplicate for mercy at his hands. But the next verse continues: Nevertheless that Lord of spirits will so press them that they shall hastily go forth from his presence, and their faces shall be filled with shame, and the darkness shall grow deeper on their faces. In 63.1 it is the Lord of spirits whom the mighty and the kings implore to grant them a little respite, but in verse 11 follow the words quoted above, in which once more the Son of man appears to be acting as judge. It is not unreasonable to infer a measure of uncertainty about the role of the Son of man in the judgement.

Matthew in general has a much more clear-cut picture of the Son of man than Mark. For Matthew the Son of Man is a king and has a kingdom, and he acts as judge (13.41; 16.28; 19.28; 25.31). There is in Mark no passage that so unambiguously states the judgeship and kingship of the Son of man. 14.62, where the Son of man sits on the right hand of the Power and comes with the clouds of heaven, perhaps implies so much, but does not explicitly claim it. We are in fact dealing here with a theme discussed – though without reference to our material – by C. F. D. Moule in *Society of New Testament Studies Bulletin*, III: 'From Defendant to Judge – and Deliverer: an Enquiry into the use and limitations of the theme of vindication in the New Testament'. It is in Matthew, not in Mark, that the Son of man becomes in a full sense the Judge and Deliverer. It would however be wrong to suppose that this transition is simply a function of developing Christology, which progressively exalts the figure of Jesus. All the gospels insist upon a Defendant figure, and do so because, they identify the Son of man with Jesus, a human figure who really did stand trial before his fellow-countrymen, not only when he appeared before the Sanhedrin but throughout his ministry as he exposed himself and his teaching – his words – to the approbation or scorn of any who chose to listen and to observe. In 8.38, Mark – and that in this he is more primitive than Matthew is scarcely open to doubt – allows this description of the Son of man to persist in the account of the heavenly trial scene. Even now, if ἐπαισχύνεσθαι is to be taken seriously, the scene is not an entirely victorious one for the Son of man, for he is ashamed, ashamed to recognize those who profess to be his disciples. That is, he is called upon as witness to answer the question: Are these men, who profess to be so, truly yours? And must answer in confusion: No, indeed; I am ashamed that they should take my name on their lips.

To go so far, however, is to vindicate Mark's allusive picture of a court and judgement scene, and thus also his ὅταν. The ἔλθῃ that accompanies ὅταν is presumably based upon Dan. 7.13. The same passage may not unreasonably be taken to supply δόξα (Dan. 7.14 LXX: πᾶσα δόξα αὐτῷ λατρεύουσα), and perhaps the angels (7.13 LXX: οἱ παρεστηκότες παρῆσαν αὐτῷ). There remains for consideration only the reference to 'his Father'. The Son of man is represented as Son of God. In this Mark is followed by Luke. The important point to observe is that Mk 8.38 stands in the course of a long and carefully worked out paragraph in which Mark sets forth the relation between the three concepts, Messiah, Son of man, and Son of God. All are fulfilled in Jesus. Peter confesses him to be the Christ; this identification is not rejected but for the moment set aside; it is hinted at again in the Transfiguration narrative. Instead Jesus affirms that he is the Son of man, and will, in that role, suffer rejection and contumely, though his suffering and death will be followed by resurrection. At the time of vindication, however, it will be impossible for disciples to join him; if they do not share his reproach now they will have no share in his glory hereafter, when he is manifested not only as the glorious Son of man but as the Son of God, in the glory of his Father. This will happen soon; some of those present, notwithstanding the impending suffering, will live to see it. At this point Mark attaches the Transfiguration, going out of his way to relate it to what precedes by a reference, unique in the main part of his gospel, to a precise interval: after six days. This narrative has been rightly explained by G. H. Boobyer as an anticipation of the *parousia*, in which the Son of man appears with the clouds, accompanied by the holy ones. In the course of it Jesus is addressed as the Son of God, whose word must be heard and obeyed. All this, however, must for the moment, until the resurrection, be kept secret. Jesus is not to be followed because of the glory to which he will eventually lead his followers, but simply for his own sake, and the Gospel's.

This is essentially a Marcan construction: 8.27–9.9 (13) sets out Mark's own Gospel more plainly than any other part of his book. How far certain parts of it correspond with historical fact is a question of notorious difficulty. Was the title Christ used of Jesus? by Jesus? was it accepted by him? Did he use the term Son of man to describe himself in his earthly life, or did he (if he used it at all) use it only of someone else? Did he foresee and interpret his impending death? What sort of role did he predict for his followers? What sort of vision was the Transfiguration? Questions such as these can only be answered, if they can be answered at all, when the passage before us is set in the context of the gospel material as a whole, and at this stage in our study (which, I must repeat, is not primarily aimed at the interpretation of the gospels for their own sake) there is only one aspect of this comparison that can be mentioned. This however is the most important. The theme of the whole paragraph is focused in Mk 8.38, and in the affirmation that there exists a unique, mysterious, but organic relation between the obscurity and humiliation of the ministry of Jesus, and the glorious future; a relation that may be indifferently described in terms of the coming of the Son of man (with features based on Dan. 7 and echoing parts of 1 Enoch) and of the establishing of the kingdom of God in power. Mark as a whole uses both methods of expressing the relation between a present, which is unique because it is bound up with a particular historical figure, and a future, which also is unique because it is the end of history. On the one hand, Jesus is the Son of man, and the compound Jesus–Son of man figure has a continuous history which begins with an earthly ministry, continues through rejection, suffering, and death to resurrection, and ultimately to *parousia* and judgement, when the elect are gathered together from the ends of the earth to rejoice with the Son of man. On the other hand, the kingdom of God, whose future coming in power is accepted in the ordinary Jewish apocalyptic manner, received a preliminary manifestation during the ministry of Jesus as he casts out demons and thus overthrows the strong man who hitherto has enjoyed undisputed control of what he has been pleased to regard as his property. The organic relation between the mysterious present and the glorious future manifestation of the kingdom is expressed notably in the parables about seeds and their growth. The ministry of Jesus may be as small and insignificant as a mustard seed, yet it is as closely related to the future consummation as the mustard seed is to the large mustard plant.

It has been pointed out in a familiar and important study, and subsequently often repeated, that these two strands of tradition, the one relating to the Son of man and the other to the kingdom of God, are distinct from each other, and from this observation historical inferences, which may or may not be justifiable, have been drawn. With such inferences we are not at present concerned. What matters is that the two great strata of the gospel tradition – the Son of man stratum and the kingdom of God stratum – are agreed in their fundamental representation of the significance of the historic ministry of Jesus. This observation may lead us back directly to Paul.

What is the theological significance of this traditional interpretation of the ministry? It is not worked out in theological terms in the synoptic gospels, and we shall therefore have to work it out for ourselves. When we have done so we shall be able to see whether the external and formal relation to the tradition of Paul's οὐ γὰρ ἐπαισχύνομαι is backed by a valid understanding of its theological substance.

The following points can be made. It will hardly be necessary to bring out step by step their relevance to Rom. 1.16.

(1) The traditional material sees a unique power, a δύναμις, at work in the ministry. This is manifested in miracles, which are characteristically described as δυνάμεις, and are regarded as signs of the kingdom of God (Mt. 12.28; Lk. 11.20). This δύναμις is at times crudely described as a kind of quasi-physical fluid operating through contact with Jesus or even with his clothing (e.g. Mk 5.27), having clear connection with magic (Mk 7.33; 8.23). It is also expressed in other manifestations of the ἐξουσία of Jesus, such as his teaching (Mk 1.22, 27), and his power to command men and secure their obedience (1.17; 2.14). This δύναμις and ἐξουσία come from God (11.27–33, in the whole context). To some extent at least they are transferable, and the disciples are sent out suitably equipped (6.7). The word δύναμις is also used in strictly futuristic eschatological contexts. The clearest examples are Mk 9.1, where it is said that the kingdom will come ἐν δυνάμει, and 13.26, where the Son of man comes μετὰ δυνάμεως πολλῆς καὶ δόξης (cf. 8.38). The power is the same, but whereas in the present it is secret, in the future it will be manifest. This future manifestation may be described as salvation. It is true that the word σωτηρία does not

occur in Matthew and Mark, and that the occurrences in Luke are not clear references to the future (though 1.69, 71, 77 are eschatological in their formulation); it is true also that the verb σῴζειν is used in a variety of senses, some of which amount to little more than 'cure'. But Mk 8.35; 10.26; 13.13, 20 have a clear reference to salvation at the last day. The man who endures to the end will come safely through the convulsive struggles of the dying age, and receive eternal life in the age to come. That is, the primary theme of the gospel tradition can be described as δύναμις εἰς σωτηρίαν – a power, at present only dimly revealed, which points toward and leads to God's final act of salvation. This δύναμις is what Jesus proclaims – his εὐαγγέλιον, if we may accept the word of Mk 1.14–15, etc.

(2) I have already said that this δύναμις is only obscurely manifested. This is perhaps an understatement. According to Mark, it was often deliberately concealed by Jesus, and when he was asked to account for his ἐξουσία he refused to do more than hint, by way of an allusion to John the Baptist, at its divine origin. More than this, the words in which he proclaimed his εὐαγγέλιον were, by the best authorities, judged blasphemous and condemned; on the ground of them he was himself condemned to death, and, when executed, proved unable or unwilling to apply the divine σωτηρία to his own case: ἄλλους ἔσωσεν, ἑαυτὸν οὐ δύναται σῶσαι (15.31). The miracles themselves could easily be discounted, and more than discounted: the man was in league with the devil and practised black magic.

From such a person – a cheap wizard, a strolling exorcist, who when put to the test could not use the powers he was supposed to claim – it was natural to turn away in disgust, and to disavow any connection with him one might ever have had. If a different, positive, attitude were taken it could not be on the basis of observed and convincing phenomena. Even the miracles, as we have seen, could prove nothing, and it is evident that most of the inhabitants of Palestine were not impressed by them. There were indeed some who pierced the anonymity of Jesus, or rather had the secret revealed to them, and not by flesh and blood. These were on the whole the babes, and the outcasts of Israel, not those who could parade learning or good works. Even these, it is true, found in the end that the strain was too great, and when the matter came to arrest, trial, and execution, ran away and even denied the Master. The opposite, however, to this negative reaction meant a willingness to trust in a divine secret (Mk 4.11; cf. Mt. 11.25 = Lk. 10.21; Mt. 16.17), to deny not the Master but oneself, to follow him at any cost, in obedience and confident trust (Mk 8.34). The single word that expresses this attitude is πίστις. The earlier synoptic passages use this word in the sense of a confidence that Jesus is able to deal with all circumstances, such as illness, storms, and the like. But the verb is used in a way that reflects the theological usage in Paul. Thus in his opening proclamation Jesus summons his hearers: πιστεύετε ἐν τῷ εὐαγγελίῳ. This is the precise opposite of being ashamed of him and his words. At 15.32 πιστεύειν denotes a false faith which requires a demonstration of power in a form which destroys the very nature of the δύναμις in question: καταβάτω νῦν ἀπὸ τοῦ σταυροῦ, ἵνα ἴδωμεν καὶ πιστεύσωμεν. Compare the refusal of a sign in Mk 8.11ff. Thus if the story of Jesus means the power of God moving towards (εἰς) salvation, it has this meaning to faith – παντὶ τῷ πιστεύοντι.

(3) The end point of the process which our material describes is judgement. Mt. 16.27 expresses this precisely, but, as we have seen, Mk 8.38 conveys the same notion clearly enough. Whether the Son of man is judge, or the Father, with the Son of man as witness or advocate, the result is the same: Judgement there will be, and the result of the judgement will be determined not by the attitude of the persons in question then (when they may cry Lord, Lord, in vain – Mt. 7.21), but by their earlier attitude to the obscure and humiliated Jesus, that is by their shame or denying, their confessing or faith. That is, there will be a future judgement, but its verdict is already anticipated in the present, and is determined positively or negatively by faith or by the opposite of faith, that is, by a positive or negative relation with Jesus. This appears to correspond with what Paul means by the manifestation of God's righteousness which is the ground of the Gospel (Rom. 1.17: the Gospel is God's power leading to salvation, δικαιοσύνη γὰρ θεοῦ ἐν αὐτῷ ἀποκαλύπτεται), and by justification by faith. No more

in Paul than in the teaching of Jesus can this lead to moral indifferentism, since faith means obedience (cf. e.g. the ὑπακοὴν πίστεως of Rom. 1.5), or following Christ with complete denial of self (Mk 8.34). The contrast cited above from Wrede breaks down at this point. The imperative of Jesus rests upon an implicit and occasionally explicit indicative of divine grace, and the Pauline indicative issues in an imperative.

(4) There is one word more to say here, but it is not easy to express it except in negative terms. The Marcan paragraph identifies Jesus, the Son of man, and the Son of God, even though in Mk 8.38 the reference to 'his Father' is probably editorial, and the verse as it stands appears to bear witness to an earlier stage in the tradition in which Jesus and the Son of man were distinguished. Even however when we go back to the earliest stage we can reach and the Christological titles become problematical, the figure of Jesus remains central, because it is by men's attitude to and relation with him that they are judged; and this is more significant than most formal Christological statements. It is reflected in Rom. 1.16f. through the doctrine of justification, which is a Christological doctrine, but for a clearer parallel we may turn back to Rom. 1.3f., which reveals precisely the same uneven continuity between him who lives a human life as the Son of David and him who after his resurrection is exalted to be the Son of God. The same person is both, and it is on the basis of historical confrontation with Jesus (in his word) that final judgement takes place. Here are the essentials of New Testament Christology. They are not in the first instance metaphysical, but show the two ways in which God confronts men; and in them Paul and the gospel tradition are agreed.

This proposition must not be exaggerated. The relation between Paul and the gospel tradition is very complicated, and raises many questions that have not been touched on in this paper. But the present investigation has added some support to the similar conclusions of Jeremias (*The Central Message of the New Testament*, p. 70: 'It was Paul's greatness that he understood the message of Jesus as no other New Testament writer did. He was the faithful interpreter of Jesus. This is especially true of his doctrine of justification. It is not of his own making but in its substance conveys the central message of Jesus, as it is condensed in the first beatitude: "Blessed are you poor, for yours is the kingdom of God"') and of Käsemann (*Versuche*, II, pp. 102f.: 'Danach (die Gerechtigkeit Gottes) hungern und dürsten diejenigen, welchen die vierte Seligpreisung gilt, nämlich nach der Verwirklichung des göttlichen Rechtes an und über dieser unserer Erde. Genau darum scheint es mir aber auch in der Paulinischen Lehre von Gottes Gerechtigkeit und unserer Rechtfertigung zu gehen'). The support is given by the measure of literary and historical contact we have observed between the gospel tradition and words which are often rightly taken to be the kernel of Paul's Gospel, which δύναμις θεοῦ ἐστιν πᾶσιν τοῖς πιστεύουσιν.

6

Paul at Athens and Paul to Rome

The question whether Paul's Areopagus speech in Acts 17 and the Epistle to the Romans, and especially the argument of chapter 1, can have been produced by the same person is an old one. Everyone who writes on Acts or Romans must consider it, and so have many others in the context of New Testament theology in general. I do not wish on this occasion simply to look afresh at a worn-out theme, though of course some of the old issues will inevitably arise – and no doubt some of the old opinions about them will be expressed. There is no avoiding this; but so far as possible I wish to see what will happen if I try to set the question in a somewhat different context.

In the new edition of my commentary on Romans I made a suggestion with regard to the origin of the epistle on which, so far as I know, no one has yet found it worth his while to comment. Why did Paul write that extraordinarily profound and wide-ranging letter? As everyone knows, that question has been much discussed in recent years; there are for example the excellent book edited by Karl Donfried, and Sandy Wedderburn's *The Reasons for Romans*. The occasion (not the same thing as the reason) for the letter is clear. After a visit to Jerusalem Paul proposes to call at Rome on his way to Spain. He hopes for help, probably both material and spiritual, from the Roman church, which evidently has come into being independently of his own mission. He must introduce himself; and since he and his apostolic status are created by nothing other than the Gospel, it is natural that he should introduce himself by giving an account of the Gospel. It was hardly natural however that he should do so to the extent of sixteen chapters; and Romans has been described as a manifesto, a testament, a summary of what he had said and written elsewhere. There is some appropriateness in all these terms, but in themselves they do not explain why Paul should have chosen this occasion to put his testament on paper. It seems reasonable to suggest that he may have done so precisely because he knew that he was not the founding teacher of the church to which he was writing. We know that there was a mission to Jews independent of Paul (Gal. 2.9). We know that there was a Judaizing mission which wrought havoc in Galatia and in Corinth, as its leaders sought to rectify errors (as they supposed) in Paul's Gospel by the application of the Law. But there was also a Gentile mission (there may have been several Gentile missions) independent of Paul's. This is proved sufficiently by the existence of a non-Pauline mainly Gentile (see Rom. 1.13; 11.13, 25) church in Rome. It is strongly hinted at by the story in Acts of Stephen and his six colleagues. It may be that the mission that founded the church in Rome and the Hellenist mission founded by Stephen were the same. Lietzmann (*Beginnings*, 267) thought so. 'It is not an eviscerated Paulinism but a Hellenistic proselyte Christianity that we meet here in a pure form, an independent growth from a root in the early church, of importance for the future. The Roman church could trace its descent back to the Hellenistic circle of Stephen.' The forthcoming visit to Rome meant that Paul must face this different version of the Gospel and come to terms with it.

Let us at least take something like this as a hypothesis that may be illuminated by, and also illuminate, a comparative study of Acts 17 and Romans 1 (with some reference to other passages also).

We need lose no time over the claim that in Romans we have Paul's words substantially as he dictated them to Tertius, who 'wrote the epistle in the Lord'. So far so good. No one is likely to claim that we have in Acts 17 a precise and accurate account of Paul's ipsissima verba as he uttered them in Athens. The most conservative is likely to claim no more than that Luke gives us in his own words an accurate account of what Paul said – an accurate summary we may add, for it is most unlikely that Paul would take up no more than two minutes of the Areopagites' time. The less conservative will be much more doubtful than that. It is in the highest degree unlikely that anyone made a careful report of what was said on this, or any other, occasion in Acts. Luke set down what he thought, with good reasons for thinking so or bad, had been said – or rather, what he thought was likely to have been said. The language was his (in the sense that he put it in his book), not Paul's. A brief analysis will confirm this. ἀναθεωρεῖν is not used by Paul; σέβασμα is used once (but in 2 Thessalonians); βωμός is not used; ἐπιγράφειν is not used; δεισιδαιμών is not used; εὐσεβεῖν is used once in the Pastorals; χειροποίητος is used once (but in Ephesians); θεραπεύειν is not used, nor is προσδέομαι, nor πνοή; ὁρίζειν is used once; προστάσσειν, ὁροθεσία, ψηλαφᾶν, and κινεῖσθαι are not used; ποιήτης is used once; χάραγμα, τεχνή, ἐνθύμησις, θεῖος, ὑπερεῖδον, are not used; οἰκουμένη is used once. Making lists is tedious, but this list is not insignificant. Unless we are to suppose (as some would perhaps maintain) that Paul adopted a special vocabulary in order to address his philosophical audience in its own terms (though by no means all the words I have considered are technical philosophical terms, though they are required by the argument) we must conclude that the language of Acts 17.22–31 is not Paul's. Perhaps even more striking than the use of different words (which the unusual circumstances might possibly explain) is the use, in v. 31, of a very characteristically Pauline word in a totally un-Pauline sense. For Paul, πίστις is *faith*; here it is something more like *proof*.

The language is not Paul's; but while we are speaking of words it may be well to go on to observe that it is not Luke's; nor is it at all common in the New Testament as a whole. Of the words I have listed above ἀναθεωρεῖν, σέβασμα, βωμός, ἐπιγράφειν, δεισιδαιμών, εὐσεβεῖν, προσδέομαι, ὁροθεσία, ψηλαφᾶν, ποιήτης, χάραγμα, ἐνθύμησις, θεῖος, ὑπερεῖδον, are used nowhere else in Acts (though it is right to note the occurrence of δεισιδαιμονία at 25.19). They are either rare, or not to be found, or found in different senses in the rest of the New Testament. χειροποίητος occurs once more in Acts; πνοή once more; τεχνή once more; θεραπεύειν four times more (but each time, as elsewhere in the New Testament, of the treatment and healing of disease); ὁρίζειν three times more outside the present speech; προστάσσειν twice more (but only once in a similar sense); κινεῖσθαι twice more (in different senses); and οἰκουμένη four times more. We may add the observation and that if Paul does not use the word πίστις in the sense in which it is used here, neither does Luke in the rest of his book.

The Areopagus speech stands out from its context in Acts. There is similar thought in the brief speech ascribed to Paul in Lystra (14.15–17), but there though the thought is similar it is not identical and the language is different. We may with some confidence draw the conclusion that Luke did not simply make up the speech for himself (though he doubtless edited it); he drew it from a source – conceivably oral, but perhaps more probably, in view of the many non-Lucan words, written. And with less confidence, but conjecturally, we may connect it with the sort of Hellenist–Jewish–Christian movement associated with Stephen – and associated, it seems, by Luke with Paul.

My concern at present, however, is not with source criticism, or, primarily, with history, but with the serious theological issue that is raised when Acts 17 and Romans 1 are compared. More important than the historical problem that lies behind the question of sources is the question whether Acts 17 (whoever is responsible for it) agrees with Paul's own account in Romans 1 of the religion, or irreligion, of his contemporaries. A serious difference here, however interesting to the historian, could be only an embarrassment to the theologian, and more than an embarrassment to the missionary whose vocation obliges him to deal with men of other faiths, or of none. In a famous little book Barth could say *Nein* to his fellow Swiss Reformed Christian Brunner; for one apostle, one New Testament writer, to say *Nein* to another would give rise to further difficulties. That there is a difference between the two passages is clear, but it is one which it is easy to mis-state, and to over-state. This is partly because there is in Acts a lack of clarity and of definiteness that is in itself quite un-Pauline. This may be illustrated by the description (v. 22) of the Athenians as ὡς δεισιδαιμονεστέρους; and to pursue the illustration briefly may

142

provide some material for the main comparison with which we are concerned.

Are the opening words of the address an accusation or a captatio benevolentiae? 'You are a superstitious crowd'; or, 'You are a most religious people'? There is no doubt that the word is capable of either meaning, though on the whole Theophrastus's Περὶ δεισιδαιμονίας and Plutarch's tractate under the same title do not present a very attractive picture. This appears also in the realm of Hellenistic Judaism; so for example in Philo, *De Mutatione Nominum* 138 ('This saying is not for all to hear, so strongly does the evil tide of superstition (δεισιδαιμονίας) flow in our minds and drown unmanly and degenerate souls' – Colson and Whittaker). In Acts the context (v. 16) describes Paul as vexed (παρωξύνετο τὸ πνεῦμα αὐτοῦ) by the sight of the city over-grown with idols, but this cannot determine for certain the way in which the speech was originally intended, that is, was intended in the source used by Luke. Of course Paul disapproves of idolatry, and if the Athenians worship idols they are superstitious idolaters. The author of the speech also very clearly disapproves of idols, but is prepared to see some soul of goodness in things evil, at least to the extent of making use of a conveniently inscribed (possibly a conveniently invented?) altar. The religiousness of the Athenians if not itself the truth may nevertheless be used to point to the truth.

I shall not take up the old question at which I have just hinted: Was there in Athens an altar inscribed Ἀγνώστῳ θεῷ, or are Jerome and many others right in the view that the nearest to this useful formula that Athens could show was 'diis Asiae Europae et Africae, diis ignotis et peregrinis', wording which Paul (or Luke, or Luke's source) changed to suit his purpose into the singular? It is quite impossible to prove the negative statement that there never was any such altar as that described here. Who knows what now lies buried beneath the track of the Athens–Peiraeus railway? Who knows what pieces of stone have in the last 1,900 years been chipped into tiny fragments? On the other hand, unless a suitable stone is one day discovered the sermon illustration must attract a measure of doubt. But our concern at present is not with archaeology but with exegesis and theology. What does Luke make of the (real or alleged) ἀγνώστῳ θεῷ? Instead of a fruitless archaeological inquiry let us look at a question of grammar. How is the clause ὃ οὖν ἀγνοοῦντες εὐσεβεῖτε be taken? Is the participle ἀγνοοῦντες simply adverbial, so that (with AV, though AV reads the masculine relative, ὅν, instead of the neuter) we shall translate, What (AV whom) you ignorantly worship? That is, You worship in a state of ignorance; you do not know, or do not know fully, in all respects, what it is that you are doing in your worship. Or is the participle a full verbal equivalent, perhaps concessive in sense: That which, though you do not know it, you worship? On the latter view, the Athenians do not know God; they practise religion, but they have no personal acquaintance with the being whom religion, their religion, presupposes. Compare Gal. 4.8, τότε μὲν οὐκ εἰδότες θεὸν – though no doubt the Galatians like the Athenians had practised religious rites of some kind. On the former view, it is the religious practices themselves that are alleged to be marked by ignorance, ἀγνοοῦντες going closely with εὐσεβεῖτε. You Athenians are at least aware of God, but you misconceive him by offering him things he does not need and supposing that he may be confined in a temple.

How should the participle be construed? I doubt whether it is possible to answer this question on a purely grammatical, stylistic basis. It is Luke's style with which we are concerned, for even if, as seems likely, he is using a source, the material has passed through his hands. But we can draw evidence – inconclusive evidence – from within the speech itself. The next verse contains two participles having transitive verbal significance, προσδεόμενος (that this verb takes the genitive makes no difference here) and διδούς: He is served (θεραπεύεται) . . . as if he needed . . . in view of the fact that he has given . . . But in v. 23 we have adverbial participles, διερχόμενος and ἀναθεωρῶν (which also has an object): It was as I was passing along and looking . . . that I saw . . . Luke – and his source – were capable of using participles in both ways. This means that we are dependent on the context; and this means essentially on the verb καταγγέλλω. Unfortunately here too we meet with ambiguity. The word may mean (in the context):

It is not a ξένον δαιμονίον (v. 18) that I am proclaiming to you, but a being whose existence you already acknowledge, though indeed as an ἄγνωστος θεός; or, The God, whom you yourselves, by your altar inscription, admit that you do not know, who is thus the ultimate ξένον, the absolute stranger, I am declaring to you. On the whole, New Testament usage seems to favour the latter meaning, but usage is not decisive. It is enough to point to Acts 3.24, All the prophets proclaimed these days – hardly an unknown quantity therefore, at least in the time of the later prophets; and 4.2, where the apostles proclaim in Jesus the resurrection of the dead – the unheard of new truth.

Usage of καταγγέλλω then, does not help, but we may find a guide to what is intended in the surprising use of the neuter pronouns ὅ and τοῦτο, for we must surely follow 𝔓⁷⁴ ℵ B D (81) 1175 pc and the Latin (quod . . . hoc) against ℵᶜ Aᶜ EΨ 𝔐 sy Clement. The external attestation of the neuter is good (B and D in agreement); and copyists had a double reason for changing the neuter into masculine: the presence of a masculine antecedent noun, θεός, and the fact that the Christian reader would assume that Paul was speaking of a personal, not an impersonal God. But in that case, why was the neuter used? Because Luke (or his source) was not thinking in technical theological terms of the knowability or unknowability of God (who was of course known by the speaker, or writer, to be personal), but of the general unreality of the kind of worship so widely practised in Athens: You are religious enough but you do not really understand what you are doing. It is, I think, fair enough to say that we are dealing here with a preacher's point, aimed at securing attention rather than at a technically sound theological statement; it is a mistake to make too heavy a theological meal of this verse. καταγγέλλω was no doubt understood by Luke to take up the noun καταγγελεὺς used in v. 18, including its connection with ξένον δαιμονίων. In one sense Paul was announcing something absolutely ξένον: the Gospel was new. In another sense the Gospel was not new, for it was the fulfilment of uninstructed Athenian aspiration. The preacher's clever introduction does imply a theology, though this must not be overstated. There is a percipient paragraph in Bultmann's *Theologie* (p. 470).

Auch insofern ordnet der Verf. der Act das Christentum als Religion in die Weltgeschichte ein, als er in der Areopagrede den Paulus an die heidnische Frömmigkeit anknüpfen lässt durch Bezugnahme auf die athenische Altar-Inschrift und auf den stoischen Gottesglauben (17.23, 28). Dadurch wird 'die heidnische Geschichte, Kultur- und Religionswelt als Urgeschichte des Christentums reklamiert' (Vielhauer), und das entspricht der Auffassung der Act vom Verhältnis des Christentums zum Judentum: die paulinische Gesetzeslehre ist nicht mehr verstanden, und die jüdische Geschichte ist einfach zur Vorgeschichte des Christentums geworden.

To this two observations may be appended. (1) Paul can say sornething similar about the Jews (Rom. 10.1–4). Israel had, and has, a ζῆλον θεοῦ, but it is οὐ κατ᾽ ἐπίγνωσιν. Christ is now τέλος νόμου to all who believe. Paul would not think of denying that there was knowledge of God in the Old Testament, and that it was the one true God who was known. But this knowledge of God was again and again misused as men supposed that God's law had been given them that they might construct out of it a righteousness of their own, made out of works done. Since Christ had come the law itself had become Vorgeschichte, and in some respects not a very creditable Geschichte. To get a known God wrong was more discreditable than to get an unknown God wrong. Thus judgement as well as Gospel came to the Jew first, but also to the Greek (Rom. 2.9). Yet the effect of Acts 17 is to move the Greek up to the same level as the Jew; and this is hardly what Paul does in Rom. 1. It is nearer to Rom. 3, with its οὐ γάρ ἐστιν διαστολή (3.22).

(2) καταγγέλλω is the word of Christian proclamation, but what we have is not quite the preaching Christ, and nothing but Christ, of 1 Cor. 2.2. It is more akin to Philo's *De Opificio Mundi*. Winding up his exposition, Philo says that by his account of creation (170, διὰ τῆς λεχθείσης κοσμοποιίας) Moses teaches five things of special beauty and importance. Of these the first is the existence, and the continuous existence of deity (ὅτι ἔστι τὸ θεῖον καὶ ὑπάρχει), the second that God is one (ὅτι θεὸς εἷς ἐστι). The being and something of the nature of God are proclaimed by creation.

It is again, however, like Philo that in the following verses (24–26) Paul (Luke) does not set out to prove the existence and nature of God from observation of the cosmos, but rather, assuming the truth about God, explains the cosmos and man's place and duty in it. Because God made the world and is lord of heaven and earth certain consequences follow. No proof of the fundamental propositions is offered; this is what Paul proclaims (καταγγέλλει). Just as there is no proof, no authority for the proclamation is cited; it is of course pure Judaism, and in the context of Judaism there is no need to point out that its authority is the Old Testament, and the language both of the basic proposition and of its corollaries – that God is not confined within human structures and is at best inadequately worshipped by the offering of gifts which by definition he does not need – is to be found in the Old Testament. A few illustrative quotations will suffice.

Gen. 1.1: ἐν ἀρχῇ ἐποίησεν ὁ θεὸς τὸν οὐρανὸν καὶ τὴν γῆν.

Isa. 42.5: κύριος ὁ θεὸς ὁ ποιήσας τὸν οὐρανόν ... ὁ στερεώσας τὴν γῆν καὶ τὰ ἐν αὐτῇ.

In Wisdom there is a hint of a move in the Greek direction, developed by Philo, in the introduction of the word κόσμος in place of heaven and earth; thus Wisd. 9.1: ὁ ποιήσας τὰ πάντα, 9: ἐποίεις τὸν κόσμον.

1 QH 1.13f., referring to land and seas, resumes the less philosophical style of the Old Testament.

But the Greeks could make the same affirmation in very similar terms. So Epictetus 4.7.6: ὁ θεὸς πάντα πεποίηκεν τὰ ἐν τῷ κόσμῳ καὶ αὐτὸν τὸν κόσμον.

Corpus Hermeticum 4.1: τὸν πάντα κόσμον ἐποίησεν ὁ δημιουργός.

In fact, in speaking as he does of God as the creator of all things Paul is proclaiming no new truth, but merely repeating what all the Areopagites, except a few sceptics, would themselves have said. They would have agreed also in principle with the conclusion that he draws in v. 24, that a God who has made the universe is not to be thought of as confined to holy dwellings of human construction.

The point is made in closer dependence on the Old Testament (citing Isa. 66.1–2) in Acts 7.48–50 by Stephen, and with much greater sharpness, since there it is said in relation not to heathen sanctuaries but to the Israelite Temple. The parallel however is significant, and helps to relate the two speeches, Stephen's and Paul's, to each other.

A second, similar deduction is made in v. 25: God made all things, God gives all things. How foolish therefore to suppose that he is appropriately served by the gift to him of sacrificial objects which he himself has in the first place given to those who worship him! These observations are familiar and there is no need to linger.

Verse 26, pointing back to human creation which begins from one first made human being, makes a further point common to both Jewish and Greek traditions (and therefore no new truth for Paul to proclaim), but continues with a more interesting ambiguity. The interpretation of ὁρίσας προστεταγμένους καιροὺς καὶ τὰς ὁροθεσίας τῆς κατοικίας αὐτῶν is a long disputed matter and from this point a more important divergence between Greek-based and Old Testament-based interpretations arises. Simply put, the areas and times referred to may signify either the geographical zones' of the earth and the seasons of the year, or the political extent and the historical rise and fall of the several races of mankind. The former is suggested by, for example, lines of Aratus's *Phaenomena* close to that quoted in v. 28 ('He telleth it, when the clod is best for oxen and for mattocks; He telleth it, when the seasons are favourable Both for the planting of trees and for the strewing of seed of every kind. For He Himself established the signs of these things in the heavens, When he ordered the stars . . .'; E. Bevan, pp. 7–11). The latter recalls passages such as Deut. 32.8 (ὅτε διεμέριζεν ὁ ὕψιστος ἔθνη, ὡς διέσπειρεν υἱοὺς Ἀδάμ, ἔστησεν ὅρια ἐθνῶν κατὰ ἀριθμὸν ἀγγέλων θεοῦ); cf. Dan. 7.1–12. That is, the wording brings together the historical religion of the Old Testament, which sees God active in the events that constitute the life of peoples and of a particular people, and natural religion, which traces God's presence in the recurring cycles of nature, and provides a means of interpreting each to the other. The wording itself makes possible, one might say equally possible, two interpretations, not necessarily incompatible but certainly distinct from each other. A similar observation can be made with regard to v. 27, where the idea of seeking God, and the idea that he is not far from any one of us, which seems superficially common to both the Old Testament and Greek traditions, are in fact differently understood in Israel and in Greece, and at the same time provide a means by which the two may approach each other. This is expressed both in man's vocation to seek God, and in the assurance that God is not far away. 'Wie schon mehrfach in der Rede, so verbindet Lukas mit dem Wort "suchen" (ζητεῖν) biblische und griechisch-philosophische Inhalte' (Weiser, p. 472). Seeking God is a theme that occurs frequently in the Old Testament: e.g. Isa. 51.1, οἱ διώκοντες τὸ δίκαιον καὶ ζητοῦντες τὸν κύριον; 55.6, ζητήσατε τὸν κύριον. Dibelius (p. 32) rightly observes that in the Old Testament seeking the Lord is a 'matter of the will'; it requires obedience. But it is not quite as exclusively so as he suggests; there is an intellectual element in it, and under Greek influence this is brought out in Hellenistic Judaism, as it is here. Thus e.g. Philo, *De Spec. Leg* 1.36, ἄμεινον γὰρ οὐδὲν τοῦ ζητεῖν τὸν ἀληθῆ θεόν, κἂν ἡ εὕρεσις αὐτοῦ διαφεύγῃ δύναμιν ἀνθρωπίνην. The εἰ ἄρα γε of Acts, with the optatives that follow it, and the choice of the word ψηλαφᾶν, *to grope*, emphasize, with Philo, the difficulty of the quest (and thereby its cognitive element), but the final clause in the verse stresses the other side. Finding God is always possible because he is not far away. Here, too, the wording is ambiguous and may be taken either in the sense of Ps. 33.19 (LXX: ἐγγὺς κύριος τοῖς συντετριμμένοις τὴν καρδίαν; cf. 144.18), where God's nearness is in mercy, and is conditioned by penitence and the fear of God, or in that of Seneca, *Epistle* 41.1 (prope est a te deus, tecum est, intus est), where God's nearness is a matter of immanence, indeed of panentheism. This twofold possibility of interpretation raises in the New Testament as it does in Philo important questions touching the author's intention. Is he unable to see the difference between the two ways of understanding man's search and God's nearness? Does he wish to assert both kinds of nearness? Does he, as a propagandist, intend to catch the interest and agreement of his hearer with something the hearer thinks he is familiar with and then to trap him into his own, different, meaning? If any of these questions is answered in the affirmative the proceeding is a doubtful one – an important observation, since it must throw doubt on a Christian missionary method adapted from Hellenistic Judaism.

Verse 28 comes out fully on the Greek side, with a quotation, possibly two quotations. τοῦ γὰρ καὶ γένος ἐσμέν is certainly from Aratus's *Phaenomena*, and is acknowledged by the speaker to come from the Greek poets. Whether ἐν αὐτῷ ζῶμεν καὶ κινούμεθα καὶ ἐσμέν also is a quotation is disputed, and this is not the time to take part in the discussion; if it is not a quotation it is at least a summary, amplifying as it inverts the close of v. 27: God is near us, within us, and we are in him. The thought if not the words is probably drawn from Posidonius, where it expresses Stoic panentheism; God, impersonal, is the environment in which we live. We are his family in that there is within us a spark of the universal, all-pervading, λόγος.

The Greek listener who heard this from a Hellenistic Jew, or Hellenistic Jewish Christian, might justifiably feel that he was being treated unfairly, since Jew and Christian, not in complete agreement with each other, did not mean by the assertion that we are God's family exactly what he meant, and were using his language (γένος οὖν ὑπάρχοντες τοῦ θεοῦ, v. 29) as the basis of a conclusion he would probably not have drawn, since the Stoics found it possible to defend the use of images. 'We attribute a human body to God, seeing in it the vessel of thought and reason. Unable to show the unimaginable and the unrepresentable by an example of it, we try to do so by means of the visible and representable. We so use this that it has the virtue of a symbol.' So Dio Chrysostom (*Oration* 12.59.61). The speaker in Acts, however, will have nothing to do with images, using invective reminiscent of Isaiah, though the main words (ἐνθύμησις, χάραγμα) are not found in the LXX; τεχνή recalls passages in Wisdom. Here at last is something truly ξένον, new and strange, not in the sense that the audience had never heard it, but in the sense that it was foreign to their own understanding of religion and religious philosophy. And they would feel that the speaker was making an illegitimate and illogical leap from a proposition they would accept to a conclusion that made no allowance for their understanding of symbolism.

Accommodation to Hellenism ends with v. 29. The earlier theme of ignorance (v. 23), hinted at in v. 29 (the Athenians evidently did think that God was in some sense like, or might be represented by, objects of gold, silver, or stone), now in v. 30 returns, but no longer in a philosophical, epistemological form; it is a fault, since it must be repented of. The moral indictment is set in a new framework, that of *Heilsgeschichte*, which was adumbrated by one way of understanding v. 26. προστεταγμένοι καιροί are marked by the rise and fall of nations; also by an age of ignorance, relatively innocent ignorance, which is now being brought to an end. This recalls Rom. 3.25f., but there is a marked difference between the two passages. There, introduced by the words *passing over* (πάρεσις) and *forbearance* (ἀνοχή), the end of the time in which God tolerantly endured ignorance was brought about by God's initiative in manifesting his saving righteousness; here his action is simply a command, and it rests with men to bring in a new age by repentance. Judgement is at hand; God's patience is at an end, though he will presumably spare the penitent. In Romans the period of πάρεσις has already ended, and ended in justification; in Acts the end of πάρεσις is foretold, and foretold in the demand for repentance in view of judgement.

There is here a close parallel to Stephen's speech in Acts 7 in that it is only in the last sentence that any specifically Christian reference is made. Even now (in Acts 17) the reference is anonymous. The Christian reader knows that the one whom God has marked out as judge by raising him from the dead is Jesus; the Areopagites of course do not know this. Not even here does a piece of Hellenistic Jewish propaganda become for them Christian preaching. There is however reason to think (see *FS* Hahn, p. 242) that Christians did from time to time take over Hellenistic Jewish pieces and adapt them by adding at the end references, sometimes as in Acts 17 veiled references, to the Christian story.

The attitude to pagan (and one may add Jewish) religion in Rom. 1 differs from this, lacking its ambiguity and obscurity. It is not my intention here simply to repeat the exegesis of Rom. 1.18–32 that I have given in my commentary; the purpose of the present exercise is comparison between the Paul of Romans and the Paul represented in Acts as preaching at Athens. That there is a difference between the two is clear, and it is not simply accounted for as the greater sharpness and incisiveness that I have just referred to. The difference has been expressed in terms of two strands that may be detected within Hellenistic Judaism, one which took a friendlier attitude towards non-Jewish religious thought, represented by Aristobulus and reflected in Acts, and one whose attitude was more critical, represented by the Sibyllines and taken up by Paul (in Romans). That such distinctions within Hellenistic Judaism may be validly made is in all probability true (though I suspect that we could find both strands in Philo), but the distinction in itself does not explain why one New Testament writer should adopt the one line and another a different line – or, if this way of putting the question is better, why Paul speaking in Athens should follow Aristobulus but when writing to Rome should abandon him for the Sibyllines. We must look further if we are to grasp and state the difference between Acts and Romans.

The real problem in Acts lies in v. 23, where Paul tells the Athenians that he is about to proclaim to them something that they do not know. He then proceeds to tell them what for the most part they knew already, that is, what educated, thinking Greeks knew already. This leads up to v. 28 and the quotation of what the heathen Greek poet had said, deliberately invoked, one would think, in order to demonstrate common ground between speaker and listeners. And even those who were prepared to defend the use of images did not assert that τὸ θεῖον εἶναι ὅμοιον, was actually *like* bits of gold, silver, or stone. Deity was spiritual; material objects might give us an idea of what he was spiritually like – beautiful, for example, and strong. The only new announcement was that God required repentance (for what?) *now* in view of the fact that he had fixed the date for judgement (in itself a notion not unknown to Greeks) to take place, and had (unknown to the Greeks) appointed the judge. The speaker takes over the kind of argument by which Jews sought to prove that all the best of Greek thought was already anticipated in Judaism. This was a much more intellectually respectable argument; at least there was something to prove, namely, that Jews and Greeks believed the same things, only Jews had known them first and held them in a purer form. But this is not how it is made to appear in Acts.

The content of Acts 17.22–29, shorn of its illogical development, is already to be seen in Rom. 1.19, 20. Acts has claimed that to the Greeks God is ἄγνωστος; the Athenians worship him without knowing him (ἀγνοοῦντες); then, confusingly, goes on not only to speak as if Gods creation of the world were common knowledge but also to quote a Greek poet's belief that we are God's family, so that to worship idols is not to be ignorant of God but to fail to draw logical conclusions from what is in fact known about him. In the light of this confusion Paul's words in Romans gain so mutch in clarity that it is a reasonable hypothesis that (along with other purposes) he is, in this letter to a church founded in all probability by Hellenistic Jewish Christians, deliberately straightening out the relation between biblical thought about God and the religions of the non-Jewish world. τὸ γνωστὸν τοῦ θεοῦ (v. 19) implies a distinction between what is and what is not naturally known about God. It is clearly beyond question that the Greeks (even the Epicureans) have an idea that God exists. Both their philosophy and their religious practices claim such knowledge, and it is communicated to them by τὰ ποιήματα – things which have been made, and not made by them, or any human hand. This γνωστόν however is limited; it is knowledge of God's δύναμις and θειότης that is, to the fact that it is God that we are talking about, and that he is not only other than man but more powerful than man, since he was able to make the sun, the moon, the earth, and so on, things which obviously we are not capable of making. It is also limited by men's reaction to God. They may worship him in the performance of religious rites (εὐσεβεῖν), but they do not offer him anything that could be called (Rom. 12.1) a λογικὴ λατρεία; they do not treat him as God, glorifying him and giving thanks to him, acknowledging, that is, their ultimate dependence on him. Their turning to idols was not simply a failure in logic but a moral disobedience, in which, unwilling to recognize any authority higher than their own, they directed their worship to images of objects which could never be their superiors or even their equals. Out of this primal sin Paul sees sins evolving, and especially the perversion of human nature. He is probably dependent on the story of the fall of Adam and Eve in Eden, but he does not develop the theme in terms of *Heilsgeschichte*; what he offers here is a radical analysis of human existence.

That Rom. 1 originated as a correction of the kind of natural theology developed in Acts 17 it is impossible to prove, though it seems to me probable. It was not Paul's way to specify his corrections of earlier Christian tradition; rather to emphasize his contact with it and to reproduce its language as far as he can. Here he analyses knowledge and ignorance as they are not analysed in Acts, and in doing so provides a ground for a summons to repentance – and faith – such as is not found in Acts. It makes good sense to say that he is deepening not only the view of idolatry that is found in Wisdom but also that of those who founded the church in Rome – just as, perhaps, he had, in 1.3, 4, deepened their Christology. The two forms of proclamation stand over against each other, not as false and true, but as shallow and profound. And the newness of the Gospel is not in its presuppositions but in its specific content, which will be effective only if *known*.

7

Pauline Controversies in the Post-Pauline Period

The theme is one that could easily be allowed to develop into a history of the apostolic age. I hope to keep it within reasonable bounds by approaching it in the main from one angle only. Like most of the great figures of the past, Paul is known to us both as a historical and as a legendary figure, and it is my intention in this paper to consider in a small way not only how the real Paul and the legendary Paul illuminate each other, but also how, between them, they cast a measure of light upon an obscure period.

There is no safer historical proposition about Paul than that his career, and the letters through which his career is known to us, were deeply marked by controversy. He was the storm-centre of his age, and even Acts, which notably dilutes the controversial element in his life, fails to remove it completely. He was a man born to trouble as the sparks fly upward, and inevitably generated controversy; at the same time, the controversies in which he was engaged helped to make him the man he was, and it was in debate that some of his most characteristic, and most important, doctrines were hammered out. It is for example doubtful whether we should have had in the form in which we know it his doctrine of justification by faith had it not been threatened before it was formulated by the Judaizing movement. It is doubtful whether he would have thought through (though presumably he would have continued to practise) his own conception of apostleship if he had not been confronted by false apostles. It is doubtful whether his Christology would have developed as it did if he had not encountered gnostic and other attempts, mostly well-meaning but not for that reason adequate, to locate the figure of Jesus in history and the universe. He was the first and greatest but not the only Christian theologian to find that controversy made him creative. So much is fairly evident, and unlikely to be disputed.

With this observation the theologian might be content to stop, and proceed to deal with the doctrinal raw material which the controversies deposited in the epistles. He would, I think, be ill-advised, for in doing so he would lose not only the context that could make his theology intelligible but also a quantity of vital theological substance, for New Testament theology is not static but mobile, and is better seen as a moving picture than as a sequence of stills. The historian will be very unwilling to stop at this point, for once he has scented a controversy a historian will, if he can, follow it to the kill. Unfortunately, however, in the Pauline controversies it is not long before he encounters a check, and line after line peters out. Again and again we simply do not know how Paul's conflicts ended. We can hardly expect to know: the epistles cannot tell us how the conflicts ended for they are part of the controversy as Paul conducted it; Acts, which in general does not tell us that the battles began, can hardly inform us of their outcome.

Perhaps the most notable example of our ignorance is the dispute with Cephas at Antioch (Gal. 2.11). What happened in the end? We may guess but we do not know. It is possible, though not altogether easy, to make out the ground and cause of the dispute, but once the theological issue has been brought to light Paul's interest in the event as such evaporates, and commentators are not even agreed where his words to Peter end and he resumes his discourse to his Galatian readers. The dispute begins with the message from James and Peter's success in bringing in on his side all his fellow-Jews, including even Barnabas. Did all the Gentile Christians side with Paul? Does his silence mean that they deserted him and accepted circumcision in order to remain in communion with the Jewish party? Did Paul retain the allegiance of the Gentiles and recapture the Jews? It would be helpful if we could be certain of the relative dates of Galatians and 1 Corinthians, where Cephas and Barnabas are referred to, though with no conspicuous warmth, as colleagues. But the date of Galatians is disputed. Tradition (questionable tradition, since Ignatius does not mention it) makes Peter bishop of Antioch before he was bishop of Rome; this might suggest that Paul was defeated. Antioch ceases to be the base of his mission, but this may mean no more than that it lay too far east, and would require too long lines of communication to serve as a centre of supply for campaigns in Rome and Spain. Possibly the dispute was not ended, and Antioch not quiet, when Paul wrote Galatians, but we can hardly suppose that Peter was simply left to stand and wait for the resumption of Paul's dressing down.

This gap in our knowledge is only one of a sequence of gaps (a sequence so extensive that it reminds one of the definition of a net as a large number of holes fastened together with string). What was the outcome of Galatians itself? Did Paul win back the Galatians, who so grieved and baffled him (4.19)? We hear in Acts 18.23 that he passed through Galatian territory and Phrygia strengthening all the disciples; otherwise only that Gaius of Derbe (20.4) accompanied him to Jerusalem; this may be significant (a) if you do not accept the Western variant Δουβέριος, and (b) if you think that Galatia includes Derbe. More important, but belonging probably to a later date, is the reference to Galatia in 1 Pet. 1.1; it seems reasonable to conclude that Christianity of a more or less Pauline kind existed in Galatia at the time this epistle was written. But this observation tells us nothing about the course of events, or about the development of personal relations between Paul and the churches, and though 1 Peter is broadly Pauline in outlook its ascription to Paul's rival in Antioch, whether genuine or pseudonymous, can hardly be insignificant.

We are a little better informed about the outcome of Paul's conflicts in Corinth. Some indeed, taking the view that 2 Cor. 10–13 is part of the 'severe letter' and that it was written before the conciliatory parts of 2 Cor. 1–9, would say that here we are actually informed by the epistles themselves and have on paper the record of Paul's reconciliation with his rebellious church: I am glad that I have every confidence in you (7.16). This conclusion must however be modified in two important respects. In the first place, it is far from certain that 2 Cor. 10–13 is to be dated earlier than 1–9; and in the second, though Paul had trouble enough with the Christians of Corinth they were not the main object of his polemic. He was desperately anxious about them because they were being duped by servants of Satan disguised as apostles, but the false apostles themselves were the real enemy. It seems, not from 2 Corinthians but from the passing remark in Rom. 15.26, that Achaea like Macedonia had made a contribution to the needs of the poor saints in Jerusalem, and thus that the Corinthians were sufficiently reconciled to Paul to trust him with their money, but it is by no means clear that the false apostles were penitent, or even that they had ceased their operations in Corinth.

The same passage in Romans that tells us that Achaea had contributed to the fund urges its readers to wrestle in prayer that the collection might prove acceptable in Jerusalem; the image (συναγωνίσασθαι) is to some extent conventional, but it would be ridiculous if Paul knew that when he reached Jerusalem he was sure to be greeted by a polite Thank you. Achaea and Macedonia had contributed – he does not say that Galatia had; but the outcome remained quite uncertain.

It would be easy, if time permitted, to take up other controversial themes, such as the dissident groups in Corinth, the problem of the resurrection and, perhaps more significant, the conflict between the weak and the strong, of which there are traces in every Pauline missionfield. If any of these disputes was settled in Paul's lifetime we do not know on what terms. I shall however close this sketch with the observation that where Paul appears to take over Christological material, which he uses presumably because it was already familiar to his readers, and perhaps had been composed by some of them, he does so with alterations. The most familiar examples are Rom. 1.3f.; Phil. 2.6–11; Col. 1.15–20. In all these passages it can be shown with considerable probability that Paul introduced comments of his own which, though verbally slight, had the effect of giving a radically new turn to the Christology he was using. In Romans 1 he brings the divine sonship of Christ into the pre-resurrection period; already as man Jesus was Son of God. In Phil. 2 the deified Second Adam of the original becomes the heavenly being who, already of divine status, begins the story by coming down from heaven and becoming man, thereby exhibiting

158

in the highest degree the humility and obedience which, as man, he continues to practise. In Col. 1 Christ is not, or is not simply, the head of the cosmic σῶμα, an ontological mediator who bridges the gap between the invisible God and the material universe, but the Redeemer who reconciles the rebellious cosmos to God through the blood he shed on the cross, conveys to men the forgiveness of sins, and becomes the head of the church. So far, so good; but what was the reply? What did those who composed the original forms of these hymns make of Paul's additions and emendations? Did they accept them as improvements? Or did they use something like the tart (and not unjustified) words of John Wesley about those who treated his and his brother Charles's hymns in this way? 'They are perfectly welcome [to reprint our hymns], provided they print them just as they are. But I desire they would not attempt to mend them: for they really are not able. None of them is able to mend either the sense or the verse.'[1] Unfortunately, we have neither this nor any other kind of comment; we do not know what happened.

If at this stage we may briefly sum up, there are two observations to make. One side of Paul's controversial activity is a frontier skirmishing with an inadequately Christianized gnosis. The clearest example of this is that which we have just considered. Behind Col. 1.15–20 is an honest attempt at Christology: take the accepted framework of cosmic speculation and give to Christ the highest place within it. The trouble is that in Paul's view this place is neither high enough nor low enough. On the one hand it leaves Christ as no more than a sort of hybrid between God and men, and on the other it fails to bring him down to the historical depth of shedding blood in death. Corinthian gnosis did well enough when it emphasized that there was but one God, that idols therefore were nothing, and that food sacrificed to idols was nothing and might be freely eaten. But it needed sharp correction when it failed to observe that I ought to be more concerned about my brother's conscience than my freedom to compile my own shopping-list and menu, drew false analogies between freedom to eat and freedom to

---

[1] Preface to the 1779 'Collection of Hymns for the Use of the People called Methodists'.

commit fornication, and applied its rationalist dialectic to the resurrection. Paul was a gnostic, but the sort of gnostic who exercised a very strict criticism on the various pieces of gnosis, speculative and moral, that he encountered and was invited to adopt.

The counterpart of this sporadic encounter with gnosis was something more like a pitched battle with the judaizing counter-mission that seems to have dogged Paul wherever he went, assuming different forms in different areas. In Galatia and Macedonia it demanded circumcision, apparently requiring that Gentile Christians become proselytes. In Corinth and the Lycus valley it entered into some kind of partnership with local religious life. Apostolic character was essential to it; hence Paul's most radical condemnation of its representatives as ψευδαπόστολοι,[2] representatives of Satan, not (as they claimed) of Christ. Or did they make this claim? Certainly they understood apostleship in a different way from Paul and may have thought of themselves not as servants of Christ but as apostles of the Jerusalem church, charged by it to bring all the new communities which were growing up in the Empire into association with the mother church. We come back here to the confrontation between Paul and Peter. In this everything was at stake: the centrality and sufficiency of Jesus, a relation with God based on faith only, and an understanding of Christian life which, though focused most sharply in the figure of the apostle, meant for all a bearing about of the killing of Jesus, transformed by resurrection. The conflict was such that Paul was obliged to fight for his life, or rather for the life of his churches and of Christianity as he understood it. As we have seen, in Galatia at least we do not know the outcome of the struggle.[3]

Within a few years the situation was completely transformed. Paul, Peter, and James died as martyrs. The evidence is not as good as one could wish, but it is sufficient. For James we have the

---

[2] See 'ΨΕΥΔΑΠΟΣΤΟΛΟΙ (2 Cor. 11.13)', in *Mélanges Bibliques en hommage au R. P. Béda Rigaux* (1970), pp. 377–96.

[3] This view seems to me much more probable than that which sees all Paul's opponents as gnostics.

explicit accounts of Hegesippus and Josephus. These are not identical, but the only point of divergence to be noted here is the date of the event. According to Josephus (*Antiquities* xx. 200) this took place just before the accession of Albinus as procurator of Judaea (διὰ τὸ τεθνάναι μὲν Φῆστον, ᾿Αλβῖνον δ᾿ ἔτι κατὰ τὴν ὁδὸν ὑπάρχειν), that is, in A.D. 62. According to Hegesippus (*apud* Eusebius, *Church History* II. xxiii.18), after James's death εὐθὺς Οὐεσπασιανὸς πολιορκεῖ αὐτούς. This is often taken to mean that Hegesippus put the event in A.D. 69, just before the siege of Jerusalem (though this was conducted not by Vespasian but by Titus), or in 66 or 67, just before Vespasian began military operations in Palestine. This however puts a heavy weight on εὐθύς, which Hegesippus may have used in the same loose way as Mark: 'and the next thing, that is, the next significant thing, was that Vespasian besieged them'. Eusbius's *Chronicle* and Jerome are in approximate agreement with Josephus, and A.D. 62 may be accepted with some confidence.

It is a surprising fact that there is no comparable early account of Peter's martyrdom. It seems very probable that Peter did reach Rome and die there as a martyr; the arguments of Lietzmann[4] have been supplemented but not disproved. The date of Peter's death is a good deal less well attested. W. M. Ramsay[5] may well be right in describing the statement that he perished in the Neronian persecution as not tradition but historical theory; his own view, that the martyrdom took place nearer A.D. 80, is also a theory, designed to reconcile the belief that 1 Peter cannot have been written in the 60s with the conviction that it must have been written by Peter. The Neronian date may be accepted, though not with complete conviction, as the more probable.

That Paul died after Peter is a belief that seems to rest on no better foundation than that Clement, in speaking of the deaths of the 'good apostles,' (1 Clem. 5.3ff.), mentions Peter first. This

---

[4] *Petrus und Paulus in Rom* (1915).
[5] W. M. Ramsay, *The Church in the Roman Empire before A.D. 170* (10th edition, no date); cf. pp. 282f.: 'While the tradition that St. Peter perished in Rome is strong and early, the tradition about the date of his death is not so clear.'

reason is hardly sufficient. Paul reached Jerusalem, bearing the collection for the poor, probably in A.D. 55; it was in the same year that Festus took office. How long Paul remained in Palestine is uncertain. His voyage to Rome started too late in the sailing season; it may have been as early as late summer 55, or perhaps a year later. According to Acts he would reach Rome in the early spring (28.11) of the next year – 56 or 57. Then began the two-year period of house arrest (28.30), ending early in the year 58 or 59.[6] How did it end? According to old tradition – as old as the Pastorals – in release and further missionary activity; but perhaps in condemnation and execution. This is a difficult question, not to be resolved in a line or two of this paper. If it is argued that the tradition in 1 Clement of preaching in the far west refers to Spain and cannot have been altogether false because at the time Clement wrote some were still alive who knew what had happened thirty years earlier, this may be countered by the tradition of the Pastorals, which represents Paul as travelling back east and says nothing about a journey to the west. According to 1 Clement Paul perished διὰ φθόνον; this is compatible rather with action by Jews or Jewish Christians than with Nero's face-saving persecution. The familiar problem of the end of Acts could be solved if there was something discreditable in Paul's death (not necessarily to him). In 2 Cor. 11.26 Paul refers to dangers he had experienced at the hands of false brothers; these occur as the climax of a list of physical perils – from Jewish and Roman beatings, from stoning, from shipwreck, from highwaymen. The false brothers were, or represented themselves as, Christians: they had already put Paul in danger of death. Did they join the Jews in accusing Paul (cf. Phil. 1.15, διὰ φθόνον καὶ ἔριν)? Did James fail to offer the support he might have given? There is no hint in Acts 21–26 that he took much positive action on Paul's behalf. It would be wrong to build much on Clement's διὰ φθόνον, which is applied also to Peter, and may be a fiction based on Acts 3–5; 12;[7] it is however not unreasonable to think that Paul died as early as 58 or 59, and

---

[6] S. Dockx, *Nov T* 13, p. 304, gives the two years as A.D. 56–8.
[7] Morton Smith, *NTS* 7, pp. 86ff. But had Clement read Acts?

even if he was released after two years of confinement he may have died as early as James and some time before the Neronian persecution.

The important fact is that Paul, James and Peter were all within a short space removed from the scene.[8] It may well be true that the more extreme members of the trio, Paul and James, died first, leaving Peter in a dominating position. This could explain many things: the emergence, or re-emergence, of Peter as in fact the rock on which the church was to stand, and the characteristics of sub-apostolic Christianity, which was not judaizing, and yet did not adopt, probably no longer understood, the radicalism of Paul. We must add the fact that 'before the war' (that is, not later than A.D. 66) the Christians in Jerusalem had left the city for Pella.[9] This must have robbed the counter-mission of its authority, for though it might be argued that all Christians should be in communion with Jerusalem, not only the scene of the Lord's death and resurrection and the seat of the first disciples but the ancient city of God's election to which the ancient promises were attached, no one could with any plausibility maintain that the Christians of, say, Philippi, Corinth and Rome owed any special obligation to the Peraean city of Pella. Thus within a few years the whole situation was transformed; not only was it transformed, the means by which the old controversies could be understood were removed.[10] Suddenly a power-vacuum came into being, which was also, and this is more important, a theological vacuum. What happened? This is the question we should like to answer, but there is no way

---

[8] There is much of importance in S. G. F. Brandon's discussion of this situation in *The Fall of Jerusalem and the Christian Church* (1951); but that from A.D. 55 Paul was out of contact with his churches, and discredited in their eyes, is contradicted by Philippians and Colossians, if these were written from Rome. Brandon is surprisingly conservative in his use of Acts 21.

[9] Eusebius, *Church History* III. v. 3. J. Munck (*NTS* 6, pp. 103f.) thinks the story a fiction – the city could not be destroyed while any of the righteous remained within it; Brandon (*The Fall of Jerusalem*, pp. 177f.) that the flight was not to Pella but to Alexandria. The latter view, does not affect my argument; the former does not adequately account for the origin of the tradition.

[10] Munck (*NTS* 6, pp. 114f.) rightly points out that later Jewish Christianity was not a lineal descendant of the Jewish Christianity that Paul encountered.

of handling it by frontal approach. We must go round to the back door, and if this is to be done effectively we must be prepared to go a long way round.

More than 100 years after Paul's death we find a distinguished Christian writer still speaking of the apostle and his place in Christian theology in a somewhat defensive manner. Irenaeus is aware that the Pauline ark has to be brought back out of the land of the Philistines.

> It is necessary to subjoin . . . the doctrine of Paul . . ., to examine the opinion of this man, and expound the apostle, and to explain whatsoever [passages] have received other interpretation from the heretics, who have altogether misunderstood what Paul has spoken, and to point out the folly of their mad opinions; and to demonstrate from that same Paul, from whose [writings] they press questions upon us, that they are indeed utterers of falsehood, but that the apostle was a preacher of the truth, and that he taught all things agreeable to the preaching of the truth. (*Adv. Haer.* IV. xli. 4)[11]

Irenaeus however marks the end of one stage, and the beginning of another. From the end of the second century Christian writers show no hesitation about the canonical status of the Pauline literature;[12] Paul, its author, was conclusively enrolled among the orthodox. The earlier defensiveness and hesitation had been due to the various pictures of Paul that circulated in the second century. We have it on the good authority of 2 Pet. 3.16 that the heretics made use of the Pauline epistles, and this evidence is confirmed by such fragments of Marcion, Valentinus, and other heretics as we possess, and by the accounts of them given by orthodox writers such as Irenaeus.

It was thus that Paul came to be seen as the proto-gnostic, the enemy, the bogus apostle, the source of error and division. The clearest of the anti-Pauline legends appears in the caricature of Paul in the person of Simon Magus, which appears in the *Kerygmata Petrou*, as this document is reconstructed from the

---

[11] Translation by A. Roberts and W. H. Rambaut, in the Ante-Nicene Christian Library. Cf. the Muratorian Canon, lines 63–8.

[12] Except, of course, Hebrews.

Clementine Homilies and Recognitions. It is impossible here to go into the complicated literary and historical problems involved; the existence of the picture is a sufficient witness to the mistrust of Paul, and to the complicated cross-currents, gnostic and anti-gnostic, Jewish and anti-Jewish, of the second century.[13]

This mistrust is reflected in the disuse of Paul by second-century figures nearer to the mainstream of Christian thought: Hegesippus, Papias, and Justin.[14] Bauer[15] cites the quotation from Hegesippus in Eusebius, *Church History* IV. xxii. 2–3, in which Hegesippus describes the true faith which he found preached in every city as that which 'is preached by the law and the prophets and the Lord'. This, Bauer says, leaves no room for Paul as an authority. In the same context Eusebius records, in connection with Hegesippus's visit to Corinth, that he knew 1 Clement, but gives no indication that he used the Pauline letters to Corinth. Bauer refers also to a passage quoted by Photius,[16] in which Hegesippus disapproves of the words, 'The good things prepared for the righteous neither eye saw nor ear heard, nor did they enter man's heart', setting over against them the Lord's saying, 'Blessed are your eyes which see, and your ears which hear.' Had Hegesippus then read 1 Corinthians (2.9) and disapproved of it? The observation is weakened by the fact that after quoting the

---

[13] On this important subject, which can only be touched on here, see G. Strecker's translation of the text in E. Hennecke and W. Schneemelcher, *Neutestamentliche Apokryphen* II (1964), pp. 76ff. and his introduction, pp. 63–9; the same author's *Das Judenchristentum in den Pseudoklementinen* (1958) L. Goppelt, *Christentum und Judentum im ersten und zweiten Jahrhundert* (1954), pp. 171–6; H. J. Schoeps, *Theologie und Geschichte des Judenchristentums* (1949); *Aus frühchristlicher Zeit* (1950); *Urgemeinde, Judenchristentum, Gnosis* (1956); O. Cullmann, *Le Problème littéraire et historique du Roman Pseudo-Clémentin* (1930).

[14] See W. Bauer, *Rechtgläubigkeit und Ketzerei im ältesten Christentum* (1934), pp. 215–30.

[15] Bauer, p. 199. For the texts of Hegesippus see M. J. Routh, *Reliquiae Sacrae* I (1846), pp. 205–19.

[16] For details see Routh, *Reliquiae Sacrae* I, p. 219. A quotation taken by Photius (in the ninth century) from Stephen Gobarus (in the sixth century) is hardly the highest authority for the views of Hegesippus (in the second century).

passage in question Paul goes on to say (1 Cor. 2.10), ἡμῖν ἀπεκάλυψεν ὁ θεὸς διὰ τοῦ πνεύματος – in this respect at least Paul and Hegesippus are on the same side. But on the whole the conclusion stands: Hegesippus was a Jewish rather than a Pauline Christian, using (according to Eusebius) the 'Syriac' Gospel according to the Hebrews and quoting it 'in Hebrew', giving particulars about Jewish as well as Christian sects and parties, and information about the family of Jesus. Eusebius, however, would hardly have used Hegesippus as he does had he been a heretical Jewish Christian, and there is little or nothing to suggest that in his disuse of Paul he was reacting against Marcion. He could not have used 1 Clement and have radically disapproved of Paul, though he may have failed to understand him.

Bauer (p. 217) notes that Eusebius quotes no information from Papias about Luke; he thinks, because this was Marcion's gospel. The extant fragments contain no reference to Paul, though Papias admired Revelation and (according to Eusebius) used 1 John and 1 Peter. This shows, says Bauer, that he confined himself to material of Palestinian origin (since he believed Mark to be dependent on Peter), and to documents of marked *Kirchlichkeit* – 1 John because it was so strongly anti-gnostic, and 1 Peter because it emanated from Rome. Paul does not figure in Papias's list of apostolic and sub-apostolic authorities (Eusebius, *Church History* III. xxxix. 4). This is indeed a noteworthy silence,[17] but it is to some extent explained by Papias's aversion to books (Eusebius, *Church History* III. xxxix.4).[18] This implies however that even in the region of Ephesus oral tradition derived or purporting to be derived from Paul had already dried up.

An even more important figure is Justin, of whom Bauer (p. 218) says, 'Bei Paulus fehlt nicht nur der Name, sondern auch jedes Eingehen auf seine Briefe.' He advances the strong arguments that when Justin claims that Christians are loyal subjects who pay

[17] It is scarcely mitigated by Routh's conjectural attribution (*Reliquiae Sacrae* I, pp. 10f.) to Papias of the passage which is ascribed by Irenaeus (*Adv. Haer*, V. xxxvi. I f.) to οἱ πρεσβύτεροι and contains a quotation from 1 Cor. 15.25–28.

[18] One must also bear in mind that, at least according to Eusebius (*Church History* III. xxxix 13), Papias was σφόδρα σμικρὸς τὸν νοῦν.

their taxes (1 *Apology* 17) he makes no reference to Rom. 13.1–7; when he discusses the conversion of the Gentiles and the rejection of the Jews (1 *Apology* 49) he does not use Rom. 9ff.; in his tract on the resurrection he makes no use of 1 Cor. 15.[19] Justin was a responsible and learned Christian who lived in Rome; why does he make no reference to Paul? E. F. Osborn[20] finds more allusions, but even so they amount to little, especially in view of the fact (which Dr Osborn brings out) that there is often common Old Testament material that may account for the resemblances between Paul and Justin. Dr Osborn offers three explanations of Justin's disuse of Paul (and of other parts of the New Testament): 'Justin's understanding of prophecy, his position as an apologist and the classical convention of indirect citation' (p. 138). These explanations are not without weight, but it must remain probable that they were strongly reinforced by a measure of mistrust; Paul was the heretics' apostle, and it was wise to be cautious in using him.[21]

With the negative results achieved for Hegesippus, Papias and Justin, Bauer does his best to accommodate the evidence to be found in Ignatius and Polycarp – not, I think, successfully. They show knowledge, he thinks, only of 1 Corinthians, 'des am lehrhaften Gehalt so armen I. Korintherbriefes' (p. 222). This judgement certainly undervalues the doctrinal content of 1 Corinthians, and probably undervalues also the number of Pauline allusions to be found in Ignatius and Polycarp. This is not the place to collect such allusions in detail; but Ignatius's reference to Paul 'who in every epistle makes mention of you in the Lord' (*Eph.* 12.2), though it need not refer to a ten-letter collection must refer to more than one letter, and it is hard not to see an allusion to the Pastorals (1 Tim. 6.10, 7) in Polycarp 4.1 (cf. 9.2; 12.3). This is of vital importance, for it means that we must reject Bauer's conclusion, 'dass die Pastoralbriefe in der Zeit, als sich Marcion

---

[19] But is there not in *De Resurrectione* 10 an allusion to 1 Cor. 15.53?

[20] *Justin Martyr* (Beiträge zur historischen Theologie, 47; 1973), pp. 135f.

[21] J. Knox, *Marcion and the New Testament* (1942), *passim*, but especially pp. 115f., supports Bauer in his view not only of Justin but of the general suspicion of Paul in the second century.

über den Umfang der Paulusüberlieferung Klarheit verschaffte, noch nicht vorhanden gewesen sind' (p. 225). Paul was used and approved before the disparaging legend became current. This is borne out by the fact that, notwithstanding the evidence from Hegesippus, Papias, and Justin, the second century, as 2 Pet. 3.16 shows, never rejected Paul altogether. For this, Wagenmann[22] gives three reasons. (1) The Corpus Paulinum already existed and was known and read in all the churches; it was now too late to excommunicate Paul, however desirable this may have appeared to some.[23] (2) From the letters it was known that Paul had been the universal missionary, responsible for establishing churches in the greater part of Christendom. It was impossible therefore to cast doubt on his doctrine and apostleship without casting doubt on one's own authenticity as church and Christian. (3) He was already too widely used for doctrinal purposes – not indeed that the post-apostolic authors really understood him, but all drew texts from his epistles (as the heretics did) to support their own doctrinal positions. These points call for some modification; Paul was not as widely read and used in the second century as Wagenmann suggests. It might be better to be content to say that the 'good' Pauline legend was in existence at least as early as the bad, and did not altogether cease to be operative, and that in influential and important quarters. Within at most a decade or so of Justin's work in Rome, perhaps earlier, there were there τρόπαια of the two great apostles,[24] and hesitant as Justin may have been in his theological writing there is no mistaking the direction of popular piety, or the weight of ecclesiastical authority behind it. That Marcion contributed much to the formation and definition of the Pauline corpus is almost certainly true; but he did not initiate the collection, and if on the one hand he furthered the legend of

---

[22] J. Wagenmann, *Die Stellung des Apostels Paulus neben den Zwölf in den ersten zwei Jahrhunderten* (BZNW 3; 1926), pp. 154f.

[23] The Clementines attack Paul under cover of Simon Magus.

[24] See the words of Gaius quoted in Eusebius, *Church History* II. xxv. 6f., and, for the date, among other publications, J. Toynbee and J. W. Perkins, *The Shrine of St. Peter and the Vatican Excavations* (1956), pp. 128f., 154f.

the gnostic Paul, on the other his contribution to the Pauline canon helped to destroy it. He was in fact operating at a relatively advanced stage in the development of the legend, which in its positive form was already full-blown in Acts and the Pastorals before the time of Polycarp. Indeed, since neither Ignatius nor Polycarp substantially adds to it we may conclude that it was virtually complete by the end of the first century.

It was – and this should be said at the outset – a legend that was by no means entirely legendary. Acts in particular contains a quantity of material of real historical value. This is not unusual: for example, the historical Tiberius, though not quite the monster of Tacitus's legendary, or tendentious, description, was nevertheless not one of the most desirable acquaintances. It is not so much large-scale falsification as subtle variation that we must observe. The main sources are Ephesians, Acts, the Pastorals, and 1 Clement; we shall not expect them all to present the same variations on the one historical theme.[25]

Ephesians is probably the oldest of the Pauline pseudepigrapha; it is precisely because the picture of Paul that it implies is so like that of the other letters, that is, is so like the historical Paul, that it continues to be possible to make a strong, though not to my mind a convincing, case for its authenticity.[26] The personal note about Tychicus (6.21–22 lifted bodily from Col. 4.7–8.) presents Paul as the busy missionary and pastor that he was, circulating among the churches, caring for those he has left behind as well as that in which he is now working, surrounded by assistants who carry news from one part of the field to another and represent the apostle in his absence. This vignette is consistent with the designation of Paul as apostle, which also is simply borrowed from the genuine letters. In particular, Paul is the apostle of the Gentiles, ὑπὲρ ὑμῶν τῶν ἐθνῶν (3.l); there is nothing strange in this, and it could be said to go no further than Gal. 2.9. In practice however, in the other epistles, and by no means least in Galatians, Paul appears as

---

[25] See R. M. Grant, *Gnosticism and Early Christianity* (1959), pp. 160f.

[26] It is reasonable to think of a Pauline school, such as E. Lohse posits for Colossians (*NTS* 15, pp. 211–20, and the same author's commentary, 1968).

the apostle of particular Gentiles, whereas in Ephesians the stress is on Gentiles as a body. As the apostle of the Gentile body Paul is the great architect of the unity of the church, for Ephesians looks back upon the gathering together in one of Jewish and Gentile Christians, all of whom are now reconciled to God in one body and have access to him in one Spirit (2.16, 18). There are other more subtle distinctions, but this achieved unity of Jews and Gentiles is perhaps the most striking feature of the Ephesian legend. In the latest epistles we have Paul was still engaged in a life-and-death struggle with judaizing envoys; in Ephesians the counter-mission has come to an end. It is recognized that Jews and Gentiles are different, and that to unite them is a signal achievement, but there is little or no hint of the internal Christian quarrel that grieved Paul himself.

No one can turn from the epistles to Acts without noting the relative absence of controversy in the account of Paul's life. He is occasionally in trouble with Roman authorities, often attacked by Jews, but the only controversy he encounters within the church is disposed of quickly and successfully in Acts 15. Serious trouble is thrown into the future in the farewell speech of ch. 20; after Paul's departure grievous wolves will harry the flock. Paul is the universal missionary, who carries the Gospel throughout the world. He is not however represented as an apostle – 14.4, 14 may be variously explained, and on the whole accentuate the failure of the book as a whole to apply the word ἀπόστολος to Paul. This unique feature of Acts (for no one else denies him the title who refers to him at length) is probably due to the fact that Luke had committed himself to a numerical identification of the twelve disciples of Jesus with the apostles; it certainly was not intended as disparagement. Paul is the outstanding bearer of the word of God; because he is the bearer of the triumphant and invincible word his own career partakes of these characteristics. Judaizers cannot pervert the Gospel; Jews cannot kill or even halt the preacher. Luke is in a difficulty here, for he knows, and knows that his readers know, that Paul died as a martyr, and he knows also that it will add to the effectiveness of his adulatory picture if he can introduce the shadows of martyrdom as they fall, not too darkly, across his hero's path, and can also indicate that Paul was aware of what was to happen. This in fact is what he does; and we may probably see here the reason why Acts stops where it does. An account of the martyrdom itself, especially if at the time Paul was deserted by his friends and the victim of some kind of treachery,[27] would not enhance the record of Paul's devotion and might detract from the sense of confidence, victory, and unity that permeates the book.

The Pastorals, in which Paul is not merely an apostle but the apostle *par excellence*, provide an important filling out of the picture in Acts (just as from another point of view Acts is a necessary completion of the Pastorals, in that it provides models for the minister who in the Pastorals is taught that it is his duty to preach). Acts avoids the controversial element in Paul's career; the Pastorals represent him as engaged in constant and violent controversy, and thus identify the grievous wolves of Acts 20.29. Paul also makes provision for the continuation of the controversy after his death, and for the teaching of the sound faith: he lays this charge upon Timothy and Titus, and they in turn must hand it on to others. Judaism, legalism, mythology, and gnosis are lumped together in a way that suggests rather that the author was concerned to omit no heresy he had heard of than that he wished, or was able, to analyse, sub-divide, and classify. Error was a mark of the last days, in which it was, or might have been, expected that men would no longer tolerate sound doctrine but turn aside after their own lusts. It is thus an eschatological phenomenon, but it is countered not by arguments based on the imminence of the end but by insistence on the form of sound words, the faithful sayings, the guarding of the deposit of faith, and its transmission to the next generation. Above all, perhaps, in the Pastorals Paul is represented as the martyr. His death, of course, cannot be described in documents purporting to have been written by his hand, but 2 Tim. 4 brings Paul as close to

[27] See above, p. 162. An alternative possibility is that Paul's imprisonment ended with the failure of his accusers to appear and his departure through the back door of the gaol – an anticlimax that would have spoilt Luke's book in a different way.

death as possible: nothing more remains but the crown of righteousness which the Lord will give him.

The martyr theme reappears in 1 Clement, where the author is able to write freely as one who looks back on the event. Peter and Paul are named together, but it is not implied that they suffered at the same time. They are the good apostles; they suffered on account of jealousy and envy (the evils that were disturbing the Corinthian church); they were the greatest and most righteous pillars – a term rather surprisingly applied to Paul in view of Gal. 2.9, but evidently it had now lost the special sense it had had two generations earlier. Paul in particular is the great sufferer for the faith, traveller, and preacher to the Gentiles (for this is probably implied when Clement says (5.7) that he taught ὅλον τὸν κόσμον). The apostles, Paul presumably among them, foreseeing trouble to come, made provision for the continuance of the preaching ministry. In addition, Paul is appealed to as a letter-writer; the Corinthians can still learn from the letter he left.

It seems clear, and it is confirmed a few years later by Ignatius, that at the end of the century, or very soon afterwards, the church had already developed a hagiographical portrait of Paul. I have pointed out above that it was by no means a wholly fictitious picture. Inevitably the later account looked back to Paul and saw him as a martyr. He could hardly see himself in this way, though his longing to be conformed to the death of Christ could, in the circumstances, hardly lead to any other end. Acts and the Pastorals represent two different ways of relating Paul to current, end-of-the-century error. Acts takes the line that in Paul's time all was well; he foresaw error, but his own time was free from it; those therefore who lived when heresy had come into being had to look back to and imitate the good old days when, under Paul's guidance, the church was pure. The Pastorals handle the same situation by bringing Paul within it and allowing him to speak to the new circumstances in which heresy was rife. Clement tells the dissident Corinthians to read 1 Corinthians.

It is the controversial element in the legendary picture of Paul that we have to consider here, just as it was the controversial element in the historical picture that we considered at an earlier point. It is perhaps in this area that the difference between the two is greatest. The battle between Paul and the false apostles has disappeared. Jewish Christians and Gentile Christians are welded together in one body. There is a relic of the old controversy in the opposition to Jews which appears in the deutero-Pauline literature, but this is a different matter. It is not simply that Acts (in the 'Apostolic Decree') and the Pastorals (especially in 1 Tim. 1.7–11) represent Paul as taking up an attitude to the law different from that which we read in the genuine letters; there is a general impression of unreality in the references to Jews: either the author of the Pastorals has simply invented the material because he knows that the historical Paul was in some sense anti-Jewish and confuses Jews with judaizing Christians, or he is writing about a new Judaism, a gnosticizing Judaism. There may be truth in both possibilities.

The vehement struggle is now between Paul and gnostics. These are probably the grievous wolves of Acts 20.29; in the Pastorals they have come out into the open and are the true enemies of the deposit of truth. The hymn of the descending, conquering, and ascending Christ (1 Tim. 3.16) bears witness to an earlier stage, when gnostic elements could be absorbed (cf. Phil. 2.6–11); the epistle itself maintains a different attitude. The generous though not unguarded concessions to the proto-gnosticism of the strong which appear in Romans and 1 Corinthians have now given place to misgiving and defensiveness.

These changes are readily explained as what might have been expected after the deaths of Paul, James, and Peter. It is impossible that Ephesians should have been written at a time when the Jerusalem church was still sponsoring an anti-Pauline mission, but when not only James but his church also ceased to exist it was possible for the integration which Luke ascribed to the Apostolic Council to come into being, and to do so on the lines described in Acts 15. Along with the rapprochement between Jewish Christians and Gentile Christians there went an alienation between Jews – Jewish Jews – and Christians of all sorts, Jewish and Gentile, for the flight to Pella emphasized the fact that not even Jewish Christians would take any part in the Jewish war against the Romans. This was a defection that Jews found hard to understand and forgive; Luke antedates it by bringing out the resistance of Jews to the Gospel in the period dealt with in Acts. Jewish Christians are ceasing to be a problem for the main body of the church. Not so gnosticism. This was the great formative period of gnosticism, when the incorporation of Jewish and Christian elements into speculative systems that had originated further east and had already made some contact with Hellenism was supplying backbone and giving firm shape to what had previously been nebulous and variable. There was some ground for greater Christian caution than Paul had shown, though the transformation of his freedom is a clear mark both of the changing environment and also of the lower potential of his successors – especially of the latter, for the next great Christian theologian, the Fourth Evangelist, was able to resume the old freedom.

The positive Pauline legend was already well developed with Ephesians, Acts, the Pastorals and 1 Clement.[28] There were complicated developments in the second century, at some of which I have hinted, and this age witnessed developed tension between the historical Paul of the letters, the gnosticized Paul, and the anti-gnostic Paul – a tension in which popular piety as well as theology played its part; but these were developments, and fresh inter-relations, of components that were already present at an earlier date and are to be found in the New Testament itself. This is perhaps the most important example of the general truth that the New Testament must 'be appraised as controversy before it can be used as history'.[29] The historical study of the last 100 years has not shown that the conflicts, tensions, and resolutions described by F. C. Baur are imaginary; it has shown that they belong to earlier dates than those to which Baur assigned them.[30] A similar observation could be made with regard to Walter Bauer's work on orthodoxy and heresy, and in particular to his distinction between Paul and the *Pauluswort*: 'Erst als Bestandteil einer in der Kirche anerkannten Hl. Schrift wird sich, nicht die Persönlichkeit des

---

[28] A full discussion would seek traces of it elsewhere, e.g. in the gospels.
[29] E. L. Allen, in *NTS* 1, p. 143.
[30] See *Durham University Journal* 64 (new series 33), pp. 198–203.

Heidenapostels und seine Verkündigung, sondern das Pauluswort, da wo man es zur Ausbildung und Sicherung der Kirchenlehre brauchen kann, einigermassen in Geltung setzen' (p. 230). Bauer himself makes this statement with reference to a period later than that with which he is expressly dealing; *mutatis mutandis* it could be applied to an earlier period, at least if by the 'Pauluswort' we may understand something like what I have called the Pauline legend. The historical development was rapid and compressed, and the period between A.D. 60 and 100 a very complicated one.

We have already seen that the legendary Paul could not have come into being except on the basis of the historical. It also serves to bring out features of the historical Paul that might otherwise have been lost. It may for example over-emphasize Paul's work as organizer and administrator; yet the historical Paul did organize and administer, even though his letters often give the impression of a disorganized and even chaotic church life. But most important is the combined light the two pictures throw on the difficult period in which the clear relation between theology and history which is manifest in the story of Jesus and of Paul, and again with John, is obscured. We know little enough of either the theology or the history of this period, and the writers who follow seem to have lost the clue to Paul's controversial theology. New controversies, which retained some of the old terminology, were described, but the old judaizing controversy with the new eschatological and gnostic controversies of the end of the century produced in combination an amalgam lacking in realism and creativity, and Christian theology does not thrive on shadow-boxing. This observation will lead to a brief consideration of our last theme. Our New Testament canonizes both the historical and the legendary Paul; what bearing has this fact on our understanding of the canon? That the legend no longer represents Paul as fighting against a judaizing agency that had ceased to exist can hardly be brought as an accusation against those who wrote rather to edify than to supply historical information. Indeed, the fiction evolved out of the fact under historical pressures that must have affected Paul himself if he had survived to witness the deaths of James and Peter, and the collapse from its centre of the organized judaizing opposition. This is not to say that Paul would in any circumstances have adopted the safe and moralizing churchmanship of the Pastorals, but that this could never have existed without Paul, and was a natural evolution from him.

More: the fictitious Paul is in a different sense 'safe', that is, harmless to the true being of Scripture and the church, because it has carried with it into the canon the genuine historical Paul. It is not for nothing that in the opening words of *Adversus Haereses* Irenacus alludes to Luke and quotes the Pastorals:

> Inasmuch as certain men have set the truth aside, and bring in lying words and vain genealogies, which, as the apostle says, 'minister questions rather than godly edifying which is in faith', and by means of their craftily-constructed plausibilities draw away the minds of the inexperienced and take them captive, I have felt constrained, my dear friend, to compose the following treatise in order to expose and counteract their machinations.

The establishing of the Pauline canon towards the close of the second century means in effect that the church corrected the Marcionite perversion of the historical Paul by adding to it the legendary Paul of the Pastorals and Acts, seeing, or perhaps instinctively feeling without understanding, that, as Dr Käsemann[31] has said, 'Das Evangelium bleibt nicht länger es selbst, wenn es allein auf dem Plan steht.' This was not merely a correction but a rescue, for apart from the legend Marcion and the gnostics might well have destroyed the historical Paul. Put in this way, it may seem that the legendary Paul is the price we have to pay for the historical; but this would be an inadequate and misleading judgement. The legendary figure contains too many historical

---

[31] E. Käsemann (ed.), *Das Neue Testament als Kanon* (1970), p. 408. Cf. p. 407: ' . . . dass es geschichtlich Jahwe nur im Streit mit Baal, Jakob nur in Bindung und Auseinandersetzung gegenüber Esau gibt, Christ und Antichrist stets gleichzeitig auf dem Plane sind, deshalb auch Glaube und Aberglaube, Kirche und Gegenkirche zwar unterschieden, aber nicht irdisch sauber getrennt werden können. Man verkennt den Kanon, wenn man sich einbildet, in ihm sei dieser Streit nicht im Gange, deshalb ihm gegenüber die Prüfung der Geister nicht notwendig.'

elements to be dismissed in this way, and in the post-Marcionite period was a step back in the direction of the historical, which it carried with it into the canon, so that the legendary stands always under the correction of the historical Paul. The process however is one that operates in both directions, and both figures exercise a critical and questioning function for the reader. Moreover, their contiguity in the canon saves us from the ill effects of canonmaking, well described by L. E. Keck[32] and summed up by him in a quotation from Harnack: 'Canonising works like whitewash; it hides the original colours and obliterates all the contours.'[33] Canon is not a set of eternal propositions; one way of describing it would be a way of perpetuating the fundamental controversies, and thus the essential mobility, of the Gospel, and of demonstrating its powers of renewal even in the hands of the epigoni.

[32] *NovT* 7, p. 224.
[33] A. von Harnack, *The Origin of the New Testament* (1925), p. 141.

8

Ethics in the Deutero-Pauline Literature

If we begin by excluding the historical Paul, known to us by means of the certainly genuine letters, there appear to be two lines of ethical tradition turning through the later parts of the New Testament. The sharp contrast between them makes it possible to take a clearer view of each, and it will therefore be rewarding to begin with a brief consideration of that line which does not constitute the major theme of this paper. This line is to be found in the gospels – we may say in the synoptic gospels; John may be excluded from the present discussion. So far as it may be said to rest upon early tradition this has been absorbed into and reinterpreted in accordance with the specifically Johannine outlook and material. In the synoptic gospels there is a vein of radical ethical material, attributed to Jesus, which is neither philosophically systematic nor adapted to the variety of practical situations. Precepts are given which have the effect not of giving the hearer directions that will enable him to choose between ethical alternatives but of placing him in the presence of a God who always requires from him nothing less than total obedience. To quote one who has given classical – and it may be, in some respects, exaggerated – expression to this understanding of the teaching of Jesus, Jesus'

> ethic . . . is strictly opposed to every humanistic ethic and value ethic; it is an ethic of obedience. He sees the meaning of human action not in the development toward an ideal of man which is founded on the human spirit . . . the concept of an ideal or end is foreign to him . . . he sees only the individual man standing before the will of God . . . This really means that *Jesus teaches no ethics at all* in the

179

sense of an intelligible theory valid for all men concerning what should be done and left undone.[1]

The requirement of obedience is from time to time illustrated in practical terms: the command to love one's enemies (which surely must on occasion mean correcting or restraining them) may be fulfilled by going an extra mile with one who commandeers one's services. But there are also commands which taken literally and universally applied would lead to the breakdown of society. Sell all that you have and give to the poor (thereby creating another penniless person); If anyone comes to me and does not hate his own father and mother and wife and children and brothers and sisters . . . he cannot be my disciple. Such commands are not serious ethics but a very powerful – and paradoxical – statement of the all-embracing claim made by Jesus in the name of God. This radical claim is made with an authority, for the most part undefined, which is the basis of all Christological development, and both the ethical content and the doctrinal foundation of the claim are accessible to inference rather than to explicit interpretation. The Christological element and the ethical element stand in close relation to each other; what we are speaking of here is Christological ethics.

This is of course not a complete account of the ethics of the gospels. As a counterpart to Bultmann's interpretation we may put E. Käsemann's essay 'Sätze Heiligen Rechtes im Neuen Testament',[2] though Käsemann does little to pursue his theme within the Synoptic Gospels. There are places where a primitive tradition, absolute in form, is accommodated to practical circumstances and thereby turned into observable law. A familiar and clear example is provided by Mk 10.2–12, on marriage and divorce. The teaching is provided by Mark with a setting (v. 2) which, describing the Pharisees as tempting Jesus, presents the material as controversial. So in itself it is, for Jesus contradicts the teaching of Moses (Deut. 24.1) and represents marriage as indissoluble. This is done by means of a reference to creation. God

---

[1] R. Bultmann, *Jesus and the Word* (ET; London, 1935), p. 84.
[2] *NTS* 1 (1955), pp. 248–60.

created man and woman to be joined together as one flesh, and the conclusion follows: ὃ οὖν ὁ θεὸς συνέζευξεν ἄνθρωπος μὴ χωριζέτω. This is the core of the tradition; Mark explains it, using an inquiry by the disciples (v. 10) as his means of introducing the piece of sacred law: If you divorce your wife and marry another you are committing adultery. Therefore, Don't do it. This was a hard command, hard not only by reason of the desires of flesh and blood but also because it contradicted Moses. Matthew accordingly modifies the teaching by assimilating it to the terms of current Jewish discussion. Moses permitted divorce; yet it disrupts families and clearly ought to be avoided if possible. We must ask therefore, In what circumstances is divorce permissible?[3] Matthew (19.9) answers, Divorce is wrong because it leads to adultery and must be avoided except where the marriage has already been broken by sexual unfaithfulness (μὴ ἐπὶ πορνείᾳ). Mark has a different addition (probably not known to Matthew and Luke). What applies to men applies also to women: If she who has divorced her husband marries another, she commits adultery. In Jewish law, women were not able to divorce their husbands; Mk 10.12 is a practical inference providing legislation for the Hellenistic world in which they had this right. As for men, remarriage meant adultery and was therefore forbidden. It was however easier to be specific over religious than over ethical requirements; easier for example to declare that no food entering the stomach could defile the eater than to be specific about those things that come out from within and do defile. Some indeed are clear enough – fornication, theft, murder, adultery, deceit, lasciviousness – but others are not. In this context however the words of Mk 7.19, καθαρίζων πάντα τὰ βρώματα, point back to the personal authority of Jesus. What Moses declares unclean he declares clean. The ethics, the ethically expressed theological assertion, is based on the assertion of the authority of Christ, in whom God in his kingdom draws near in judgement and mercy.

The historical Paul was prepared to handle specific ethical problems when they were presented to him, whether by those who

---

[3] Cf. the well known disagreement between Hillel and Shammai (Gittin 9.10).

sought instruction in what they should do or by those who were able to report problems that had arisen in the churches. Thus 1 Cor. 7 contains treatment of the problems of marriage and divorce analogous (though not identical) with that in Mk 10. But it is more characteristic of Paul that he too deals (though in a way different from that of the synoptic tradition) with the Christological roots of ethics. The essence of the matter is that one died for all in order that those who are alive should live no longer for themselves but for him who on their behalf died and was raised (2 Cor. 5.15). His lists of vices (works of the flesh, Gal. 5.19–21) and of virtues (fruit of the Spirit, Gal. 5.22–23) are similar to those of Mk 7. We are given no examples of the ways in which love, joy, peace, and the rest are to be manifested. As soon as we step into the Deutero-Pauline letters a change is apparent. Colossians and Ephesians both contain sets of household rules: for husbands, wives, children, parents, slaves, and masters. Neither of these epistles is unaware of the spiritual depth and ethical spontaneity of life lived in Christ, but in these passages (Col. 3.18 – 4.1; Eph. 5.22 – 6.9) Christians are provided with a code; and there is other ethical material of the same kind.

The tendency to codify Christian behaviour appears much more strongly in the Pastorals. According to M. Dibelius[4] the Pastorals are characterized by 'Bürgerlichkeit', a word that defies translation: it describes the character and attitude of the good, honest, decent, ordinary citizen. Household rules reappear, though the family is now the church rather than the natural family: thus 1 Tim. 5.1 (how to treat an older man, younger men, older women, younger women) and Titus 2.2–6 (rules for old men; rules for older women, who must instruct younger ones; rules for younger men). Most important in this respect are the social and moral qualifications required in church officers – bishops (or elders) and deacons. These, as has long been recognized, present many parallels with the qualifications that were looked for in candidates for civil office; see for example Dibelius pp. 42–8. There is certainly nothing to complain of here. It was – and is – desirable that Christian ministers

---

[4] *Die Pastoralbriefe* (HNT 13; Tübingen, 1955), p. 7.

should be as upright and as intelligent as members of the civil service. The lists of qualifications are both more explicit and less inspiring than 'We preach not ourselves but Christ Jesus as lord, and ourselves as your slaves for Jesus' sake' (2 Cor. 4.5). The minister must be 'free from reproach, faithful to his one wife,[5] sober, sensible, dignified, hospitable, good at teaching, not given to wine or violence, but gentle, peaceable, no lover of money, presiding well over his own household, having children who are kept in order and fully respectful, . . . not a new convert . . . he must have a good reputation with those outside the church'. These are the requirements of an ἐπίσκοπος in 1 Tim. 3.2–7; διάκονοι must show similar virtues (3.8–12). They are admirable qualities, whether in Christian ministers or in city councillors. Paul would (perhaps unwisely – people sometimes let him down) have taken them for granted. In addition to these passages the Pastorals are full of good, sensible advice, calculated to produce Christians who will win the respect of all honourable and intelligent men. There is no space here to give it in detail.

In Acts there is little explicit ethical teaching. It is true that hearers of the apostolic message are urged to repent (Acts 2.38; *et al.*), but apart from the implication that those responsible should repent of killing Jesus we are not told of what sins they should repent. Nor are we told with what virtues they should replace their vices. It is clear enough that some people are regarded as 'good' and others are not. Barnabas does well in selling his property for the benefit of others (4.36–37); Ananias and Sapphira are not good when they try to deceive the Holy Spirit (5.1–11). It is clearly implied that to flog and imprison Paul and Silas was a bad thing[6] and that to wash their wounds and feed them was good (16.19–34). This however is scarcely advanced casuistry, though, as ethics, it may perhaps be regarded as being on the same level as the simple but adequate theology of Acts. Christians who look to God for forgiveness should perform works worthy of

---

[5] There are other interpretations of this obscure phrase.

[6] But why? because they were innocent? because they had no judicial hearing? because they were Roman citizens?

repentance (26.20). And it is assumed that we all know well enough what that means.

These observations are superficial, but they may lead to a further step in the discussion. In our glance at the synoptic gospels it was possible to use Bultmann's perhaps exaggerated understanding of the tradition. Here we may make a similar critical use of E. Haenchen's comment on Acts 23.1 (ἐγὼ πάσῃ συνειδήσει ἀγαθῇ πεπολίτευμαι τῷ θεῷ ἄχρι ταύτης τῆς ἡμέρας). He writes,[7] 'Diese Theologie des "guten Gewissens" wird in der nachapostolischen Literatur beliebt', and in a footnote refers to 1 Tim. 1.5, 19; 3.9; 2 Tim. 1.3; 1 Pet. 3.16, 21; Heb. 9.14; 13.18. Earlier in his note he has referred to the close parallel in Acts 24.16 (ἀσκῶ ἀπρόσκοπον συνείδησιν ἔχειν). It is not clear what Haenchen means by 'this theology of the "good conscience"', or indeed whether *theology* is an appropriate word. In the two passages quoted Paul is simply asserting that he has at all times behaved as a good Jew, though his understanding of what being a good Jew meant had suffered a violent change when he discovered that God had raised Jesus from death. This is an important factor in Paul's view (or what Luke believed Paul's view to have been) of the relation between Christianity and Judaism, but neither Luke nor Paul asserts that Paul's relation with God depends on his having maintained a good conscience (though Acts contains no such vigorous disclaimer as 1 Cor. 4.4). The word συνείδησις occurs nowhere else in Acts; it does occur six times in the Pastorals (1 Tim. 1.5, 19; 3.9; 4.2; 2 Tim. 1.3; Titus 1.15), but it occurs also fourteen times in Romans and 1 and 2 Corinthians, so that as a word it cannot be regarded as post-Pauline. It is true that the conscience does in the Pastorals play a somewhat different part from that which it has in the genuine letters; this provides at least a partial justification (as Acts does not) for Haenchen's view of its popularity and distinctiveness. Love, faith, and a good conscience commend us to God; beware lest your conscience become seared or defiled. Too much should not be made of this. The 'good conscience' may have the effect of devaluing love and faith, but

---

[7] *Die Apostelgeschichte* (KEK III; Göttingen, 1977), p. 609.

the reverse process also is in operation. 'Das gute Gewissen ist somit . . . mehr als das schlichte reine Herz der alttestamentlichen Frommen . . . So sind an diesem Punkte die Pastoralbriefe nicht nur das Produkt christlicher Bürgerlichkeit, sondern ebenso das bewusste Echo des paulinischen Rechtfertigungsbotschaft, aus der heraus sie gewachsen sind.'[8] What we may take out of the two verses in Acts and use as the starting-point for future inquiry is not so much the use of τυνείδησις as of the verbs that accompany it, πολιτεύεσθαι and ἀσκεῖν. These in turn suggest a number of others:[9] ἀγών (+ ἀγωνίζεσθαι); ἀθλεῖν; γυμνάζειν (+ γυμνασία); ἐγκράτεια (+ ἐγκρατεύεσθαι, ἐγκρατής); προκοπή (+ προκόπτειν).

Most of these words have their primary reference to the games, to the life and effort of the athlete; in the New Testament they are of course used metaphorically, or in similes. Paul himself had done this; for example: at 1 Cor. 9.25–27, and probably at Phil. 1.27, 30. The Deutero-Pauline use however is different. In 1 Corinthians and Philippians the thought concentrates upon the fierce and disciplined contest itself. You must run hard, fight hard; behind the exhortation lies Paul's awareness of a contest into which he has to enter with himself; ὑπωπιάζω μου τὸ σῶμα. In Philippians (cf. Colossians) the ἀγών is rather with external circumstances. Paul's own circumstances are made clear in the epistle itself. He is in prison (1.13, 17) and facing the possibility of death (1.21–23); and he has reason to think that his readers are in a comparable situation; they are sharing the same ἀγών (1.30) and in it he urges them to join unitedly (συναθλοῦντες) in the contest.[10] This basic sense is of course inseparable from the language used, but the general image of athletics is wide, and, on the whole, the later writers choose to emphasize another aspect of it.

In the two Acts passages referred to above the verbs are πολιτεύεσθαι and ἀσκεῖν. The former may not be significant. Though it referred originally to the conduct of the citizen in relation

[8] C. Maurer, *TWNT* 7.917 – putting the matter perhaps a little too strongly.
[9] More could be added; those mentioned here suffice for a brief sketch.
[10] Cf. also Col. 1.29; 2.1; 4.12, where Pauline authorship cannot be reckoned certain.

to his πόλις it came to mean no more than *to conduct oneself*. Here it need not mean more than this. It does however seem to have been used with special reference to behaviour in relation to the Jewish πολιτεία, and this seems to be the sense that Luke is putting into Paul's mouth. From the beginning up to the present day he has conducted himself conscientiously in strict accordance with the Jewish way of life, which he follows as understood by Pharisees (23.6). This has nothing to do with a 'theology of the good conscience', or with the point that will emerge as ve proceed.

ἀσκεῖν, which occurs nowhere else in the New Testament, is different. It may mean *to work curiously, to form by art, to dress out, to trick out*, but its most characteristic meaning is *to practise, exercise, train*, 'properly of athletic exercise'.[11] From this the metaphorical use developed, and it was used of training, exercise, in truth, righteousness, virtue. 'Diese Bedeutung von ἀσκεῖν ist schon dem klassischen und hellenistischen Griechisch geläufig.'[12] 'I see that as those who do not train their bodies (τοὺς μὴ τὰ σώματα ἀσκοῦντας) are not able to do the things proper to the body, so those who do not train the soul (τοὺς μὴ τὴν ψυχὴν ἀσκοῦντας) are not able to do the things of the soul.'[13] This use of ἀσκεῖν (and of ἄσκησις) continued into the post-classical age; thus for example in the Cynic Epistles,[14] *Epistle* 19, to Patrocles (68.26), . . . ἐπὶ τῷ τὴν ἀρετὴν ἀσκῆσαι ἀνδρεῖον, . . . courage in the practice of virtue. Acts 24.16 goes further than 23.1. Paul does not simply assert that his conscience is clear; he trains his conscience in order to keep it clear, a particularized version of Xenophons training of the soul.

The imagery of other words is even more explicit. Thus in 1 Tim. 4.7, 8 there occurs the pair γυμνάζειν, γυμνασία. Their

[11] Liddell and Scott, p. 257. See also F. Pfister, Ἄσκησις, in *Festgabe für Adolf Deissmann* (Tübingen, 1927), pp. 76–81; H. Dressler, *The Usage of ἀσκέω and its Cognates in Greek Documents to 100 A.D.* (Washington, 1947).

[12] H. Windisch, in *TWNT* 1.492.

[13] Xenophon, *Memorabilia* 1.2.19; see the whole paragraph, 1.2.19–28.

[14] It is interesting that neither the New Testament nor any of the other works covered in Bauer-Aland's *Wörterbuch* makes any use of ἀλείπτης, the trainer, or coach.

original sense requires no illustration. There is a neat parallel to 'Paul's' use with the reflexive pronoun in Epictetus 2.18.27, where Epictetus is emphasizing the importance of attention to what is true over against mere appearance. 'This is the athlete concerned for truths (ὁ ταῖς ἀληθείαις ἀσκητής – see ἀσκεῖν above), he who exercises himself (ὁ . . . γυμνάζων ἑαυτόν) against such appearances.' Over against σωματικὴ γυμνασία, which has its uses, 1 Timothy sets piety, εὐσέβεια, and the practice of piety involves serious training. Verse 8 is to be connected with v. 10, to which v. 9 provides an emphatic pointer – You know this is true, and you must accept it. To this end we labour and strive (κοπιῶμεν καὶ ἀγωνιζόμεθα – the latter another word derived from athletics); the attainment of piety is not easy, and the training for it includes hope and faith.

The Pastorals use another related word, ἀθλεῖν (2 Tim. 2.5). The literal meaning of the verb is *to take part in the games, to contend for a prize*. No athlete can win unless he contends νομίμως. Again there is a parallel in Epictetus, 3.10.8: God speaks: δός μοι ἀπόδειξιν, εἰ νομίμως ἤθλησας. The words that follow bring out the meaning of νομίμως: εἰ ἔφαγες ὅσα δεῖ, εἰ ἐγυμνάσθης, εἰ τοῦ ἀλείπτου ἤκουσας. That is, to contend *lawfully* is to observe the rules of training. It is implied that there are rules of training for the Christian athlete, and he will not receive the promised crown if he does not observe them. This is interesting and important in itself, in that it indicates an attitude to and understanding of Christian life. It is important too in that it points out the correct interpretation of 1 Tim. 1.8: the law is good ἐάν τις αὐτῷ νομίμως χρῆται. That is (one may suggest), the law is good if one uses it as a means of training in the good life, the life of piety. The law is no threat to a good man who thus uses it for instruction in the way of obedience; it is a threat only to those who disregard it, who are ἄνομοι, and express their lawlessness in the various ways listed in vv. 9, 10, which (as we say) 'break training'. It is in agreement with this that a vital constituent in training for the Christian life is ἐγκράτεια (Acts 24.25), and that the *episcopus* must be ἐγκρατής (Titus 1.8). Self-control, self-discipline, is an essential quality of the Christian athlete, whose aim must be to fight the καλὸν ἀγῶνα (1 Tim. 6.12; 2 Tim. 4.8; cf. 1 Tim. 1.18). The use of ἀγών and ἀγωνίζεσθαι points, in the Pauline fashion, rather to the contest itself than to the training undergone in preparation for it.

This sketch of some of the background material is enough to show that the Deutero-Pauline works, especially Acts and the Pastorals, are related to earlier and contemporary moral philosophers in their concept of training for the good life. They have of course a somewhat different (not entirely different) concept of what the good life is, but they agree that it is not achieved automatically or without effort. As the athlete exercises self-control and obeys the rules laid down by his trainer (ἀλείπτης), so the Christian must obey the laws that God has given and be prepared to deny himself and stand firm in faith in order to make sure of receiving the crown that God has promised to all who have set their hearts on Christ's appearing (2 Tim. 4.8). To this must be be added a further observation.

This language and this framework of thought had already been taken up in Judaism. To complete the quotation from Windisch (*TWNT* 1,492) given above (p. 186), 'Diese Bedeutung von ἀσκεῖν ist schon dem klassischen und hellenistischen Griechisch geläufig, ebenso dem jüdischen Hellenismus.' Windisch rightly adds, 'Begriff und Sache hat dann Philo in die theologische Ethik eingeführt' (1.493). The evidence is plentiful, notably in Philo's description of Jacob as ὁ ἀσκητής. Among the patriarchs Abraham represents μάθησις, Isaac φύσις, Jacob ἄσκησις. He is the one who learns by practice, who trains himself in virtue; ἀσκητής, the man in training, is suggested by ἀθλητής, the man who practises athletics, and Jacob is shown to be such a man by the story of Gen. 32.24–32, Jacob's wrestling match with the mysterious figure at the brook Jabbok. The outcome of the process of ἄσκησις is Jacob's change of name; he becomes Israel, which Philo interprets as ὁρῶν θεόν, the one who sees God. The end of moral and spiritual training is the vision of God. Thus for example *Mig.* 200, 201: παλαίοντος γὰρ καὶ κονιομένου καὶ πτερνίζοντος Ἰακώβ ἐστιν ὄνομα . . . ὅταν δὲ τὸν θεὸν ὁρᾶν ἱκανὸς εἶναι δόξας Ἰσραὴλ μετονομασθῇ . . . This spiritual advance is προκοπή, progress. At *Ebr.* 82 Jacob is introduced as ὁ ἀσκητής; his is a name for learning and progress (μαθήσεως καὶ προκοπῆς); but Israel is a name for perfection (τελειότητος); ὅρασιν γὰρ θεοῦ μηνύει τοὔνομα. Other words that have been considered can be found in Philo. *Spec. Leg.* 2.183 will cover at once two words. The priests' privileges may be γέρας ἀγώνων, οὓς ὑπὲρ εὐσεβείας ἀθλοῦσιν, a reward for the contests they take part in for the sake of piety. Philo comes near to a more literal understanding of training when he says that the Law is concerned περὶ τοῦ γυμνάσαι καὶ συγκροτῆσαι ψυχὴν πρὸς ἀνδρείαν (*Virtut.* 18). In *Mos.* 1.48 he combines the theoretical and the practical (θεωρητικὸν καὶ πρακτικόν) in a sentence full of relevant words: τοὺς ἀρετῆς ἄθλους Μωυσῆς διήθλει τὸν ἀλείπτην ἔχων ἐν ἑαυτῷ λογισμὸν ἀστεῖον, ὑφ' οὗ γυμναζόμενος πρὸς τοὺς ἀρίστους βίους. Moral traininq, ἄσκησις, requires self-discipline. Those who obtain true wealth, the wealth that is the result of controlled desire, are ὀλιγοδεῖαν καὶ ἐγκράτειαν ἀσκήσαντες (*Praem. et Poen.* 100).

So far I have quoted only Philo; given the extent of his works within the field of Hellenistic Judaism this was inevitable. Other examples of the use of the words that have been considered here are not easy to find, no doubt in part because athletics was a suspiciously Greek and un-Jewish pastime. There are however a number of examples in the Epistle of Aristeas of the use of ἀσκεῖν. Thus at §168, the Law commands us to do evil to no one, ἀλλ' ἵνα δι' ὅλου τοῦ ζῆν καὶ ἐν ταῖς πράξεσιν ἀσκῶμεν δικαιοσύνην πρὸς πάντας ἀνθρώπους. Cf. §225: ἠσκηκὼς πρὸς πάντας ἀνθρώπους εὔνοιαν καὶ κατεργασάμενος φιλίας; §255: . . . τὴν εὐσέβειαν ἀσκοῦντι; §285: . . . πᾶσαν ἠσκηκὼς καταστολήν. Josephus uses γυμνάζειν in the literal sense of bodily training, but gives to ἀσκεῖν a moral sense, for example at *Antiquities* 3.309, where τοῖς ἀρετὴν ἠσκηκόσιν are soldiers trained not only in military skills but in courage and determination; 4.294 is similar, though the construction is different. It is worth while to note also the words of Trypho, in Justin, *Dialogue* 8.3. It would be better, he says, for Justin to adhere to Plato or to some other philosophical discipline, ἀσκοῦντα

189

καρτερίαν καὶ ἐγκράτειαν καὶ σωφροσύνην, ἢ λόγοις ἐξαπατηθῆναι ψευδέσι . . .

The upshot of this study is that the Deutero-Pauline works in the New Testament (and these could have been extended to include 1 and 2 Peter and Hebrews) differ from the genuine Pauline letters in their concern for disciplined training in the ethical and spiritual life, in which progress, προκοπή, is made in ἀρετή and εὐσέβεια. This is not to say that Paul would have actively disapproved of such ἄσκησις. Faith includes obedience, and he was aware of the fact that obedience is not easy. He was probably aware also of the fact that the professional athlete (in moral matters) is in danger of generating a good opinion of his achievements which may be more perilous than the occasional cropper of the enthusiastic but unthinking amateur. The course however was set for the following generation, and the Apostolic Fathers take up the language of disciplined progress. A few examples must suffice.

1 Clement, 2 Clement, and Barnabas all use ἀγωνίζεσθαι in an exhortation. 1 Clem. 35.4 shows that what is in mind is a continuing effort: ἀγωνισώμεθα εὑρεθῆναι ἐν τῷ ἀριθμῷ τῶν ὑπομενόντων αὐτόν. This is the way to share in the promised gifts. 2 Clem. 7.1–5 sketches the whole process: ἀγωνισώμεθα . . . ὁ ἀγών . . . οὐ πάντες στεφανοῦνται εἰ μὴ οἱ . . . καλῶς ἀγωνισάμενοι. In Barn. 4.11 the struggle is to keep the commandments: φυλάσσειν ἀγωνιζώμεθα τὰς ἐντολὰς αὐτοῦ. ἄσκειν is used with a number of objects: δικαιοσύνην (Hermas, *Mandate* 8.10); πᾶσαν ὑπομονήν (Polycarp 9.1); ἀκακίαν (Papias, fragment 8). Surprisingly, the *Epistle to Diognetus* uses ἀσκεῖν in a bad sense: Christians do not practise a distinctive manner of life (βίον παράσημον, 5.2); γνῶσις is an appropriate way to pursue (12.5). In the *Martyrdom of Polycarp* 18.2 ἄσκησις is especially training for martyrdom. The 'birthday' of the martyr is observed εἴς τε τὴν τῶν προηθληκότων μνήμην καὶ τῶν μελλόντων ἄσκησίν τε καὶ ἑτοιμασίαν. ἀθλητής and ἀθλεῖν are used in 1 Clem. 5.1f. of the martyrs Peter and Paul. This application of the language of athletics reaches its climax when it is applied to Christ himself: ὁ εἰς πολλοὺς ἀγῶνας ὑπὲρ ἡμῶν

ἀγωνιζόμενος καὶ νικᾶν ποιῶν ἡμᾶς ἐν πᾶσι. ὁ ἀληθὴς ἀθλητὴς ἡμῶν καὶ ἀήττητος (*Acts of Thomas* 39).

These observations about the contrast between the ethical teaching of the historical Paul, with his 'sin shall no more have dominion over you' and his 'become what you are', and Deutero-Paul, whose converts are expected to enter into training for the ethical and spiritual life cannot of themselves prove but fit well into an historical situation which on other grounds seems probable. The author of Acts seems to have regarded Paul as a successor to, a replacement of, the Hellenist Jew Stephen; the Areopagus speech which he puts into Paul's mouth is best explained (as also is Stephen's speech in Acts 7) as a Hellenistic Jewish sermon, turned into a Christian Jewish sermon by the addition of a somewhat obscure reference to Jesus. If this is true, it suggests that in the generation after Paul's death there was a tendency to understand him as a member of the Hellenistic Jewish Christian group. This he was not; he was not a Hellenist but a Hebrew, as he himself asserts. The mistake was probably an honest one. The Hellenistic Jews already before they became Christians exercised a mission to the Gentiles; as Christians they became more ardent missionaries. Paul was notoriously the apostle of the Gentiles. It was an almost inevitable, though in part it was a mistaken, conclusion that he had himself been one of the Hellenistic Jewish Christians. If so, he will have shared their approach to the Gentiles; hence the Areopagus speech. If so, he will not have left his churches to themselves to sort themselves out and settle their problems under the guidance of the Spirit; he must have set out a clear-cut organization based on the ministry of presbyter-bishops and deacons. If so, he will not have left his young churches to the guidance of the Spirit under such basic commands as 'Love your neighbours'; he will have instituted training programmes in ethics and spirituality. The historical Paul was not a Hellenistic Jew,[15] and had not absorbed Stoicism on the way to Christian faith.

---

[15] He was, of course, a Hellenistic Jew in the sense that he was a Jew born in the Hellenistic city of Tarsus (according to Acts 22.3); I refer here to his attitude.

It is not strictly relevant to this paper, but I cannot forbear to add that this observation helps me with a problem. M. D. Goulder's *Tale of Two Missions* (London, 1994), though popular in style is a very serious restatement of something like the position of F. C. Baur. It is to be taken seriously, and welcomed. Most of it I believe to be true, but I have, found difficult the assertion that in the conflict between 'Paulines' and 'Petrines' it was Paul who won. This puzzles me; it seems to me that Paul lost. If however we may take the 'Paul who won' to be not the historical Paul but the unhistorical, or, more accurately the not quite historical Paul, the difficulty disappears, or at least is diminished. But this is a matter that I have discussed and hope to discuss further in other places.

9

The Christology of Hebrews

A study of the Christology of Hebrews may be given direction and precision by a hypothesis concerning the background and origin of the epistle. If the resultant Christology is convincing the hypothesis may at the same time be to some extent confirmed.

Long ago W. Manson[1] argued that there was a close relation both historical and theological, between Hebrews and Stephen, for whom Manson regarded the material in Acts 6 and 7 as trustworthy historical evidence. He made much of a community of eschatological belief, and saw Stephen and his fellow Christian Diaspora Jews as initiating a Gentile mission responsible, among other things, for the spread of Christianity not only to Antioch (Acts 11.19–26) but also to Alexandria and to Rome. At the time when Hebrews was written the Roman church (if in those early stages the word ἐκκλησία is appropriate for it) was still a section of the synagogue and over-emphasized the Jewish element in Christianity. It needed to be made aware of the wider horizons and deeper implications of the new faith.[2] Hebrews was addressed to them[3] with this aim. In achieving this the author showed something of the influence of Alexandrian Hellenism.

---

[1] W. Manson, *The Epistle to the Hebrews* (London, 1951).

[2] One wonders what they may have made of Romans.

[3] The destination of Hebrews is a notable puzzle. Rome, or somewhere in Italy, may well be correct; other possibilities mentioned by Kümmel (*Einleitung*) are Corinth, Ephesus, the Lycus Valley, Antioch, Cyprus, Jerusalem or elsewhere in Palestine.

Not a little of this may be affirmed, even if the evidence of Acts is rated somewhat less highly. Luke seems in fact to distinguish less clearly than is desirable between Paul and non-Pauline missions to the Gentile world. He knows, or wishes to tell, nothing of the unhappy event at Antioch (Gal. 2.11–21), and represents the dispute over circumcision as quickly settled. Paul is represented as an agent of the church of Antioch; so perhaps at first he was, but in the period of the latter part of Acts he was acting as an apostle 'not from men or through man'. There was a non-Pauline mission (there may have been more than one), and the Seven of Acts (6; 7; 21.8) and the church at Antioch played parts in it. This mission, though ready to address Gentiles, was less critical of the Law than Paul (or perhaps we should say, less critical than the critical element in Paul's thought, less affirmative than the affirmative element) and was probably responsible for the Decree of Acts 15.29.[4] Pioneer mission work in Alexandria and Rome is an interesting possibility to keep in mind, but it is unlikely to contribute much to our present task. More relevant is the hypothesis that the speeches of Acts 7 (attributed to Stephen) and of Acts 17 (attributed to Paul) originated with this group of Christians.[5]

The most striking feature of both speeches is their extremely slight Christian content. The greater part of Stephen's speech is devoted to a review of Old Testament history, beginning with Abraham and the patriarchs, continuing with Moses and the Exodus, and going as far as Solomon, his Temple, and some prophetic comments on the Temple. Notwithstanding repeated emphasis on the power of God to overcome suffering and apparent defeat, and to bring positive good out of them, for example in the story of Joseph (Acts 7.9–16), a theme which it would have been easy to apply to the crucifixion and resurrection of Jesus, and the

---

[4] See *Jesus Christus als die Mitte der Schrift* (*FS* Hofius), ed. C. Landmesser, H.-J. Eckstein, H. Lichtenberger (Berlin and New York, 1997), p. 338; *Context* (Essays in Honour of P. J. Borgen), ed. P. W. Børkman and R. E. Kristiansen (Trondheim, 1987), pp. 19–33; in the present volume, pp. 37–54.

[5] See my *Commentary on the Acts of the Apostles* (ICC), I (Edinburgh, 1994), pp. 334–40; II (1998), pp. civ, 825f.

application to Moses of terms (e.g. *ruler* and *redeemer*, 7.25) which, on the lips of a Christian preacher, might have seemed more appropriately applied to Jesus, no attempt is made to relate the Old Testament material directly to the Christian story. The Law was 'living oracles' (7.38); there is no suggestion of any sense in which a Christian might be 'dead to the Law' (e.g. Gal. 2.19). The Temple, however, was a mistake; God was more at home in a moving tent; he had no wish for a house. The lesson of Jeremiah 7 had been learnt; God sought obedience to his word rather than cultus. It is only in the last few lines of the speech that Jesus is alluded to (he is not named), and that for no positive value that his life and teaching might have contained but as the final example of the failure of God's people to hear and obey his word. If we omit the seven words of 7.52b (οὗ νῦν ὑμεῖς προδόται καὶ φονεῖς ἐγένεσθε) the speech could have been delivered by a Jew in any Diaspora synagogue. Some might have disapproved the disparagement of the Temple (though it is based on Scripture); all would have approved the praises of Moses and the Law; some might have been moved to penitence for their neglect of God's word in Torah and resolved to be more faithful members of God's people. It is an attractive hypothesis that this was in fact the origin of the speech. If the original speaker became a Christian there was no reason why it should not be preached in a Christian context; it needed only a hint at the end to give it a new point.

In many respects the Areopagus speech is different. There is no allusion to the history of Israel. There is however a striking resemblance in the slight Christian touch with which the speech ends. That God intends to judge the whole of mankind is not a uniquely Christian belief; it is not specifically Jewish. There are Greek parallels. Again we have what could have originated as a lightly Christianized version of a synagogue sermon. The body of the sermon is indeed different from that of Acts 7, but it is equally suitable for synagogue use. The speaker treads the border-line between Old Testament prophecy and Greek religious philosophy, showing how close they are to each other. Each is opposed to idolatry, knowing that God is not to be represented by human art working on wood or stone. Each knows that God is close to his human creatures; in him we live and move and have our being. He is not in need of our gifts; on the contrary, he not only gives us all that we need but controls history, and appoints to the various races periods of authority and areas for residence. The speaker declares that he is about to inform the Areopagites of what they do not know as they worship an unknown God, but most of what he says would be familiar enough in the Stoa Poikile or the Garden of Epicurus, or both. To rehearse it however might persuade a tolerant Greek of the virtue of Judaism and encourage a doubting and hellenizing Jew to remain loyal to the faith of his fathers.

The Diaspora Jews who began their preaching in these ways became, when converted to Christianity, in some respects the most influential group of early Christians.[6] Luke, who was a good enough historian to recognize the importance of Paul, seems nevertheless to have confused the two Gentile missions, Paul's and that of the Seven. He probably thought of Paul as deeply influenced by Stephen and as continuing his work (Acts 7.58; 8.1–3; 22.20). The Areopagus speech was theirs, not his (he had a different approach, without 'wisdom', concentrating on the cross: 1 Cor. 2.1–5), the Decree of Acts 15.29 was theirs, not his (and not James's). Authors of the Decree, they controlled and directed the great Gentile expansion of the church in the 70s, 80s, and 90s. They lacked the theological sharpness and profundity of Paul, this may to some extent have accounted for their success. But there were gaps in their statement of the Christian case. It is easy to name two. One was the Temple. There was in the Diaspora no single view of the Temple.[7] Some, because of its inaccessibility, valued it the more, but there must have been some who reflected, We have to practise Judaism, and do practise, Judaism, without the Temple; therefore the Temple is not indispensable. The destruction of the Temple in A.D. 70 must have made this thought bite more deeply and more widely. Yet, though there are prophetic passages critical of the

---

[6] See *Mighty Minorities?* (*FS* J. Jervell), ed. D. Hellholm, R. Moxnes and T. K. Seim (Oslo, etc. 1995), pp. 8f. Reprinted here as Chapter 10.

[7] See *Templum Amicitiae* (*FS* E. Bammel), JSNTSS 48, ed. W. Horbury (Sheffield, 1991), pp. 357–62.

Temple, the Temple was, until, and, in a different sense, after its destruction, a major part of the Israelite inheritance. Prophetic books were full of the hope of its reconstruction, and a considerable part of the Law itself was given up to instructions for the conduct of the Temple's sacrificial system. The Mishnah tractate Middoth recalls (perhaps here and there invents) countless details of Temple procedures and dimensions which there was little point in memorizing apart from the hope that they might some day be put again to practical use. The Temple and the sacrifices (many would think) cannot have counted for nothing in God's call and guidance of his people; and now (so at least a few would think) that we are Christians we must believe that the true meaning of the Temple has been fulfilled in Christ – an article of faith which those to whom the Temple was something of an embarrassment[8] might welcome with relief.

This observation points immediately to a second gap in the Christian Diaspora group's theological system. It was (if we may judge by Acts 7 and 17) sadly deficient in Christology. Jesus had marked the unhappy climax in the story of Israel's disobedience, its readiness to neglect the word of God in the interests of its religious institutions, and the moment when God chose to announce the final judgement of mankind and to indicate the ground and principle of judgement by appointing the last and greatest prophet as Judge, demonstrating his status by raising him from death. This was true as far as it went; but it did not go very far, and the author of Hebrews was on hand to supply what was lacking. I do not mean by this that the author surveyed the field of current theology, noted its gaps, and saw the opportunity to present a prize-winning dissertation. Theology, like nature, abhors a vacuum, and there was a vacuum waiting to be filled.

The two outstanding characteristic themes of Hebrew are the work of atonement in the heavenly Temple, and Christ as its priestly officiant. Consideration of these themes prompts a further, more speculative, observation. If the Areopagus speech gives a fair and representative insight into Hellenistic Jewish use of Greek

[8] Cf. *Templum Amicitiae* (n. 7), pp. 356f.

philosophy, this was on the whole limited to Stoicism and Epicureanism.[9] This is a large assumption, and we must not build too heavy a structure upon it, but it may at least permit the suggestion that these two practical lines of philosophy were being practised to the neglect of more speculative Platonism, which thus remained as a field waiting to be explored. It may be no accident that the author of Hebrews makes use of a popular Platonism (not unrelated to apocalyptic[10] as Stoicism and Epicureanism were not unrelated to prophecy) as his means of developing at the same time an interpretation of the Temple and its practices and an advanced Christology.

So much by way of introduction. It remains to examine the data of the epistle itself, considering its Christological statements in the light of its quasi-platonic interpretation of the Temple and its cultus. Within the compass of this paper it will be possible to examine, and that briefly, only some of the most important passages.

It is consistent with these observations that the epistle begins with a very emphatic assertion of a high Christology, which both fulfils and antiquates the Old Testament. God had indeed spoken in the past to the fathers of the Jewish people, but he had done so πολυμερῶς and πολυτρόπως. His message had been delivered through a number of prophets, piecemeal and with no consistent formulation. This partial communication of truth belongs to the past, from which the present is distinguished as the ἔσχατον τῶν ἡμερῶν, a LXX expression[11] which often means little more than *finally*, *now at last*, but here can hardly mean less than a claim that the author is writing in the closing period of human history, the end of these days, this period, in which we live. There can therefore be no further revelation beyond that which is now given ἐν υἱῷ, in one who in his essential nature is a son, and thus a member of the divine family. To affirm this at the outset will not prevent the

---

[9] See *New Testament Christianity for Africa and the World* (*FS* H. A. E. Sawyerr), ed. M. E. Glasswell and E. Fasholé-Luke (London, 1974), pp. 72–7.

[10] See *The Background of the New Testament and its Eschatology* (*FS* C. H. Dodd), ed. W. D. Davies and D. Daube (Cambridge, 1956), pp. 363–93.

[11] It renders באחרית הימים.

author from recognizing the true humanity of the incarnate son, but it makes clear what he is in himself. The Father–Son relationship will be taken up in v. 5. Its roots are in belief about the King (including the supreme final King) of Israel; it is messianic terminology, though as the next lines show it goes far beyond conventional messianic belief. It appears too (though the word is not used here)[12] that the Son is also the Word. The prologue of Hebrews is not without resemblance to the Prologue of John.

The status of the new agent of revelation is emphasized in a sequence of honorific clauses, which lay down an initial framework and standard for the Christology of Hebrews. The surprising order (final inheritance coming before creation) is probably determined by the association of creation with the allusions and images to come in v. 3, though eschatology will return in v. 4. The result is a chiastic structure. At the beginning, when the Son was the agent of creation, God had already planned that he should in the end be the Lord of creation. He would be the first and the last (cf. Rev. 1.17; 2.8; 22.13). The spanning of creation and consummation is characteristic of the more advanced Christological passages in the New Testament, e.g. John 1.1–18; Phil. 2.6–11; Col. 1.15–20.

The Son is thus the Word throughout history, God's self-communication from the beginning to the end of time. To describe his being and its significance the author picks up another concept, but, surprisingly, does not use its key word. It is hard to doubt that the word ἀπαύγασμα points to the figure of Wisdom; see especially Wisdom 7.25 (ἀπαύγασμα γάρ ἐστιν φωτὸς ἀιδίου). Wisdom (σοφία) is God's agent, in creation (Prov. 8.22), and continues to uphold that which is made.

Almost every word in v. 3 is heavy with meaning. It would of course be anachronistic to read into ὑπόστασις the meaning (or meanings) it acquired in the Christological debates of the fourth and fifth centuries, but it points to the underlying being of God, as ἀπαύγασμα and χαρακτήρ point to what is visible in light and shape. The Son is God in his audibility (ὁ θεὸς . . . ἐλάλησεν) and also in his visibility. The two channels of revelation are

[12] See Heb. 4.2, 12.

combined here as they are in John[13] though there is no ground for positing a literary relation between the two works. There is no immediate contiguity between creation and consummation; there must intervene God's way of dealing with the human sin that has perverted creation. Here too the Son–Word–Wisdom is the agent of divine action. He effects purgation of sins: how he did this will receive so much attention later in the epistle that at this point we may be content to pass it by as a simple affirmation. The ascent and heavenly session of the Son (v. 3d) may also be considered later, though we should note the contact here with the important Jewish question: who (if anyone) may share God's throne in heaven?

At this point a new theme, which will fill the rest of the chapter, is introduced. He who is Son, Word, and Wisdom is contrasted with angels; the contrast is developed by means of Old Testament quotations from v. 4 to the end of the chapter. The Son is better (κρείττων) than the angels, as he has inherited (from his Father?) a more excellent (διαφορώτερον) name; he is distinctive as a son, begotten by the Father; the angels are to worship him; they are ministering spirits whereas he shares the throne of God; he laid the foundations of the earth, and when all else changes he will remain unchanged; God invited him to sit at his right hand, with his enemies beneath his feet. In all this there is nothing with which any New Testament writer would be likely to disagree, but one wonders why it was necessary to lay so much weight on the Son's superiority to angels. The thought springs to mind that the author wished to discredit a Christology in which Jesus appeared as an angel appear-ing in the form of man. One can easily imagine the development of such a Christology, no doubt arising out of excellent motives. It might seem to be a suitable way of defining the person of one who was certainly understood to be greater than human beings; he must have been an angel taking the form of man. The difficulty is that there seems to be no evidence for such an angel-christology in the first century or soon afterwards. A few passages

---

[13] The use of λόγος, especially in the Prologue, for audibility; for visibility, 14.9.

in the Shepherd of Hermas[14] might be relevant; the Elchesaites claimed[15] that revelation had been given by an angel of enormous size who was the Son of God; Justin Martyr[16] applies to Christ the title of Isa. 9.5 (LXX), Μεγάλης βουλῆς ἄγγελος, but he can hardly be said to make a Christology out of it, and if he did it would not be properly called an angel-christology but simply one that rested on (supposed) messianic titles in the Old Testament. All this material is in any case too late to provide a background to Hebrews. The heavily underlined contrast in Hebrews 1 must have an internal explanation, and there is no need to look further than Heb. 2.5f. Angels mediated a Law that had to be observed (cf. Acts 7.53), but Christ was the bringer of the Gospel. The fact that the Son of God was so greatly superior to angels serves also to emphasize his voluntary and gracious humility in accepting a position lower than theirs.

Hebrews 2.1–4 then uses the comparison between the Son and angels in an exhortation to give heed to the Christian message, no angelic word, important as that could be, but one spoken by the Lord himself and passed on with the confirmation of signs and portents and spiritual gifts by those who heard him.

This warning leads to a fundamental statement of the theme to which it draws attention. This is expressed, we must observe, not in Platonic but in eschatological terms. What we are speaking about is the world (οἰκουμένη) to come. It is true that it will appear, as we proceed, that this is a term that holds the door open to a measure of Platonic, or quasi-platonic, interpretation, for that which to us is the world to come is the world that already exists in heaven, where it may be seen by those who are willing to be guided by the Christian revelation.[17] We may, therefore, speak about the world to come though we live in the present world, which if it is in any sense a copy of the heavenly world is a defaced copy, awaiting cleansing. The opening verse of the new paragraph (2.5) contains

[14] Notably *Similitude* 9.12.7f.
[15] See Hippolytus, *Philosophumena* 9.13.
[16] *Trypho* 76, 125; Hebrew פלא יועץ. See also *1 Apology* 63; *Trypho* 56, 58, 59.
[17] For the background of this see especially C. Rowland, *The Open Heaven* (London, 1982).

its own problems, though on the whole these are cleared up as we follow the argument. Who, we may ask, is the subject of ὑπέταξεν? For the present it is sufficient to observe that the subject of ὑπέταξας is undoubtedly God; no one else could in the Psalm be addressed as *thou*. And why should the world to come be subjected to anyone? Perhaps it is a position that that world would itself choose to occupy. It has not been subjected to angels; if not to them, to whom? The answer sometimes given, based upon the quotation of Psalm 8 that follows in 2.6–8, is, It is subjected to man, to the human race. This answer is, I think, mistaken. The figure who stands over against angels is, as ch. 1 makes unmistakably clear, not man in general but the Son of God; it is to him that the world to come is made subject. He is here described as Son of man (υἱὸς ἀνθρώπου); modern readers of the Psalms are of course familiar with parallelism as the fundamental form of Hebrew verse and recognize that ἄνθρωπος in v. 6b and υἱὸς ἀνθρώπου in v. 6c are in synonymous parallelism and that both refer to human beings (collectively). But the use of parallelism in Hebrew poetry was first recognized by Robert Lowth (1710–1787), and, whatever the Psalmist may have meant we have no right to suppose that the author of Hebrews took υἱὸς ἀνθρώπου to mean merely *man*. He had a clear pointer in a different direction. Ps. 8.7 (quoted in 2.8) concludes with the affirmation, Thou hast put all things in subjection under his feet. This cannot fail to call to mind the similar affirmation of Ps. 110.1, quoted in Heb. 1.13, where God addresses his Son, who shares his throne, sitting at God's right hand, and promises that his enemies shall be set as a footstool for his feet. It is the same person to whom all things, including his enemies, are put under his feet, and he is the Son of God and the Son of man.[18]

Out of Psalm 8 we learn the story of the Son of God–Son of man. It is in three stages. (1) God made him for a little while[19] lower than the angels – an extraordinary paradox in view of what

---

[18] Psalms 8 and 110 are similarly combined in 1 Cor., 15.25, 27.

[19] It would be possible to translate the words βραχύ τι, a little (lower), but this is less suitable to the context

is said about the angels in ch. 1, where their inferiority to the Son is repeatedly emphasized. To be made lower than the angels is to be made man; the reference is to the incarnation of the Son of God. (2) God crowned him with glory and honour. In view of what follows (v. 9) we may say that his humiliation, suffering, and death are presupposed. Because of his voluntary acceptance of these he is highly exalted. The reference is clearly to the resurrection (to which Hebrews refers explicitly only once) and to the ascension (which of course presupposes the resurrection) of Jesus. (3) As the final stage of his exaltation, when the history of mankind has run its course, all things are put in subjection to him.

These three points, with their interpretation, are set out clearly in vv. 8 and 9. We see Jesus made lower than the angels (for he becomes a man), suffering death, and crowned, in resurrection and ascension, with glory and honour. It is however recognized explicitly that we do not yet see all things set in subjection under him; the story is not complete. The final state of universal sovereignty belongs to the world to come, of which we are speaking (2.5).

The paradoxical element in this story, to which many will have instinctively objected, is that it involves one who might seem to be nothing less than immortal, in suffering and death. The justification for this begins with a plain, and unsupported, affirmation. It became him (ἔπρεπεν αὐτῷ – God) in bringing many sons into glory to perfect their leader into salvation through suffering. For the present this must remain unexplained, except insofar as there is an explanation in the very word *leader* (ἀρχηγός): if he is to lead the way he must start where the human race is. For them the way is bound to lead through suffering, including the suffering of death; if he is to lead them he too must tread that path. Another way of putting this is to say he is brother to the human race (v. 11); that he who is sanctified and they that are sanctified are of the same human origin. So if they are partakers of blood and flesh so must he be; and blood and flesh mean suffering and death. By his voluntary experience of suffering and death however he will overcome the devil, who held the power of death, and thus set mankind free from bondage and fear. His own suffering and death are the means of liberation for those whom he has accepted as brothers. It is at this point that Hebrews' distinctive designation of Jesus as high priest enters the exposition. It is his readiness to be made in all aspects identical with his brothers, his readiness therefore to accept with them the experience of suffering and death, that qualifies him to act as a merciful and faithful high priest (2.17). Because of his unique relation with God (which his relation with humanity does not destroy) he can act in relation to God and can expiate (ἱλάσκεσθαι) the sins of his people. Having been tested by suffering he can help those who are tried; it is not angels but the seed of Abraham[20] whom he helps.

The figure of the high priest, reached at the end of ch. 2, is set on hold for two chapters while two related matters are developed. One is directly Christological. The Son, who has already been shown to be greater than angels, is now seen to occupy a higher position than Moses. Moses was a faithful servant in God's household; Christ, as God's Son; is over the household (3.5). This would seem to be too obvious to be worth saying were it not that priesthood is bound up with covenant and law – theological themes that will occur later; and Moses is the brother of Aaron, first high priest and head of the whole priestly operation. There is a further connection that will appear shortly.

The second matter is only indirectly Christological. It will be recalled that Psalm 8, quoted in Heb. 2.5–8, sets out a timetable for the work of the Son of God–Son of man: he will be made lower than the angels; he will be crowned with glory and honour all things will be set under his feet. The first two stages have already been accomplished; the third has not. This means that the Christians are living in the final eschatological period of history. Part of God's plan has already been completed, part has not. Human beings are thus confronted with the final outworking of God's purpose, and are thereby challenged to accept their place in it. This situation is analogous to that contained in the story of Moses and the exodus, especially as this is set out in Psalm 96 (quoted in Heb. 3.7–11). There remains, as yet unachieved, a rest, a κατάπαυσις, for the

---

[20] However the 'seed of Abraham' may be constituted, cf. Gal. 3.28.

people of God;[21] the old story shows that it is possible, by disobedience and lack of faith, to miss this rest. The new, Christian, story shows that men are still subject to the same decision of faith, and this decision has to be made in relation to the person of Christ.

Chapters 3 and 4 contain other themes that are not unrelated to Christology, but a decisive step is taken at the end of ch. 4 and in ch. 5. The theme of highpriesthood is taken up at 4.14 with a general emphasis on its importance, on the ability of the Son of God as high priest to sympathize with our weaknesses, and the parenthetical and at this point unexplained statement that he 'passed through the heavens'. In the opening verse of ch. 5 the theme begins to be developed. At first there are general propositions about the functions and office of a high priest. His work is done in matters relating to God; he has to make sacrifices for sins; he offers for himself as well as for others. He does not seize the office for himself but must be called and appointed by God. At this point (5.5, 6) the author returns to Psalm 2, which speaks of the divine begetting which constitutes the Son of God (Thou art my Son, this day have I begotten thee), and to Psalm 110, which contains the divine appointment which makes the Son of God high priest (Thou art a priest for ever in the order of Melchizedek). The latter passage provides a fresh point of departure for the treatment of highpriesthood[22] in Hebrews. The first point of departure is Psalm 8, in the representative role of the Son of man. This may not appear in literary guise as a piece of Hebrew parallelism, but it appears in Scripture as a theological factor. It is a familiar observation that in Daniel 7 the Son of man vision is interpreted as a representation of the people of the saints of the Most High; if he receives a kingdom, that means that the people do. If this means that in any sense or at any stage he is identified with the Messiah the same interpretation applies, for the king is the representative of the people; in their

---

[21] On this see O. Hofius, *Katapausis: Die Vorstellung vom endzeitlichen Ruheort im Hebräerbrief* (WUNT 11; Tübingen, 1979).

[22] There seems to be no difference in Hebrews between priests and high priests. The use of priest is probably dependent on the Melchizedek passage in Psalm 110.

king the people as a whole experience defeat or victory. In the gospels the Son of man (whatever precisely the term may mean) acts representatively for the people; he gives his life a λύτρον ἀντὶ πολλῶν. In the Pauline literature the curious expression ὁ υἱὸς τοῦ ἀνθρώπου does not occur, but (in better Greek) Jesus is the New Adam, the second representative Man, and as in Adam all die, even so in Christ shall all be made alive (1 Cor. 15.22). Of this representative function the high priest is a specialized figure; the high priest acts, sacrifices, on behalf of the people as a whole. When the term high priest is first used in 2.17 this is the background against which it has to be understood. Now however Psalm 8 leads to Psalm 110, connected by way of the picture of universal sovereignty, and the triumphant figure – all things set under his feet – is said to be a priest for ever in the order of Melchizedek. This is another great figure, greater than Abraham, as the epistle points out at 7.4–10, greater than Levi, and one might add greater than Moses and his brother Aaron, the first high priest. The important thing about the Aaronic high priest is precisely that he is Aaronic; that is, he is from the beginning integrated into the structure of the people on whose behalf he is to act. Aaron himself is the brother of Moses, and from their time Torah and Abodah, Law and Temple worship, are brothers, together constituting the life of God's people.[23] It is true that Jesus stands a little aside from this pattern because he does not belong to the tribe of Levi, but, as we shall see, his actions reduplicate precisely (though on a different level) those of the Aaronic high priest. The essence of Melchizedek is that all this is what he is not: he has no country, no father, no mother, no beginning, no end. Scripture has made him like the Son of God (Heb. 7.3). He appears suddenly on the biblical stage and is seen for a moment as its supreme figure, recognized as such even by Abraham. The two high priests provide an illustration of J. L. Leuba's theme in *Institution et Événement*.[24]

---

[23] Cf. Aboth 1.2; also Rom. 9.4.
[24] J. L. Leuba, *L'Institution et L'Événement* (Neuchâtel, Paris, 1950). Unfortunately the author offers no discussion of Hebrews in this important book.

Jesus fulfils the Aaronic high-priestly institution, but fulfils it in a quite unexpectedly radical way because he does so as the non-Aaronic, non-Israelite, non-institutional Melchizedek.

At the end of ch. 5 the argument of the epistle breaks off (5.11), and the author exhorts his readers. They must press on, giving careful heed to what he writes, and show ceaseless vigilance, lest they become sluggish and lose the hope that has been set before them.

With ch. 7 the author returns to Melchizedek, emphasizing his greatness and importance. Much of the material in this chapter I have anticipated; but exaltation of Melchizedek leads to criticism of the alternative, the Levitical priesthood. If this had led to perfection (τελείωσις) there would have been no need and no room for another priesthood, and God would not have supplied one (7.11). It is here that the family connection between the priesthood and Moses the lawgiver – if it may be so described – becomes important. It is on the basis of the Levitical priesthood that the people νενομοθέτηται (7.11). It is not easy to find a precise rendering for this verb, especially when its somewhat different use in 3.6 is borne in mind. *To constitute legally, to give a legal constitution to*, will do perhaps as well as any. The word has the importance of bringing together the Levitical priestly system and the Law; also (from 8.6) the covenant. At the same time, it means that if for the Levitical high priest the Melchizedekian high priest is substituted, the Law and the covenant must be radically changed. In this way the deficiencies of the old Jewish Christian Diaspora are on the way to being dealt with. Christology, which was lacking, is introduced by the entry of a new high-priestly figure, already appearing in the roles of Son, Word, and Wisdom, and not a functionary (as was the Levitical high priest) of the old Law. The new high priest means a new legal enactment, a change in the old legal basis of the people. And with the new law is bound up a new covenant, replacing the old. Again we are anticipating material, with which we shall catch up in ch. 8. For the present it is important to note the distinctiveness of the new high priest, though this proves to be inseparable from the question of the law. The old high priest was established by a law consisting of a fleshly commandment; the new priest by the power of an indissoluble life (7.16). This leads to a statement about the law as radical as anything written by Paul, though the language is completely different. 'There is an annulment of a foregoing commandment because of its weakness and un-profitableness – for the Law made nothing perfect – and the introduction of a better hope, through which we draw near to God' (7.18, 19). Appointed by the divine oath of Ps. 110.4 Jesus is the surety of a better covenant, and he was appointed for ever, unlike the many successive Levitical priests appointed by the Law who offered sacrifice after sacrifice. He is able to save for ever (*or*, completely) those who approach God through him (7.20–28).

The operations of the new high priest are thus hinted at and will be developed in more detail later, but the writer now proceeds in ch. 8 to point out the κεφάλαιον, the summary or main point (there is something of each sense in the word) of the whole argument. This begins with the contrast between those priests who serve what is but the image and shadow of the true tabernacle and the ministrant of the Holy Place and true tabernacle which the Lord pitched, not man, but the basis of the exposition is not a Platonic figure of ideal and phenomenal but biblical eschatology and its fulfilment. Inevitably the paragraph is cast in terms of covenant, not simply because it includes a long quotation from the new covenant prophecy in Jeremiah 31 but because covenant means the relation between two parties, here God and man, and this is at the heart both of the Christian message and in particular of the work of a high priest. When Scripture speaks of a new covenant it has antiquated the old one; and that which is antiquated and growing old is near to disappearing (8.13).

From this point what may be called the eschatological Platonism of the epistle is developed. I discussed this briefly long ago[25] and must here consider it only from the point of view of Christology. The raw material of which it is composed is the Old Testament account of the Levitical high priest and his activity, especially on the Day of Atonement; the mysterious figure of Melchizedek; and the hint, recorded especially in Exod. 25.39, 40, of a heavenly

[25] See *FS* Dodd (n. 10); also *SJT* 6 (1953), pp. 136–55, 225–43.

antitype of the earthly tabernacle. We must trace its development in the concluding chapters of the epistle.

Hebrews 9 contains an account of the actions of the earthly priests in the earthly tabernacle, with occasional hints, and more than hints, of a better liturgy in a better sanctuary. An account of the tabernacle and the way it was used (9.1–10) leads to the devastating criticism (descended from the polemic against the Temple contained in Stephen's speech?) of material sacrifices. Such gifts can never perfect the worshipper in his conscience; they relate merely to foods and drinks and washings. Their value is that they point forward to a time when something better will be provided. This paragraph is followed by 9.11–14, in which the thought of the epistle is summarized. It begins inevitably, and verbally, with Christ. He is defined by his role of High Priest, and in one sentence he is set in historical and theological terms as the High Priest of the good things that have now come into being, not with the blood of bulls and goats but with his own blood, and in quasi-platonic terms as one who has entered into the holy place – the holy place of the tent not made with hands, the holy place that is not of this creation (9.11–12). Because this High Priest has thus acted in this place he has found for us a redemption that is eternal. If animal blood can convey an external purification, how much more will the blood of Christ cleanse our conscience from dead works? The rest of the chapter justifies, amplifies, and applies the image.

Chapter 10 begins with a sharp but speedily qualified reassertion of Platonic terminology: The Law has a shadow of good things, not however their very image (αὐτὴν τὴν εἰκόνα), the three-dimensional representation of the actual realities. The shadow sacrifices are repeated again and again – itself a proof of their inadequacy and inefficiency. If they really achieved their object in cleansing the worshipper they would have ceased to be offered; why should they be repeated if their work was done? We may pass the bad logic of the argument – new sins were committed year by year, requiring the annual ceremony of the Day of Atonement. For the annual sacrifice had at least the virtue of reminding the worshipper that sin exists and that sin needs to be forgiven; the virtue also of providing terminology suitable for use in speaking of the one effective sacrifice. But material sacrifices create rather than deal with 'conscience of sins' (συνείδησις ἁμαρτιῶν, 10.2). It is conscience, an inward thing, that needs cleansing. The blood of bulls and goats belongs to a different category of existence, and a sacrifice must be sought that operates in the sphere of the conscience. Here the writer is able to pick up an important Old Testament passage, critical of the operations of the old, earthly sanctuary.[26] Sacrifices are commanded in the Law (κατὰ νόμον, 10.8), but at this point the Law has to be not merely criticized but plainly contradicted. 'Sacrifice and offering thou didst not desire, but thou didst prepare for me a body; whole-burnt-offerings and sin-offerings did not please thee. Then I said, Behold, I have come (in the roll of the book it is written about me) to do thy will O God' (Ps. 40.7–9); Heb. 10.4–7). This is so important that the writer repeats it and states its meaning in the boldest terms. He (the one who is speaking in Scripture, the representative of God – it is of course Christ who is meant) takes away the first-named matters (sacrifices as performed κατὰ νόμον) in order that he may establish the second-named (the doing of God's will). The goal is still (but in a profounder sense) sanctification, and two words are taken up from the quotation, defining each other. By the will of God, accepted and completely performed by his Son, we have been sanctified through the offering (not of the blood of bulls and goats but) of the body of Jesus Christ, which was devoted without remainder to the will of God.

It would be easy, in view of the way in which in 10.1 the Law and the sacrifices it commanded are described by the quasi-platonic 'shadow', to conclude that in the offering made by Jesus Christ we have the true, ideal, parallel to the earthly, phenomenal, high priest and his work in the earthly, phenomenal, tabernacle. It is not however so simple. The work of Christ is inseparable from material and historical circumstances. The conscience itself is an inward spiritual entity, but the sins by which it is defiled are earthly enough. The devotion of Jesus to the Father's will is an inward spiritual

---

[26] We may recall once more Stephen's criticism of the Temple.

entity, but our author is careful to select and quote an Old Testament passage that insists upon his body.[27] The sacrifice is that of a completely obedient will, but it finds concrete historical expression in a death as real as that of any bull or goat offered in the Temple. There is in fact a threefold set of relationships within which the work of Jesus, which is the core of the Gospel, operates. It operates on a simple historical level in the crucifixion of Jesus. Secondly, this crucifixion is a moral act, in which Jesus offered to God his completely obedient will, a moral act which had the effect, thirdly, of cleansing the defiled consciences of those who had not seen fit to offer their wills in obedience to God but used them in pursuit of their own self-centred ends. These three operations are bound together by a fourth dimension, which is related at once to history, to the Old Testament Temple and the regulations that governed it, and to what may be called a platonic way of conceiving reality. This is most simply set out in the form of a table, summarizing on the one hand the account in Leviticus 16 (helped out by the Mishnah tractate Yoma) of the events, especially the actions of the high priest, on the Day of Atonement,[28] and on the other the acts ascribed to Jesus in the story of the cross. Thus

Leviticus 16 (Yoma)

(a) Sacrifice publicly carried out, outside the shrine, visible to all.

(b) Entry of the high priest into the holy place, with blood, the visible and effective evidence that sacrifice has been offered.

(c) Intercession and atonement made by the high priest within the holy place, where he alone may enter. He represents the people before God.

(d) Return of the high priest to the waiting public, outside the holy place. He is able to tell them that their sins are forgiven.

---

[27] The Hebrew text differs: אזנים כרית לי, for LXX ὠτία δὲ κατρτίσω μοι. So Rahlfs, but for ὠτία (G 3), B S A have σῶμα. There can be little doubt that our author found σῶμα in his text.

[28] Our author finds no use for the scapegoat, sent away bearing sins to Azazel. He does not freely create doctrine by allegorizing the Old Testament text, priority is with doctrine.

All these points appear in *Hebrews*.

   (a) Christ suffered publicly, in an act visible to all mankind (13.12), offering his obedient will expressed through his body, obedient to death (10.10). This was a once-for-all act (9.13–14) – historically, the crucifixion.

   (b) After his death Christ ascended into heaven, with his own blood, the sign of his sacrificial death. Hebrews scarcely refers to the resurrection, though the author certainly believed in it (13.20). It is the ascension that matters because this is the Son's entry into the heavenly sanctuary.

   (c) In the heavenly sanctuary Christ makes an act of atonement. This is eternal (7.25), in the sense that the atonement effected is eternal in its application and results (10.14), and in the simple chronological sense that up to his return Christ is continuously in heaven.

   (d) Like the returning high priest, Christ will appear ἐκ δευτέρου (9.28). The second coming is εἰς σωτηρίαν – to complete and apply the results of atonement. These are already anticipated in access to God, and in the enjoyment of the powers of the age to come (6.5).

All this may be said to retain of Plato's famous cave[29] only the stage-set and the stage machinery. The whole is rotated from a horizontal to a vertical position – not 'inside the cave and outside the cave' but 'below and above'. And we have not objects standing or moving without and casting shadows, stationary or moving, on the wall within, but one being who acts both outside and within, moving from the visible world of historical event to the interior hiddenness of heaven, dying a human death and from his death going to plead the cause of his fellow human beings (for he is one of them, though much else also) with his Father in heaven. It is the Temple and the Law that are shadows, indicating as it were the shape of reality, but – though this introduces a new factor into the imagery – they are shadows that disappear as the new day of the new covenant dawns.

[29] *Republic* vii. 514a–517a.

There is a further sense in which the historical event, recognizable to us in this world as the crucifixion of Jesus, has a double interpretation. It is an event that belongs at once to the realms of the visible and the invisible, of the phenomenal and the ideal; it also belongs to both time and eternity. It is of its nature that it happened once; its effects persist. 'By one offering he has perfected for ever those who are sanctified' (10.14). The Son, after the sacrifice of himself, has no more to do, in the visible world, till his return. He makes intercession (7.25) and waits till all his foes are subjected to him (10.12–13).

Having reached this conclusion the author has little more Christology to offer, he draws practical consequences and exhorts his readers to live the life of faith, running with endurance the race that is set before them, their eyes fixed on Jesus. Into the details of this exhortation we cannot follow him; it has not been possible to go into the details of this appropriation of the sacrificial system of the Old Testament. He has drawn on an aspect of the Old Testament neglected in most of the New, on traditional eschatology, and on his knowledge of Greek thought, to make up any deficiency there may have been in the Christology of his predecessors.

10

Effective Forces in the Late First Century

It may seem paradoxical and indeed discourteous to accept, and to accept with great pleasure, the privilege of contributing to a number of *Studia Theologica* designed to honour one for whom I have the highest regard, and then to propose a brief study whose title sets a question mark against the theme not only of the Festschrift but of one of Professor Jervell's most notable essays, an essay from which every New Testament historian has much to learn. I have in fact more than one question in mind – and I shall be very happy if my questions provoke from Professor Jervell a vigorous reply that will make me think again.

My first question is one that may seem to be mere playing with words, though I think it is more than that. Is it possible in the period that we have in review – the first Christian century, let us say, especially A.D. 70–100 – to identify minorities and majorities? It may be due to the relics of an original training in mathematics that I prefer to avoid such words as minority and majority when we have no numerical information. 'We do not have exact figures for those years of Jewish and Gentile Christians.'[1] The fact is that we do not have any figures at all, exact or approximate, for the period A.D. 70–100 of which Dr Jervell is speaking in this sentence. Nor do we have exact figures for the earlier years. True, we have 3,000 in Acts 2.41 and 5,000 in Acts 4.4; but no one is likely to take these figures as exact, and Acts 6.7, with its πολύς τε ὄχλος τῶν

[1] J. Jervell, *The Unknown Paul* (Minneapolis, MN: Augsburg, 1984), p. 33, in the essay 'The Mighty Minority'.

215

ἱερέων, contains no figures at all and is valueless from the numerical point of view – and perhaps from other points of view also. It may well be true (and this I presume is all that Dr Jervell wishes to assert) that if the numbers of Jewish Christians and of Gentile Christians were plotted against years on the same piece of paper the curves would probably intersect at a point somewhere between A.D. 70 and 100; they would probably intersect a number of times before the Gentile curve decisively took off and left the Jewish curve behind. This, however, would be an over-simplification. We should need a fresh sheet of paper for every centre of population; the rates of change would not everywhere be the same. This is not merely pernickety purism; it is one way of bringing out the fact that we know very little about the racial and social make-up of the earliest Christian churches. Even the interesting and important results of sociological study give us little that we can build on here. Recognition of our ignorance opens the way to further questions.

Indeed, one is tempted to throw a charge of paradox back at Professor Jervell. The theme of his essay on the Mighty Minority is that in the last decades of the century the influence of the Jewish Christians was out of all proportion to their numerical strength. He traces this influence in a series of fascinating studies. There is not only plain opposition to Paul, there is an effect upon Paul's own thinking: Paul's understanding of Israel and of Israel's destiny in Romans 9–11 is different from his earlier teaching. The influence persists and is to be traced in later books of the New Testament. Dr Jervell sums up his argument:

> The problem of the validity of the Mosaic torah and of Israel as the elected people of God dominates the apologetic in the controversies with the synagogue. We find this, inter alia, in the gospels of Matthew, Luke, and John. And precisely in the years from 70 to 100 we find a most lively discussion of the mission among Gentiles. Long ago the Gentile mission started and only after some years, especially between A.D. 70 and 100, do we find the discussion of how this mission can be understood theologically and justified. I can only see the *Sitz im Leben* for this lively discussion in what happened to the Jewish Christians after they had to live in Gentile surroundings, separated and isolated

from their own people, still claiming to be Israel. Precisely in the years from A.D. 70 to 100 the Jewish influence in the church reaches its climax. This is not only due to the influx of Jewish thoughts and ideas, but also to literary influences. We can mention here the Letter to the Hebrews, the Apocalypse of John, and the first use of Jewish pseudepigrapha as Christian documents by the means of interpolation.[2]

The paradox is clear: 'Precisely in the years from A.D. 70 to 100 the Jewish influence in the church reaches its climax' – as the proportion of Jews to Gentiles decreases. It must be said at once that though paradoxical this is by no means impossible. Influence is not necessarily (though it often is) proportionate to numerical strength. But ought we not at least to query the assumption (for assumption is what it appears to be) that this period of Jewish Christian influence is one in which Jewish Christians were in a diminishing minority? Perhaps we should question also the statement that Jewish Christians 'had to live in Gentile surroundings'. True, they no longer lived in Jerusalem.[3] But outside Jerusalem, outside Palestine, how greatly did their environment change? It is not easy to give a confident answer, and no doubt (if we had the evidence) every centre of population would call for a different answer. Where there is evidence, it seems that Jewish communities in Asia Minor led a stable existence, enjoying on the whole good relations with their Gentile neighbours. This has been demonstrated, for example, with regard to Sardis, where the fine and centrally situated synagogue survived till the seventh century.[4] This of course tells us nothing about the relation between Jewish

---

[2] *The Unknown Paul*, p. 39.

[3] Or at least not many of them did. For the continuation of Jewish practices in Jerusalem after A.D. 70, see K. W. Clark, 'Worship in the Jerusalem Temple after A.D. 70', *NTS* 6 (1960), pp. 269–80.

[4] For a recent account see P. R. Trebilco, *Jewish Communities in Asia Minor* (SNTSMS 69; Cambridge: Cambridge University Press, 1991), pp. 40–51, with his bibliography, especially A. T. Kraabel, ANRW 2.19.1 (Berlin/New York; de Gruyter, 1979), pp. 477–510. For Antioch see W. A. Meeks and R. L. Wilken, *Jews and Christians in Antioch* (SBL Sources 13; Missoula, MT: Scholars Press, 1978), especially p. 18.

Christians and Gentile Christians. There is no archaeological evidence for the existence of Christians in Sardis, but there is the literary evidence not only of Rev. 3.1–6 but Melito's tract *On the Passover*. From the former little is to be deduced except on the basis of silence. The churches of Pergamum and Thyatira are warned against those who eat food sacrificed to idols and commit fornication. Those who do these things are presumably either Gentiles or Jews who have been infected by Gentile freedom; they do not observe the decree of Acts 15.29. There is no such complaint in the letter to Sardis. Melito's Homily however contains a vigorous attack on the Jews;[5] it was hardly written by a Jewish Christian, and does not suggest a mixed church with good relations between its Jewish and Gentile components. Much can happen in a hundred years.

Professor Jervell's discussion of the works he mentions in the passage quoted above are of great interest and for the most part convincing; the writings of the period A.D. 70–100 do show awareness of the problems that must have arisen in mixed, Jewish and Gentile, communities. We may take as perhaps the clearest examples Matthew and Acts. On Matthew: 'We have in this gospel a clear antisynagogue sentiment *and* a preference for Jews.'[6] Professor Jervell refers to 10.5f. ('Go nowhere among the Gentiles') and implies a reference to 28.19 as he makes the point that 'the church behind the gospel in which it is said "not a dot will pass from the law" (5.18), is a church for the Gentiles' (p. 47). In it Jews may live along with Gentiles because the old law is still valid, though it receives (in Matt. 5–7) a new, true interpretation. It is a mixed church with a mixed theology, in which the Jewish Christians played a dominant part (p. 48).

A similarly pervasive influence is to be seen in Acts. Professor Jervell's two most important points refer to Luke's understanding of the church and to his portrait of Paul. 'The church in Jerusalem lived in complete obedience to the law of Moses. The outcome was that the church in the beginning rejected any mission to the

---

[5] See especially §§ 72–99.
[6] *The Unknown Paul*, p. 47.

Gentiles, but God forced Peter to address the Gentiles and acknowledge them (Acts 10–11). The apostolic decree is in itself a manifestation of the law insofar as it expresses what the Mosaic torah (Leviticus 17–18) demands of Gentiles . . .' (p. 40). Most important is the Acts picture of Paul, a law-observing Pharisee, 'not the ex-Pharisee, because he remains a Pharisee after his conversion' (p. 41). This is correct observation (see Acts 23.6), but it is important to go a little further; for example in regard to Acts 21.21–24. Does this passage imply that 'Paul teaches Jews and Jewish Christians in the diaspora to circumcise their children and observe the law'? (p. 41). It does not say so much; it goes no further than 'Paul does not teach Jews and Jewish Christians not to circumcise their children and not to observe the law'. He probably regarded such matters as adiaphora (Gal. 6.15) and those who made a fuss about them as *weak*. This is probably the historical truth (if we may depend on Paul's letters) and may be what Luke intended; but it does not control the motivation behind Acts, in which Paul is on the whole represented as a law-abiding Jew. The Jewish Christians whose work Dr Jervell sees in Acts represented him as conforming to their own position.[7]

There is much in this that is convincing and of the greatest value, and all must be grateful to Dr Jervell (a mighty minority even on his own?) for emphasizing these aspects of the Christian literature of the last third of the first century. Some questions however remain. Is the picture of Paul that has just been reviewed that which Jewish Christians wished to promote? It is not the picture with which they ultimately emerged from the dark period in which there is no evidence and only inferences are possible. A little later Paul will appear under the guise of Simon Magus, the origin of evil in the church. After the pairs, such as Cain and Abel, Esau and Jacob, have been listed the *Kerygmata of Peter* continues,

> He who follows this order can discern by whom Simon (= Paul), who as the first came before me to the Gentiles, was sent forth, and to whom I (= Peter) belong who appeared later than he did and came

[7] See Romans 9–11; and in *The Unknown Paul*, pp. 41, 42.

in upon him as light upon darkness, as knowledge upon ignorance, as healing upon sickness.[8]

This of course takes us beyond the period with which we are concerned. But we must ask whether Dr Jervell's account of Matthew (for example) goes far enough.

Matthew's Jewish Christian attitude is painted in brighter colours in a recent book by M. D. Goulder,[9] a book to which I shall have occasion to return. Professor Goulder contrasts the attitude of Matthew, a 'Petrine' gospel, with Mark, a 'Pauline' gospel, with regard to the family of Jesus (pp. 8–15) and with regard to Peter himself (pp. 16–23). He contrasts the attitude to the Law of Matthew with that of Paul and Mark

> Disciples of Paul like Mark are a serious menace, suggesting that the food-laws have been abrogated, or the Fourth Commandment repealed. Nothing of the kind: the whole *Law and the Prophets* are valid, every *iota* . . . , every crown on a letter, and they are valid *till heaven and earth pass away, till all is accomplished.* So teachers like Mark who go about relaxing even the least commandment (let alone the Ten Commandments!), and *teaching men so* in their Gospels, can hardly expect to go to heaven even; while people like Peter and James who have stood up for the validity of God's Law will be honoured there. The basis of religion is given by God in the first five books of the Bible, and of course this has to be kept (p. 32).

If Dr Goulder is right, Matthew is much more aggressively anti-Pauline than Dr Jervell allows. This tells us nothing about relative numbers; minorities are not infrequently aggressive. But Dr Goulder's picture suggests a minority that is aware that it is losing, or is in danger of losing the battle whereas Dr Jervell suggests a minority that knows that it can and does exercise influence and is conscious of strength rather than weakness.

---

[8] W. Schneemelcher, *New Testament Apocrypha*. Eng. ed. R. McL. Wilson, London 2nd edn, 1991, vol. 2 (Cambridge: James Clark), p. 535 (= Clem. *Hom.* 2.17).

[9] *A Tale of Two Missions* (London: SCM Press, 1994).

If, when Matthew was written, there were those who defended the Law and believed that it was the business of Christians to observe it, there was a party which, without denying a kind of validity to the Law, opposed them, taking a view of the Law that superficially, but only superficially, resembled Paul's. The upholders of the Law are clearly in view in 1 Tim. 1.7–10. They wish to be known as teachers of the Law (νομοδιδάσκαλοι), but they do not understand the Law or recognize that it is to be applied not to the virtuous but to those who need correction.[10] Legal controversies reappear in Tit. 3.9, and in Tit. 1.10 disorderly persons are found particularly among οἱ ἐκ τῆς περιτομῆς. These seem to be dissident members of the church and are therefore to be thought of as Jewish Christians. They are blamed (1.14) for giving heed to ἐντολαῖς ἀνθρώπων (cf. Mark 7.7).[11]

If we are to speak of majorities and minorities in the last decades of the first century we have a good deal of guessing to do, but there is no need to guess at the continuation of the controversies that marked Paul's career in the 40s and 50s,[12] though Acts itself suggests a context of consensus.[13] These observations are not contradictory; they are worth pursuing. Everyone knows that F. C. Baur based his understanding of early Christian history on the existence of controversy (if that is a strong enough word). Baur's account of the history has been widely abandoned; understandably, since Baur set it out in relation to the dates that he ascribed to New Testament documents. Since Baur's time many of these dates have been shown to be mistaken and with them Baur's whole view of New Testament history has been jettisoned – understandably, but in error. Baur was not the only scholar to observe the disputes that lie behind the

---

[10] If in v. 7. περὶ τίνων is taken as masculine rather than neuter there is an allusion to persons of whom the would-be νομοδιδάσκαλοι disapprove.

[11] For ἐντολαί F G have ἐντάλματα, possibly influenced by the Marcan passage.

[12] See my 'Pauline Controversies in the Post-Pauline Period', *NTS* 20 (1974), pp. 229–45; in this book, pp. 155–77.

[13] See my 'Acts and Christian Consensus', *Context*. Festskrift til Peder Borgen (Trondheim: Tapir, 1988), pp. 19–33.

New Testament; Lightfoot for example could see them too,[14] and Professor Goulder has now taken up the theme – exaggerating it, I think, in places,[15] but demonstrating it convincingly. He recognizes Baur as a forerunner;[16] so also does Dr Jervell,[17] though he makes the point that Baur's view of early Christian history is not that presented by Luke in Acts. Baur of course never claimed that it was.

I too believe that Baur was right in principle. The first age of Christianity was an age of conflict, and it is out of that conflict that the – more or less – settled church of the second century emerged. I am more than grateful for the version of Baur that Dr Jervell and Dr Goulder have given us. They are not, however, in full agreement with each other, and I am not in full agreement with either, indebted as I am to both. Dr Jervell seems to me to have difficulty with Acts. Can Luke's evident enthusiasm for the Gentile mission be accounted for as bearing witness to the way in which the influential Jewish Christian minority found itself obliged to come to terms with the mission and at the same time impose its own conditions upon it? And was Luke subtle enough to invent a Pharisee Paul to gratify the Jewish Christians? Or stupid enough not to see that they were foisting such a figure upon him? Acts is best explained

[14] See e.g. his *Galatians* (London: Macmillan, 1865 and many reprints), p. 374; and cf. W. G. Kümmel, *Das Neue Testament im 20. Jahrhundert* (Stuttgarter Bibel–Studien 50; Stuttgart: Katholisches Bibelwerk, 1970), p. 73: '. . . am Ende des 19. Jahrhunderts hatten sich diesem modifizierten Baurschen Geschichtsbild auch konservative Forscher wie . . . J. B. Lightfoot angeschlossen'.

[15] For example, I do not think that Paul on his second mission 'had to submit to the indignity of being supervised by a Jerusalem Christian, Silas' (p. 183). Is there any good reason for questioning the ἐπιλεξάμενος of Acts 15.40? Pages 70, 71 are hardly strong enough. Or do we, with D, read ἐπιδεξάμενος?

[16] 'The theory I have proposed . . . is not new in principle: it was in fact suggested in outline by Ferdinand Baur, Professor at Tübingen in Germany, in an article of 156 pages in 1831, and it was broadly accepted during most of the last century' (*A Tale*, p. 194). In this quotation the word *broadly* has to bear much weight; there was a good deal of opposition, especially perhaps in England, among those who had as well as those who had not read him.

[17] 'In spite of all criticism of Baur, especially with regard to Jewish Christianity after A.D. 70, his categories are still determinative – and rightly so' (*Unknown Paul*, p. 13).

as the honest but not always accurate product of an age of consensus,[18] written at a moment of peace when the old conflicts were no longer understood and new ones had not yet broken out. The point of principle over which I stumbled in Dr Goulder's book is stated most plainly on pp. 8, 9:

> The pillars had the authority of having been chosen by Jesus, and the authority of the Bible, which both sides agreed to be infallible; and in 48 they were running a scatter of churches with perhaps five thousand members, while Paul was pastor of a single church at Antioch with perhaps fifty. But Paul was better educated than they were, and he was a brilliant thinker; and he was possessed by an overmastering conviction that he was called by God. Convictions are always more powerful than institutions, and it was Paul who triumphed.[19]

Did Paul win? It is not only that institutions seem to have a good record against principles; we must not be misled by the number of Pauline epistles in the New Testament canon. Paul may have won in the long run (though that is questionable); in the short he did not.

The two main battles described within the New Testament itself are the affair at Antioch (Gal. 2.11–18), of which Dr Goulder (p. 3) says, 'The Peter party, the *Petrines*, had won the round', and the Council of Acts 15. Here (and this applies elsewhere also, where the story is not so clear) both Dr Jervell and Dr Goulder seem to have over-simplified the story – so too perhaps did Baur, whose long essay 'Die Christuspartei in der korinthischen Gemeinde, der Gegensatz des petrinischen und paulinischen Christenthums in der ältesten Kirche, der Apostel Paulus in Rom',[20] at least in its title omits one of the Corinthian parties. The earliest stages of conflict were fought out between not two but three groups. Of these, two groups, though they stood on opposite sides, both called themselves Hebrews (Ἑβραῖοι) and were radicals, though they stood at opposite ends of the spectrum. There was a Jerusalem

---

[18] See n. 13.

[19] Cf. p. 3, 'In the long run the Paulines won.'

[20] *Tübinger Zeitschrift für Theologie*, 1831, pp. 61–206.

group that used the title: they were Hebrews, Israelites, the seed of Abraham. They also spoke of themselves as servants of Christ (2 Cor. 11.22, 23); Paul denies them none of these titles, merely claiming that they applied to him also. He was more a servant of Christ than they, in that he had worked harder, suffered more. The irony with which Paul refers to them[21] identifies them with the similarly treated *pillars* of Galatians 2. But he too is a Hebrew; cf. also Phil. 3.5.[22] By Ἑβραῖοι Paul seems to mean one who is deeply concerned for the identity and destiny of his people, though it need not be said that he and James would understand the identity and destiny of the people of God in different ways. That they could understand and agree with each other, provided they went their separate ways, appears in Galatians 2, where Paul makes it clear that he will have no dealings with the false brothers whose aim was to bring his Gentile Christians into slavery (Gal. 2.4, ἵνα ἡμᾶς καταδουλώσουσιν) but was willing to accept the arrangement of two separate missions (2.7, 8). It was a superficially attractive arrangement, but it was bound to break down in a church with a mixed congregation, such as Antioch, and that it did break down is clear in Gal. 2.11–14. It is also clear that there were Jewish Christians (false brothers, therefore claiming – though in Paul's opinion falsely – to be Christians) who insisted not only on food laws but on circumcision (2.3, 4). This insistence was to be found not only in Jerusalem but in Galatia also (6.12 *et al.*). There was, as Baur saw long ago,[23] no hope of full agreement between the radical left and the radical right. It may have been after the affair at Antioch that a centre party arose; according to Acts it had been in existence much earlier. At that earlier point (Acts 6.1) Luke calls them Hellenists, a word of no fixed meaning (cf. Acts 9.29; 11.20), and finds their founder in the martyred Stephen, a Jew of

[21] See my commentary on *The Second Epistle to the Corinthians* (London: A. & C. Black, 1973), p. 278.

[22] Cf. Rom. 11.1, where Paul does not use the word Hebrew; he is not dealing with opponents who used it.

[23] James was prepared at most to tolerate Paul's mission to the Gentiles; he was not prepared to take part in it. See F. C. Baur, *Paulus* (Stuttgart, [1]1843, [2]1855), pp. 125/142f.

the Dispersion. There is no reason to doubt that this group existed; in some respects Jews of the Dispersion may have been easier to win for the new faith than Jews of Palestine. And the vacuum in the church called for filling. It was filled by Jews (and Gentiles, no doubt) who were prepared to compromise: No circumcision, but no offence at table to Jews who felt themselves obliged to observe the food laws; with complete repudiation of idolatry and loyalty to the one true God. This compromise, the 'Apostolic Decree', is represented in Acts 15 as proposed by James, and not merely accepted but disseminated by Paul. It is certain not only that Paul in his extant correspondence does not mention the Decree but that his teaching on food sacrificed to idols contradicts it. It is certain also that an influential party continued to assert the Law. As far as the New Testament goes it is unknown whether James accepted the Decree, but Hegesippus' account of his death represents him as venerated for his (Jewish) piety and righteousness (apud Eusebius, *HE* 2.23.4–18; cf. Josephus, *Ant.* 20.200f.).

Paul did not win and James did not win. The centre party with their compromise Decree won. No doubt they began as a minority, but in the period A.D. 70–100 they were on the way to becoming a majority. It is their view of Paul that appears in Acts, where Paul is a kind of successor to the man whose death he approved (22.20); their Decree was recognized in the churches of Asia in which the Apocalypse circulated (Rev. 2.14, 20) and became universal Christian practice.[24] In other respects too their understanding of Christian doctrine prevailed. It is hardly correct to call them (as Dr Goulder does) 'Petrines', for though they may have adopted Peter as a useful figurehead the man himself seems to have been too unstable and changeable to be a true leader; see Gal. 2.14 and other passages. This is a somewhat more complicated picture than the invaluable sketches drawn by Dr Jervell and Dr Goulder, but it seems to do more justice to the facts.[25]

[24] See *Australian Biblical Review* 35 (1987). Special issue in Honour of Professor Eric Osborn, pp. 54–9 (where there was space only for some of the evidence).

[25] Of these only a few have been mentioned in what is no more than an attempt to enter into conversation with Professor Jervell. I hope to do more justice to the argument elsewhere.

11

Paul and the
Introspective Conscience

It may seem ungracious to resurrect a controversy in which two distinguished theologians engaged a quarter of a century ago, a controversy which, at least in explicit terms, seems in these days to awaken few echoes. Perhaps it should be regarded as settled. But it calls to mind not only two of the most important New Testament theologians of our own age but also the greatest theologian of the first Christian generation (and perhaps of any generation) and another who comes not far short of him. And I doubt whether the last word on the matter has been said yet. It is probably true that it has been obscured by more recent controversies, not identical with it but related to it, and these cannot be entirely excluded from this discussion.

Everyone knows that in 1976 (a year later in Great Britain) Krister Stendahl republished in *Paul among Jews and Gentiles* (pp. 78–96) a paper which had previously appeared in the *Harvard Theological Review* (56; 1963); It had originally been published in Swedish in *Svensk Exegetisk Årsbok* (25; 1960). This was 'The Apostle Paul and the Introspective Conscience of the West'.The publication in *HTR* provoked a vigorous response by Ernst Käsemann in one of the lectures printed in *Paulinische Perspektiven* (1969; pp. 108–39). This volume was later (1971) translated into English, and Dr Stendahl printed a rejoinder in an appendix to *Paul among Jews and Gentiles* (pp. 129–33).

Dr Stendahl's starting-point (and I cannot in this paper go very much further than his starting-point) may be given best in a sentence of his own. 'Especially in Protestant Christianity – which, however, at this point has its roots in Augustine and in the piety of the Middle Ages – the Pauline awareness of sin has been interpreted in the light of Luther's struggle with his conscience. But it is exactly at that point that we can discern the most drastic difference between Luther and Paul, between the 16th and the 1st century, and, perhaps, between Eastern and Western Christianity' (p. 79). This is not merely a matter of psychology, for 'Paul's statements about "Justification by faith", have been hailed as the answer to the problem which faces the ruthlessly honest man in his practice of introspection' (p. 79). What then are the roots of Paul's doctrine of justification by faith, and is the doctrine rightly regarded as central in his understanding of the Gospel? The questions may be given historical and theological sharpness if they are reworded as, Did Luther understand or misunderstand Paul? In answering the need of those who, like himself, asked, 'How can I find a gracious God?' did he, as an interpreter of Paul, and did the Protestant tradition as a whole, lead the seekers astray? (pp. 82f.). The doctrine of justification did not arise out of the troubles of Paul's conscience (which was 'robust' (p. 80)); it was rather his way of vindicating his mission to the Gentiles, a theme worked out with special force and clarity in Romans 9–11, chapters which thus constitute essentially Paul's *Heilsgeschichte*.

It must be remembered that Dr Käsemann's reaction to this is contained in one of four lectures on Paul delivered in America, where Dr Stendahl's lecture had recently been published and might be expected to be especially influential. The title of the lecture is 'Rechtfertigung und Heilsgeschichte im Römerbrief', and one suspects that the theme may have been settled independently of the essay. Dr Käsemann could see that what he had to say about justification and *Heilsgeschichte* would be nullified if Dr Stendahl's thesis were accepted, and therefore felt obliged to attack it, though without offering the detailed exegetical reply that Dr Stendahl evidently felt (p. 131) that he had a right to expect. To some extent this deficiency is made up in Dr Käsemann's commentary on Romans (of which Dr Stendahl speaks [p. 129] with great respect), but only to some extent. I have noted only two references to Dr Stendahl in the commentary. His name does not appear in the general bibliography. His article 'Rechtfertigung und Endgericht'[1] is mentioned in the bibliography to 2.1–11 (p. 49) but it is not taken up in the exposition that follows. 'The Introspective Conscience' occurs in the bibliography to 9.6–13 (p. 251) and again in the argument (pp. 254f.), but the point at issue is the relation between justification and *Heilsgeschichte*; on this see below. In any case, Dr Stendahl supports his view with the observation that though we read much of righteousness and justification in Romans and Galatians, there is little of them elsewhere in the Pauline corpus. Dr Käsemann however, both in *Perspektiven* and in the commentary maintains the centrality of justification in Paul's thought and its importance as a key to his writings.

It could hardly be said that the two primary contestants had said everything that is to be said on the issue, though as far as I am aware little has been done to follow it up since 1977. There have been not a few articles and books on Paul, including a group of major commentaries on Romans, but though 'the introspective conscience of the west' has become a familiar phrase this application of it has tended to fall out of sight.[2] This is partly because it may seem to have been absorbed in the discussion of the Law generated by E. P. Sanders and taken up by many others.[3] If the Law was a covenant of grace what room was there for a tormented conscience? What could it be but an unnecessary aberration? Perhaps on this matter also there is more to be said, though here only allusively. I have touched briefly on the main issue in one or two other places,[4] but it seems a suitable theme with which to salute one who is expert in both biblical and Luther studies.[5]

---

[1] *Lutherische Rundschau* 11 (1961), pp. 3–10.

[2] See however J. M. Espy, 'Paul's "Robust Conscience" Reexamined', *NTS* 31 (1985), pp. 161–88.

[3] The discussion begins with E. P. Sanders, *Paul and Palestinian Judaism* (1977), which is still of fundamental importance.

[4] See M. D. Meeks (ed.), *What Should Methodists Teach?* (1990), pp. 41f., and a book, *St Paul: An Introduction to His Thought*, to be published by Geoffrey Chapman in 1994.

[5] And I do not forget that James and I first met at a gathering of the Luther-Akademie at Goslar in 1953.

Did Paul have an introspective conscience? The answer is that he certainly did, but the question before us is not immediately settled by this answer. A conscience is nothing if not introspective; there is nowhere else it can look but within, that is, into an awareness of previous actions (which of course must include words and thoughts) and of their relation to some accepted standard of right and wrong. A conscience operating in this way is implied in 1 Cor. 4.4, where the verb (σύνοιδα) is the etymological partner of the noun συνείδησις and the sentence is properly translated, 'I have nothing on my conscience', that is, I can see in my remembered actions (in the area under consideration) nothing that I now believe to be wrong.[6] Such passages must not be over-interpreted or taken outside the field to which they belong. Paul means that in his dealings with (for example) the Corinthians he has no regrets. What he has done he would in like circumstances do again. His words make no claim to total moral perfection. Paul assumes too that others equally have consciences and may legitimately pass judgement on his (as well as their own) behaviour. Thus he commends himself to the consciences of all (2 Cor. 4.2): let them judge fairly how he has conducted himself. They may not judge correctly, for conscience in itself is not infallible. There were in Corinth those who passed a judgement different from his own on Paul's apostolic conduct. There are those whose conscience is weak, those for example who judge that to eat meat that has been offered in sacrifice to an idol is to participate in idolatry and is thus a wicked act which is displeasing to God. They are mistaken: to eat εἰδωλόθυτα is not in itself wicked but indifferent. The conscience of the weak is in error, but the conscience of the strong is deficient too, because it fails to tell him that wilful disobedience to whatever is believed – however mistakenly – to be God's will, and to act with loveless disregard of others, are both sinful.[7] These passages are of great importance, not only because they show that the conscience, though important, is a fallible moral guide, but because they point beyond

---

[6] Cf. Acts 23.1; 24.16. These sentences may or may not have been spoken by Paul; they show an understanding of συνείδησις current in Pauline circles.

[7] See 1 Cor. 8–10; Rom. 14; 15.

conscience to a higher, to the only absolute, authority. The point is made explicitly by a fuller consideration of 1 Cor. 4.4 in its context: To me it is a matter of the smallest importance that I should be examined by you, or by any human assize; nay, indeed, I do not even examine myself. For though I have nothing on my conscience it is not by that that I am justified. He who examines me is the Lord. It is not the verdict of my conscience or the verdict of the moral examination conducted by others that I should be either pleased or distressed about. There is only one Judge, and it is his verdict that I must dread – unless I have good reason for doing otherwise. The same point is made in a different way in 1 Cor. 8, where it is clear that the conscience of one Christian declares, It is wrong to eat εἰδωλόθυτα, and of another, This is an adiaphoron; eat what you please. It is clear that the conscience of one of these fellow Christians is misleading him; it is mistaken. The truth is with God.

To say this is not to say that conscience is of no importance or that its judgements may be ignored. Man's 'conscience is not so much the bar at which his conduct is tried, as a major witness, who may be called on either side as the case may be'.[8] This is the meaning of Rom. 2.15–16, where the conscience plays its part not in directing behaviour during a man's lifetime but on Judgement Day (the day when God judges the secret things of men – hidden from others and to some extent from themselves). The conscience bears witness jointly with the Law[9] to wrongdoing. The operation of the conscience is described in the clause that follows – their inward thoughts in mutual debate accuse or else excuse them. In this thought, and in the use of the word συνείδησις, Paul is following Stoic models.[10]

The conscience then is essentially (but it cannot be claimed that Paul's use of the word is rigidly consistent) not judge but witness, and a forensic process will normally begin only with some

---

[8] C. K. Barrett, *The Epistle to the Romans* (2nd edn, 1991), p. 51.

[9] συμμαρτυρεῖ; Paul does not say with what or whom the conscience bears joint testimony, but it is hard to understand anything other than the Law.

[10] For a wide range of material see C. Maurer, *TWNT* 7.897–906.

external judicial authority to set it in motion. This will most evidently happen at the Last Day, at Judgement Day, and it is God who holds assize and summons the witnesses. But since God is always Judge (whatever else he may be) his presence will always have the same effect of setting judgement in motion. Did Paul know this for himself? That he had an introspective conscience has been claimed simply on the basis of the observation that conscience is always and necessarily introspective since there is nowhere else for it to look: my conscience examines and assesses my behaviour, including of course its inward motivation. We must now go on to ask, Did the inward investigating gaze of his conscience cause Paul acute unhappiness, a sense of hopelessness, of perdition?

Dr Stendahl considers Rom. 7.7–25, a paragraph that has divided interpreters in more ways than one.[11] It is important to remember that Paul did not set out in this paragraph to present a psychological analysis of the soul in its sickness. His intention is to answer the question, made inevitable by 7.1–6 and other passages, Is the Law sin? It is so closely associated with sin that it might seem to be identified with it. The question has to be taken seriously, but there is no doubt about the answer: μὴ γένοιτο (Rom. 7.7). Yet there is more to say. The Law, holy, righteous, good, spiritual as it is proves to facilitate the entrance of sin and becomes its agent. The evil I would not do, yet practise, is the work of sin which dwells within me. Dr Stendahl rightly makes, with great emphasis, the point that the paragraph contains 'a defence for the holiness and goodness of the Law' (p. 92). From this he proceeds to an evaluation of the anthropological references in Rom. 7 as

> means for a very special argument about the holiness and goodness of the Law. The possibility of a distinction between the good Law and the bad Sin is based on the rather trivial observation that every man knows that there is a difference between what he ought to do and what he does. This distinction makes it possible for Paul to blame

[11] For the history of interpretation see the Commentaries of C. E. B. Cranfield (pp. 340–7), U. Wilckens (Vol. II, pp. 101–17), E. Käsemann (pp. 183–204), and J. D. G. Dunn (Vol. I, pp. 378–99).

Sin and Flesh, and to rescue the Law as a good gift of God. 'If I now do what I do not want, I agree with the Law [and recognize] that it is good' (v. 16). That is all, but that is what should be proven (i.e., that is what Paul means to prove) (p. 93).[12]

There are, as we shall observe, questions to raise in regard to the setting of the inward struggle (note the words ἀντιστρατευόμενον and αἰχμαλωτίζοντά in v. 23) described in this paragraph, but it is hard to see how anyone can draw from v. 17 the conclusion that 'the argument is one of acquittal of the ego, not one of utter contrition' (p. 93), as if Paul were saying, The Law is good, I am good, it is only these impersonal factors, Sin and Flesh, that cause the trouble. It need not be said that there are details of Dr Stendahl's interpretation of the passage that are perceptive and true; but his treatment is selective. Sin worked in me πᾶσαν ἐπιθυμίαν; sin came to life and I died; sin . . . killed me; I am a man of flesh (σάρκινος), sold as a slave so as to be under the power of sin; what I hate (not, what I mildly disapprove), that I do; no good thing dwells in me, that is, in my flesh; sin that dwells in me; there is imposed upon me, who would do what is good and right, a law, to the effect that evil shall always attend me. A war between two laws is raging within him, and the better part is taken prisoner by the law of sin. No wonder he cries out, ταλαίπωρος ἐγὼ ἄνθρωπος. If this passage does not depict a man profoundly conscious of division and conflict within himself it is hard to know what it is about. True; it is about the virtue of the Law. True, therefore, that the anthropological material is in a sense incidental. But it is not accidental that the anthropological material is introduced. Paul is capable on occasion of using mythological language, but he knows that in fact the scene of the battle between good and evil is the human heart, and that he had been – or was – involved in it.

I have discussed the interpretation of Rom. 7.7–25 elsewhere[13] and must not here simply repeat myself. The one exegetical point that it may be worthwhile to pick up is the meaning of the word

[12] The 'rather trivial observation' gave Luther years of hell.
[13] *Romans*, 2nd edn, pp. 130–44.

flesh, σάρξ. It is essential to Dr Stendahl's argument that 'the "I", the *ego*, is not simply identified with Sin and Flesh' (p. 92). This will perhaps stand if the word *simply* is emphasized as strongly as possible, but it is nearer to the truth to say that σάρξ denotes not an alien body and not a part, a 'lower' or 'unspiritual' part of the self; it is rather the self devoted to itself,[14] neglectful of God and of the neighbour because it is devoted, as by nature it is, to its own interests and concerns. The clearest of all passages is Gal. 5.13–24, where the double contrast, between flesh and love and between flesh and (Holy) Spirit, is made explicit. The contrast with love indicates that flesh denotes egocentric existence; it is not a contrast with or denial of the ego but an unbridled affirmation of it. The contrast with Spirit means that the ego has no means of ejecting itself from the centre of its own existence; the most it can in the nature of things achieve is a transformation of irreligious self-centredness into religious self-centredness, and the latter is usually more objectionable than the former, and harder to eradicate. Transformation is possible only when the ego is replaced as the controlling centre by the Spirit of God. The nature of the trans-formation is determined by the way in which ego–centricism has previously been expressed. Of fornicators, idolaters, adulterers, catamites, sodomites, thieves, the rapacious, drunkards, the abusive, robbers, Paul can say only, ταῦτά τινες ἦτε (1 Cor. 6.11): that is what you were but have now ceased to be. The old way of life has gone. It is not so easy to point out a difference in the way of life of the man who lived under the rule of the religious flesh. The practices of religion may be little changed, if changed at all, but they acquire a new meaning. When to the Jews Paul the apostle became as if he were a Jew (1 Cor. 9.20) the religious practices that he observed he observed with a new motive, that of winning his fellow Jews for Christ.

---

[14] Cf. Luther's famous phrase, *cor incurvatum in se*; also his comment (WA 56.347) on Rom. 7.25: 'Non enim ait: mens mea servit legi Dei, nec: caro mea legi peccati, sed: ego, inquit, totus homo, persona eadem, servio utranque servitutem. Ideo et gratias agit, quod servit legi Dei, et misericordiam querit, quod servit legi peccati.'

The transformation is never described by Paul in psychological or moral terms – that is, in regard to himself. The passage just quoted from 1 Corinthians gives a clear indication of the moral transformation experienced by some of the Corinthian Christians. The change in Paul from persecutor to preacher (Gal. 1.23) might be described as a moral transformation but it was not of the same kind: before it and afterwards he believed – with good conscience – that he was acting in obedience to the will of God. The righteousness in which he was faultless (ἄμεμπτος, Phil. 3.6) certainly included obedience to Thou shalt not steal and Thou shalt not commit adultery; and if there was a sense in which he did not observe Thou shalt not kill (Acts 8.1; 26.10) it was done in the best of causes and for the glory of God. The moment of conversion[15] is described unambiguously in Gal. 1.15–16 – unambiguously, but without content beyond the central fact that it meant God's manifestation of his risen Son, Jesus Christ. No moral or psychological accompaniments or consequences (beyond Gal. 1.23) are mentioned. The same is true of other references to the appearance of the risen Christ (1 Cor. 9.1; 15.8).[16] There is more information in Phil. 3, but it is almost confined to the two words κέρδος and ζημία (3.7, 8; with ζημιοῦν and σκύβαλα). To reverse one's estimate of a significant feature of one's life from positive to negative is a revolutionary act which belongs to the realm of the conscience and can hardly fail to be profoundly disturbing; incidentally it casts a good deal of light on the way in which Paul understood the righteousness that is based on and arises out of law. His Jewish descent, his Pharisaic attitude to the Law, his zeal for Judaism, expressed in persecution of the church, his law-based righteousness, were credits (κέρδη) in his account, which clearly he had in the past regarded as desirable assets. The abandonment of this outlook must have caused a measure of distress – even if also of relief.

---

[15] Which was at the same time a commissioning to apostolic service.

[16] The narratives in Acts (9.1–18; 22.6–16; 26.9–18) describe supernatural phenomena – light, blindness, a fall, and so on – which must have been inseparable from, if they are not mythological objectifications of, inward psychological reactions, but they are not related to the conscience. Somewhat surprisingly, the words 'I am Jesus whom you are persecuting' do not elicit a prayer for pardon.

Yet Paul had a conscience; and he knew something of the torments that religion can inflict upon its devotees. The old debate about Rom. 7 – does it refer to Paul's pre-Christian or to his Christian life? – is an over-simplification, and Origen's compromise (*inter regenerandum*) is not the way out. Paul is writing, with the vividness and in the personal terms of one who had himself passed that way, of the relation of human life to the Law of God when this is seen *coram Deo*. Of course the Law is gracious and good, but the holiness of the Law is my condemnation, and the judge who condemns is a more formidable dicast than my conscience. It is God himself, and the Law (which indeed has other functions too) compels me to take him seriously, joined as it is by its fellow witness, conscience. Paul had always been a religious man, but it was a fresh encounter with God, taken seriously as never before because now apparent in the crucified (crucified with his own consent and approval if not by his action) yet now living Jesus, that opened his eyes to the full meaning of life as it had been, and, even after the thanksgiving of Rom. 7.25a still was. Paul knows the terror of the Lord, exposed as he is to God (2 Cor. 5.10, 11: θεῷ δὲ πεφανερώμεθα).

It is at this point that we may turn to Luther. Important though this aspect of the question is, I shall follow the examples of both Dr Stendahl and Dr Käsemann in treating it more briefly. Dr Käsemann of course is much less concerned with the psychological issue and more concerned with the alternatives, if they are alternatives, justification and *Heilsgeschichte*.

Every student of Luther is aware of the *Anfechtungen* with which he was constantly beset. This is no place for a full discussion of the *Anfechtungen*, nor am I competent to give one; a few points only need be made. The German word is almost unavoidable; there is no English word that adequately expresses its meaning. *Temptation* is sometimes used, but it is misleading. *Depression* is worse. Rupp[17] suggests that we 'may employ John Bunyan's tremendous phrase "the bruised conscience"', and it is true that there are analogies between Bunyan and Luther (differences, too), true also that the

---

[17] G. Rupp, *The Righteousness of God* (1953), p. 105.

conscience is involved in *Anfechtungen*, but a bruised, wounded, conscience is rather the effect of *Anfechtungen* than *Anfechtungen* themselves. *Fechten* is *to fight*, *anfechten* is *to attack*, and *Anfechtungen* are attacks made from whatever quarter upon the inward being and the peace of man. Luther was subject to them through the whole of his adult life; and without them his theology would have been far less profound than it was. It owed its strength to the fact that it had been fought for. Paradoxically, the adversary was sometimes the devil and sometimes God; it is bad enough when the devil questions a man's relation with God, worse still when God himself questions it. 'The whole meaning of "Anfechtung" for Luther lies in the thought that man has his existence "Coram Deo", and that he is less the active intelligence imposing itself on the stuff of the universe around him, than the subject of an initiative and action from God who employs the whole of man's existence as a means of bringing men to awareness of their need and peril.'[18] The familiar story of Luther's first mass gives the essentials of Luther's position in vivid form. To recite the words beginning *Te igitur clementissime Pater* was almost too much for him.

> At these words I was utterly stupefied and terror-stricken. I thought to myself, 'With what tongue shall I address such Majesty, seeing that all men ought to tremble in the presence of even an earthly prince? Who am I, that I should lift up mine eyes or raise my hands to the divine Majesty? The angels surround him. At his nod the earth trembles. And shall I, a miserable little pygmy, say "I want this, I ask for that"? For I am dust and ashes and full of sin and I am speaking to the living, eternal and the true God.'

'The terror of the Holy, the horrors of Infinitude, smote him like a new lightning bolt, and only through a fearful restraint could he hold himself at the altar to the end.'[19]

---

[18] Rupp, *Righteousness*, p. 106. I cannot forbear to add here a reference to that profoundly theological novel, G. K. Chesterton's *The Man who was Thursday*.

[19] I take the translation and the comment from R. H. Bainton, *Here I Stand* (1955), p. 30.

Conscience does indeed enter the process, but (just as with Paul) primarily as a witness, not as judge. 'Ihm [Luther] blieb in aller seiner Verwirrung sein Gewissen allein der unverrückte Massstab, nach dem er sein Verhältnis zu Gott beurteilte.'[20] But important as the conscience is he can appeal against the conscience to God. 'Der Aufrichtige muss glauben, dass ihm in der Anfechtung Gott selbst begegnet ist, er muss gewissenshalber glauben, dass das Gericht über ihn Gottes letztes Wort wäre. Und trotzdem soll er wiederum glauben, dass das Gericht über ihn nicht das letzte Wort sei, dass der Gott, der ihm in gerechtem Zorn gegenübertrat, doch nicht der "wirkliche" Gott sei . . . .'.[21]

Anfechtungen did not end with Luther's discovery of the true meaning of righteousness and justification, but they did to some extent change their character and took the form partly of the opposition he had to endure[22] and partly the nagging fear lest he, standing alone as he had so often been obliged to do, had after all been mistaken and had led half Christendom astray. He was encouraged and to some extent consoled by the reflection that many of the great men of the Bible had been in the same position. It is in this period that *Anfechtungen* are mainly the work of the devil.

The fact that *Anfechtungen* persisted to the end of his life is a clear indication that to treat them as a condition for the understanding of justification, and as brought to an end when justification is received by faith, is a serious misunderstanding, though it is a misunderstanding that has deep Lutheran roots. It is found as early as the Confessio Augustana.

> Quanquam autem haec doctrina contemnitur ab imperitis, tamen experiuntur piae ac pavidae conscientiae plurimum eam consolationis afferre, quia conscientiae non possunt reddi tranquillae per ulla opera, sed tantum fide, cum certo statuunt, quod propter Christum habeant placatum Deum, quemadmodum Paulus docet Rom. 5: Iustificati per

---

[20] K. Holl, *Gesammelte Aufsätze zur Kirchengeschichte, I: Luther* (1921), p. 24.
[21] Holl, *Ges. Aufs.*, p. 61; with n. 4.
[22] See the passages quoted in J. Atkinson, *Luther, Prophet to the Church Catholic* (1983), pp. 206–11.

fidem, pacem habemus apud Deum. Tota haec doctrina ad illud certamen perterrefactae conscientiae referenda est nec sine illo certamine intelligi potest. (XX 15–17)

The last sentence is not contained in the German text; and one looks in vain in both the Large Catechism and the Small for any suggestion that to be a true Christian one must pass through the struggle that the Confessio describes. Perhaps the word *intelligi* must be stressed: the fact that some have passed through the *certamen* enables the rest of Christians to understand and value the justification that they have received at less cost to themselves.

This discussion has shown that there is a difference between the experiences of Paul and of Luther on their way to and in faith. For pointing out the existence of a difference we must be grateful to Dr Stendahl. But the difference is more complicated than his description of it, and there is a resemblance which he did not observe, and which Dr Käsemann, whose interest was somewhat different, did not point out. Both Paul and Luther had introspective consciences and each of them found his conscience awakened at the point of the discovery that he stood *coram Deo*, and in the presence of a God defined in terms that were new to him. Paul, in the first Christian generation, made the discovery in the last (1 Cor. 15.8) of the resurrection appearances; for him, from the moment when God revealed his Son (Gal. 1.15–18), God could be understood only as the one who raised from death the Friend of sinners and thereby manifested a love otherwise unknown (Rom. 5.8). Before this there had been no occasion for *certamen*; there was now, and the clear evidence for it arises with (Phil. 3.7–9) and after the moment of conversion. The infant Martin Luther was baptized into the Christian tradition. It was a tradition that was in need, as few would now deny, of some kind of reformation, but at least it told him of a God who claimed him and would on certain terms accept him. They were terms that many could accept and apply; but they were terms that, as he understood them, called for perfect *contritio* and more than Augustinian ascetic discipline. His blameless behaviour as a monk corresponded to Paul's blameless righteousness of law (Phil. 3.6), but precisely because of the tradition in which he stood Luther himself knew that monastic perfection did not suffice. His *certamen* (or some aspects of it) came to an end where Paul's began, with the discovery of a gracious God.[23] For both, the way ahead meant 'unus et idem homo simul servit legi Dei et legi peccati, simul justus est et peccat!'.[24]

No more for Paul than for Luther was justification an instrument for validating the line of missionary work that he had adopted. Not that it was unrelated to the mission to the Gentiles. The doctrine and the mission ran side by side, each supporting and each deepening the other. As for *Heilsgeschichte*, it is a term that can be made to mean almost anything the user wishes,[25] and we might be better off without it. If it is construed to mean that the principle of justification was one that served its turn at a certain point – an important point – in the first century, it is misleading. If it means that justification by faith is a basic principle of God's dealing with his creatures, worked out in different ways in the story of a Paul and the story of a Luther, it is, near enough, the whole of *Heil* and the better part of *Geschichte*.

---

[23] No doubt – we are grateful to E. P. Sanders for emphasizing it – the gracious God was there in Judaism; but that is not where Paul found him. My own gratitude for this goes back to H. M. J. Loewe, many years ago Reader in Rabbinics at Cambridge.

[24] In the passage quoted above, n. 14.

[25] Käsemann, *Perspektiven*, p. 112: 'Ich habe nichts gegen das Wort "heilsgeschichtlich", obgleich mir seine Verwendung oft fragwürdig erscheint, und meine sogar, dass man die Bibel im allgemeinen und Paulus im besonderen ohne die heilsgeschichtliche Perspektive nicht begreifen kann. Umgekehrt sollte man dieses Wort nicht aus der mit ihm verbundenen Problematik herausnehmen und wie alle gefährlichen worte möglichst genau definieren.'

Index of Modern Writers

241

Index of Ancient Persons
and Places

Index of Ancient Writers

Select Index to the Pauline Epistles